Democracy and Public Choice

Gordon Tullock

Democracy and Public Choice

Essays in Honor of Gordon Tullock

*Edited by and
with contributions from*

CHARLES K. ROWLEY

Basil Blackwell

Copyright © Basil Blackwell 1987

First published 1987

Basil Blackwell Ltd
108 Cowley Road, Oxford, OX4 1JF, UK

Basil Blackwell Inc.
432 Park Avenue South, Suite 1503
New York, NY 10016, USA

British Library Cataloguing in Publication Data

Democracy and public choice: essays in
honour of Gordon Tullock.
1. Social choice 2. Political science
I. Rowley, Charles K. II. Tullock, Gordon
320.01'9 JA77

ISBN 0–631–15029–3

Library of Congress Cataloging in Publication Data

Rowley, Charles Kershaw.
Democracy and public choice.

Includes index.
1. Social choice. 2. Democracy. 3. Tullock, Gordon.
I. Tullock, Gordon. II. Title.
HB846.8.R68 1987 302'.13 87–6402
ISBN 0–631–15029–3

Typeset in Ehrhardt on 10/12pt
by Alan Sutton Publishing Limited
Printed in Great Britain by T. J. Press Ltd, Padstow

To Marjorie
with Love

Contents

Contributors

PETER H. ARANSON Professor of Economics, Emory University, Atlanta, Georgia

JAMES M. BUCHANAN Nobel Laureate in Economic Science, General Director, The Center for Study of Public Choice, George Mason University, Fairfax, Virginia

MICHAEL A. CREW Professor of Economics, Rutgers University, Newark, New Jersey

CHARLES J. GOETZ Professor of Law, University of Virginia, Charlottesville, Virginia

MARGARET A. MONACO Undergradate Major in Economics, George Mason University, Fairfax, Virginia

WILLIAM C. MITCHELL Professor of Political Science, University of Oregon, Eugene, Oregon

DENNIS C. MUELLER Professor of Economics, University of Maryland, College Park, Maryland

WILLIAM A. NISKANEN Chairman, The Cato Institute, Washington, DC

DOUGLASS C. NORTH Professor of Economics, Washington University, St. Louis, Missouri

MANCUR OLSON Professor of Economics, University of Maryland College Park, Maryland

CHARLES C. PLOTT Professor of Economics, California Intstitute of Technology, Pasadena, California

SUSAN ROSE-ACKERMAN Professor of Law, Columbia University, New York

CHARLES K. ROWLEY Dean of the Graduate School and Research Associate of The Center for Study of Public Choice, George Mason University, Fairfax, Virginia

WARREN F. SCHWARTZ Professor of Law, Georgetown University, Washington, DC

ARTHUR SELDON, CBE Editorial Director, The Institute of Economic Affairs, Westminster, London

ROBERT D. TOLLISON   Director, The Center for Study of Public Choice
George Mason University, Fairfax, Virginia
RICHARD E. WAGNER   Professor of Economics, Florida State University
Tallahassee, Florida

Preface

This book is the outcome of a conference held at Colonial Williamsburg 9–11 April 1986, entitled 'Towards a Freer Society: Some Unintended Consequences of Tullock's Scholarship'. This conference was generously funded by The Liberty Fund in honor of a great scholar of public choice. My particular thanks are due to Dr. Neil McLeod, then President of The Liberty Fund, who assisted me at all stages in the organization of the conference. I am grateful also to Carol Robert and Betty Tillman who both helped with the organization of the conference. I am especially indebted to my secretary, Ellen Ladow, who skillfully typed much of the text of this book and helped to carry it through to publication. I wish finally to acknowledge the continuing support of my wife, Marjorie, without whom the book would not have been completed, and to whom it is dedicated.

Charles K. Rowley

1

Introduction
CHARLES K. ROWLEY

The essays presented in this book originated from a Conference in Honor of Gordon Tullock held at Colonial Williamsburg in April 1986 and attended by many of the world's most distinguished scholars in public choice and related disciplines. The conference centered attention on areas of study pioneered by a leading scholar of public choice, placing his contributions in a more general *ex post* perspective. The topics covered etch across most of the field of public choice in its contemporary form–and this itself is testament to Tullock's prolific and finely-sensed contributions.

It is especially fitting in 1987, given the recent recognition accorded to public choice by the Swedish Academy in awarding James M. Buchanan the Nobel Prize in Economic Science, that the work of his colleague and co-author of *The Calculus of Consent* (Buchanan and Tullock, 1962) should be revisited. The revisitation provides a rich menu of insights and perspectives which in turn offer an invaluable introduction to public choice, both for those inside the academy and for those without who wish to become knowledgeable about this thriving discipline. Those who already practice will find many original contributions opening up a rich agenda for the second 25 years of the public choice research programme.

Public choice uses the methodology of economics to study questions traditionally investigated by political science. As such, it is rightly regarded as the economics of politics. The key element in this approach is the assumption that political man, like his economic counterpart, is a rational, self-interested being. This assumption emphasizes the individualistic utilitarian thrust of neoclassical economics with important distinctive implications for its evaluation of behaviour in political markets.

Scholars both in economics and in political science frequently criticize public choice for its emphasis upon self-seeking in political markets and for its rejection of the public interest thrust of the new welfare economics that had characterized the decades of the mid-twentieth century. They castigate those who research in public choice as excessively cynical in their view of human nature, and excessively pessimistic in their prognoses of the future of democracy. Gordon Tullock, more than most, has been a focal point of such criticism.

The critics, for the most part, misdirect their aim, confusing the protected core of a theory in the sense of Lakatos, (1970) with assertions about the real world. The self-seeking postulate is employed in positive public choice essentially as an "as if" proposition which, when combined with relevant auxiliary conditions, generates testable predictions concerning the response of political variables to exogenous change (Popper, 1968). To the extent that such predictions differ from those of alternative approaches, and conform more closely to the evidence, so the self-seeking postulate is justified, whether or not it reflects the reality of the political market behavioral calculus.

Even within this perspective, however, the critics remain on the attack, claiming that positive public choice is vulnerable to the generalized Heisenberg principle. If political actors are analyzed as self-seeking, they may well take their cue from theory and adjust their behavior from altruism to selfishness. Public choice thus stands condemned as a self-justifying paradigm imposing grave cost upon citizens and irreversible damage upon the institutions of the political market place. Those who criticize public choice on this ground typically do not advocate false science as a substitute. Rather, they take a strong presumptive position against public choice and in favor of the public interest approach.

Although protected core assumptions may be unrealistic in good predictive theory, there is no necessity that such will be the case. Citizens are much more cynical than they were in 1960 concerning the motives of their political representatives, much more willing to probe beyond the rhetoric of platform speeches into the actual behavior of political actors. Of all the presidents since Eisenhower, only Ford emerges relatively unscathed from such a searching skepticism. The myth of Camelot, shattered with the assassination of Kennedy, is now seen as illusion. The disillusionment of dystopia (Buchanan, 1986) has replaced illusion with the "as if" postulates of public choice widely viewed as a realistic representation of political market motivation. The Virginia School has played no small part in this unification of positive theory with political market realities.

The term "Virginia School" was first coined by Mancur Olson to encompass a brand of scholarship emanating from the Center for Study of Public Choice, then located in Blacksburg, Virginia, with tendrils extending across the Western world. The Virginia School earned its title by sharing three characteristics, namely a common methodology, a distinctive ideology and a burning enthusiasm for the development of its discipline (Mueller, 1985).

The methodology of the Virginia School that distinguishes it from rival scholarships is the systematic application of neoclassical economics to all aspects of the polity. Other scholars, such as Black, Arrow and Downs have led occasional forays into the field; but only to retreat into other more conventional areas of economic analysis. The ideology of the Virginia School in essence is one of profound skepticism concerning the role of government, a systematic preference for market over non-market decision-making which permeates almost all of the writings of its scholars. The enthusiasm is self-evident in any visit, however brief, to the Center, and is witnessed by the quite remarkable publication rates of those closely associated with it, most notably, James M. Buchanan, Gordon Tullock and Robert D. Tollison. (Breit 1986)

Tullock, the co-founder with Buchanan of the Virginia School, was to play a pivotal role in its development. His classic article (Tullock, 1959) which demonstrated how majority rule can lead to an excessive expansion of government, first awakened interest in public choice at The Thomas Jefferson Center. His work on the basic constitutional model sparked off team production with Buchanan culminating in *The Calculus of Consent* which itself established the logical foundations of democracy. Together with Buchanan, he founded the Public Choice Society in 1963. Shortly afterwards, he introduced a new journal, *Papers in Non-Market Decision-Making*, which was the forerunner of *Public Choice*. He co-founded the Center for Study of Public Choice in 1968 following the location shift to Blacksburg. He has carried the public choice message throughout the Western World with unending zeal and enthusiasm.

Widely regarded as an extremist in his use of the self-interest axiom, Tullock in fact is less inclined than many of his Virginia School associates to push the axiom to its ultimate limit. Indeed, the "law" that he has promulgated as "Tullock's Law" states that individuals are altruistic, *5 per cent of the time*. His own work on income redistribution reflects the insight that this retreat from solipsism provides. Economists within the Chicago School would classify Tullock as a sociologist for this concession. Few economists working anywhere within the neoclassical framework are as prepared as Tullock to divert from wealth maximization assumptions.

Moreover, unlike much of public choice analysis, which offers a very pessimistic perspective on in-period politics, *The Calculus of Consent* provided a much more optimistic vision. Gains from trade are available to citizens via constitutional choice; constitutional rules can inhibit negative sum games within the legislature; indeed they can protect the legislature itself from the wealth-destructive behavior of interest group politics. This insight, essentially the gift of Tullock to *The Calculus of Consent*, offers hope of consensus, of contractual outcomes, in an environment that otherwise appears to be characterized by conflict and to be ruled by guns.

The essays in Part I of this book offer sharply differing insights into the method of public choice, both in its general application and with respect to Tullock's contributions. The reader whose appetite is whetted by this discussion may wish to browse through Tullock's works which are listed in the Appendix. The essays in Part II reflect on the original contribution to public choice in Tullock's co-authoring of The Calculus of Consent. Once again, subtle disagreements are apparent which may stimulate the research interests of scholars specialized in the history of thought and/or in the logic of scientific revolution.

The essays in Part II shift attention away from the process of constitutional choice to the political market-place itself, revisiting the paradox of voting, arguably with only limited success. The essays in Part IV focus upon the role of interest groups, including bureaucracy, which are seen to impose demands upon the in-period polity. The relevance of constitutional constraints in canalizing interest group pressures into wealth enhancement is carefully explored. Part V concentrates upon the theory of rent seeking, arguably one of Tullock's most important insights, emphasizing the wealth destructive implications of institutions that are vulnerable to rent seeking behavior.

Part VI shifts attention away from political markets and towards the law and legal institutions. These essays suggest that Tullock may have failed to utilize public choice analytics successfully in this field, perhaps because his training in the law preceded his discovery of public choice. Part VII concentrates on institutional reform, applying public choice insights to two of the most pressing economic issues that face the Western democracies.

It is remarkable that a set of essays designed to honor a single scholar should end up by spanning the entire field of public choice. That they do so is perhaps the highest testimonial that can be offered. Surely Tullock's insights permeate every aspect of the discipline that he has helped to forge. His unworked ideas offer a remarkable research agenda for the last years of the twentieth century.

Tullock requires no written testament to his quarter century of contributions to public choice and to the Virginia School. His testament is in his life and work. It is also in the enthusiasm of those who attend the meetings of the Public Choice Society, and those who seek him out at the Center. It is fitting therefore to end this chapter with the epitaph engraved on the tomb of Sir Christopher Wren "si monumentum requiris, circumspice" (if you seek his monument, look around). Fortunately for public choice and for the Virginia School, this is no epitaph. Tullock is alive and well and full of original ideas. This book is only the end of the beginning.

References

Breit, W. (1986) *Creating the "Virginia School": Charlottesville as an Academic Environment in the 1960s.* Center for Study of Public Choice, George Mason University.

Buchanan, J.M. and Tullock G., (1962) *The Calculus of Consent: Logical Foundations of a Constitutional Democracy*. Ann Arbor: University of Michigan Press.

Buchanan, J.M. (1986) *From the Illusion of Camelot to the Disillusionment of Dyspopia*. Institute for Humane Studies.

Lakatos, I. (1970) "Falsification and the methodology of scientific research programs", in I. Lakatos and A. Musgrave, (eds) *Criticism and the Growth of Knowledge*, Cambridge University Press.

Mueller, D.C. (1985) *The "Virginia School" and Public Choice*. Center for Study of Public Choice, George Mason University.

Popper, K.R. (1968) *The Logic of Scientific Discovery*. Harper Torchbooks (revised edn).

Tullock, G. "Problems of majority voting", *Journal of Political Economy*, 67, December, pp. 571–79.

I

On Method

2

The Qualities of a Natural Economist
JAMES M. BUCHANAN

2.1 Introduction

There are very few natural economists, and most of those who claim professional competence in economics as a discipline are not, themselves, "natural". They tend rather to be reformers, revolutionaries, paternalists, and more frequently of late, mathematicians. Gordon Tullock is an exception to most of his peers in this important respect, and his qualifications as a "natural economist" cut through and thoroughly dominate his own professional training in law. I use the term "natural" here in a manner that is precisely analogous to its usage when applied to baseball players, musicians, and comedians. To designate someone a "natural" is to suggest that he or she has intrinsic talents that emerge independently of professional training, education, and experience. A "natural economist" therefore, is someone who more or less unconsciously thinks like an economist.

But how does an economist think? I leave my designation ambiguous until and unless I answer this preliminary question. An economist, in the sense of the term used here, views human beings as self-interested, utility-maximizing agents, basically independent one from another, and for whom social interchange is initiated and exists simply as a preferred alternative to isolated action. Psychologically, persons remain in a Hobbesian setting, or, as Tullock perceptively suggested in his title for a revealing essay, "The Edge of the Jungle" (Tullock, 1973), despite the political–legal–institutional trappings of civic order. To the economist who looks at persons in this way, there seems little room for moral or ethical precepts in either positive or normative exercises. Persons are observed to behave in certain patterns, and the economist's task is to offer an explanation-understanding of that behavior in terms of his model of self-interested utility maximization. And, because he considers himself successful in this positive aspect of his science, the economist offers normative guidance grounded on his own self-interest as a participating member of the inclusive political community.

All those of us who "do economics" necessarily take on the economist's perspective, as sketched out above, when we engage in analytic enterprise. Those of us who do not qualify as "naturals", however, tend to stop short at the several subjectively-determined boundaries of personal behavior. Many of those who call themselves economists are quite willing to incorporate self-interested utility maximization on the part of participants in organized market activity – as consumers, investors, labor-suppliers, owners, enterpreneurs – while at the same time they object, sometimes quite vociferously, to extensions of the *same* motivational–behavioral model to persons as participants in non-market interactions – as politicians, bureaucrats, voters, agents for nonproprietary institutions, criminals, revolutionaries, university administrators, teachers, research scholars, family members, preachers, and judges. It is the "natural economists" such as Gordon Tullock, Gary Becker, and Armen Alchian who have opened up several new areas of interaction to inquiry by extending the economist's standard model. In so doing, they have "dragged" some of us along in the process, despite some initial reluctance on our parts.

My discussion of the qualities of a natural economist will concentrate on Gordon Tullock, and, in part, my discussion must be autobiographical due to my long association with Tullock as a co-author and colleague. Aside from this relationship, however, some treatment of Tullock's influence on my own work can be helpful in developing my central theme. As I noted in the acknowledgment to one of my volumes of collected essays (Buchanan, 1977), my debt to Gordon Tullock stems in part from his long-continuing insistence on the economic view of man, which has served to check my own tendencies to wander off into ethical and moral discourse. On the other hand, and by contrast, I think that my own continuing reluctance to view man, always and everywhere, as self-seeking, explains my search for ways and means of reconciling self-interest with broader norms for social interaction. Appreciation of the essential tension between these two perspectives provides, I think, some understanding of the success of our major joint effort, *The Calculus of Consent* (1962). Independently of some emphasis on rules, on constitutional structures, straightforward extensions of economic models of behavior to politics might have seemed Schumpeterian (Schumpeter, 1944), in the sense that they offer no basis for constructive reform. On the other hand, independently of something like Tullock's economic reductionism, my own analyses of politics might have failed to attract the attention of either economists or political scientists. The separate directions of our works after this initial major joint effort illustrates the divergence in our perspectives. My own efforts have been toward the elaboration and development of what we now call "constitutional political economy", the analysis of alternative structures of rules which constrain man's self-seeking. By comparison, Tullock's efforts have involved, for the most part, still further imaginative extensions basically employing the same natural economist perspective on human behavior.

In what follows, I shall discuss several of these extensions briefly to illustrate my main theme. Gordon Tullock's work is, of course, no exception to the general rule that consistency in terms of any classificatory standard is not to be expected. He has, on occasion, applied his imaginative insights to the resolution of analytical problems that cannot readily be brought within the "natural economist" rubric. Such "deviant" contributions will not be surveyed here because, in my judgment, these do represent digressions from Gordon Tullock's more characteristic and consistent path of inquiry.

2.2 The Politics of Bureaucracy

When I first met Gordon Tullock in 1957, he had in hand a voluminous manuscript on bureaucracy that he had tried, unsuccessfully, to publish. What I took home with me from Philadelphia turned out to be a fascinating analysis of modern governmental bureaucracy that was almost totally buried in an irritating personal narrative account of Tullock's nine-year experience in the foreign service hierarchy. (Then, as now, Tullock's work was marked by his refusal to *write* (everything is dictated) as well as by his apparent inability to separate analytical exposition from personal anecdote). The substantive contribution in the manuscript was centered on the hypothesis that, regardless of role, the individual bureaucrat responds to the rewards and punishments that he confronts. This straightforward, and now so simple, hypothesis turned the whole post-Weberian quasi-normative approach to bureaucracy on its head. The bureaucrat becomes an economist actor in his own account, rather than the economic eunuch enshrined in the standard treatment. The economic theory of bureaucracy was born, one that has since been considerably enriched by Downs (1967), Niskanen (1975), Breton and Wintrobe (1982), and others.

Tullock's book, *The Politics of Bureaucracy*, the ultimate version of the 1957 manuscript, was published in 1965, after our collaboration on *The Calculus of Consent*. The former was hammered into acceptability to a publisher only after my own heroic scissors-and-paste effort completed during a rain-soaked holiday week in a West Virginia state park – an effort that involved excision of much personal narrative. The rather intensive reading of the initial Tullock manuscript, however, forced me into a much deeper appreci-ation of the categorical difference between market and political organization – a difference that I tried to elaborate in my own Foreword to the book. This difference, which I discussed in terms of the power relationships among persons, emerges clearly only if one does, indeed, adopt the natural economist's perspective. The implications of the differences between the receipt of opportunity-related wages and situation-related rents for individual well-being and psychological security were clarified. My own tendency is to think in terms of organizational principle, but, even for those for whom political philosophy holds little or no interest, there could be little or no satisfaction in a rent-dependency status. A reading of Tullock on bureaucracy leaves no mystery concerning his own profound disaffection with government as a monopsonist employer.

2.3 Voter Abstention and Voter Ignorance

Gordon Tullock (1967), along with Anthony Downs (1957), is credited with having emphasized the basic paradox exhibited in voting behavior in large-number electorates in which majority or plurality rules are utilized to determine the ultimately selected outcome. The paradox emerges directly when the natural economist looks at the behavior of the individual who faces the voting and non-voting options. Attention comes to be placed directly on the privately differentiated costs and benefits anticipated for each of the two alternatives. Because of the extremely low probability that any individual vote will affect the ultimate electoral result, the value differential to the individual between participation and non-participation in the election must be large indeed if rationality considerations are to dictate going to the polls, even if such action involves a minimal cost.

Note that the prediction of rational abstention that emerges from the economist's model of behavior here does not depend on the dominance of individually-defined, measurable self-interest, such as net wealth, in the ultimate comparison of the electoral alternatives. A person may well desire that Party A win over Party B for purely ideological rather than identifiable "private" reasons. Nonetheless, unless the differential value weights are very large, rational behavior may still suggest abstention from voting participation. The prediction of rational abstention does require the presumption that, when the individual chooses between participation and non-participation in an election, he acts in accordance with self-interest, rather than in terms of "duty", "civic responsibility", or similar standards. It is useful to distinguish between the relevance of identifiable self-interest in the individual's ranking of the ultimate electoral alternatives (candidates, issues, or parties) and the relevance of identifiable self-interest in the ranking of the participation and non-participating options.

The logic of the paradox of voting extends, of course, to the behavior of the individual in determining the level of personal investment in acquiring information about the electoral alternatives. The absence of the direct linkage between the potential act of voting and the final electoral result introduces an element of irresponsibility in the political process that is absent in the comparable market process, where there is one-to-one relationship between individual choice and final result (see Buchanan, 1954). Even if the individual votes, therefore, he is unlikely to be well informed about the predicted properties of that for which he votes, the pattern of behavior of a candidate, the effects of a particular referendum proposal, or the working out of a party's platform pledges. And note that, in this informational element, there is no distinction to be made between those persons who do choose to vote and those who do not. Those persons who violate the paradox and go to the polls may behave consistently with the economist's model in remaining uninformed about the voting options. Rational behavior dictates that those who do vote should remain "rationally ignorant".

The basic logic here can be extended further to emphasize the possible dominance of expressive, fashion, or whim motives in the actual behavior within the polling booth. The individual may use voting as means of expressing his whim rather than his genuine ranking over the alternatives because the very institution of the large-number election allows such expression at relatively low cost (see Brennan and Buchanan, 1984).

To those who do not accept the economist's model of rational choice, the twin hypotheses of voter abstention and voter ignorance do not warrant serious consideration because they neglect motivational influences that cannot be brought within the rational choice framework. And, empirically, we do observe that many persons vote in large-number settings – an observation which seems to refute the central abstention hypothesis. The basic contribution of Tullock, Downs, and others who have developed the hypothesis lies, however, precisely in the challenge posed to those who would offer alternative explanations. Why do individuals vote? The observed results may well suggest limits to rational choice approaches to behavior, but until and unless the critics of these approaches produce an alternative explanation, we remain with the paradox.

There are important implications here for any normative theory of democracy. If the act of voting must be "irrational" in many settings, and if, in voting, the individual expresses merely an uninformed and whim-driven attitude rather than a genuinely measured preference over the electoral alternatives, how is democratic process to be defined? The natural economist stops at this point and says to all of us "the ball is in your court". It is precisely at this point that the "constitutional economist" draws perhaps most closely on the analysis of the natural economist in his search for institutional changes that may limit the potential for excess in the extension of non-constrained majoritarian politicization.

2.4   Revolution, War, and Crime

From the perspective of what I have here called that of the natural economist, perhaps the most difficult, and most questionable, extension of the model is to the behavior of those persons who initiate and participate in revolutionary activity, along with those persons who seem to sacrifice themselves voluntarily in wars. Gordon Tullock has not flinched from such a challenge, however, and has made valiant efforts toward incorporating all such behavior into his inclusive analytical structure (with an apparent delight at the shock effect on his peers).

There is no room for the hero in the Tullock world, and ideology motivates behavior only to some second order of smalls. Yeats description of the worst persons as those "full of passionate intensity", finds no sympathetic reading by Tullock, who tends to shun literary metaphor. The revolutionary leader in the Tullock canon is an entrepreneur, analogous to other entrepreneurs, who recognizes an opportunity for potential personal gain (which may be status – rather than weath-based), and who sets about to exploit it. Lenin's interest in "saving the world by Communism" was not measurably different from that of anyone else; his interests were his own. The followers of the revolutionary leader, those who actually make the revolution, reach their decisions on the basis of a self-interested utility-maximizing calculus, just as do those who elect to remain non-revolutionaries. The soldier-hero who sacrifices his life for his comrades may, of course, make errors in judgment, but his decision calculus can still be brought within the natural economist's explanatory umbrella.

In my assessment, these are the extensions of the model that are the most vulnerable to criticism, and it is in his willingness to make these extensions that Gordon Tullock has exposed himself to sometime strident attack. By seeming to go too far, these efforts may well have tended to reduce appreciation for Tullock's work in more acceptable applications. (Much the same point might be made with reference to the work of Gary Becker.) In part, the vulnerability here stems from a methodological ambiguity, which was again a tension in *The Calculus of Consent*. Tullock has never clearly distinguished between predictive and explanatory models of behavior. If defined in sufficiently general terms, all human behavior can be "explained" in some utility-maximizing framework, that is, if the arguments in the utility function are left totally unspecified, even as to sign. The utility-maximizing hypothesis becomes tautological, or nearly so, in this setting, although it may remain of some heuristic value in analysis.

On the other hand, if the arguments in the individual's utility functions are defined, along with the assignment of positive and negative signs, operational content beyond formal tests for rationality is put into the model, and refutable implications may be derived. At this level of generality, a significant contribution may be made by looking at non-economic behavior from the economist's perspective, even if it is fully recognized that this perspective is not, in itself, dominant in "explaining" behavior. Even if an individual revolutionary is motivated primarily by ideological conviction rather than measurable net wealth, so long as the latter is positively valued, it follows that changes in the constraint structure can affect behavior in predictable ways. *Some* revolutionaries will respond to increases in rewards for defection or increases in penalties of capture. To the extent that the economist's analytical inquiry concentrates on such exploitable trade-off margins, there is both explanatory and normative value in having this perspective extended to include overtly non-economic aspects of behavior.

The proponents or advocates of the economist's perspective, including Tullock, have made their efforts more vulnerable to criticism by failing to make clear the operationality of the model, even in such limited motivational settings. Instead, advocates of an "economic" explanation of revolutionary and patriotic behavior tend to go further and to substitute, implicitly if not explicitly, some version of a wealth-maximizing for a utility-maximizing hypothesis. That is to say, and as Tullock has indeed argued, a revolutionary is hypothesized to act so as to increase the expected value of his private net wealth – a much more severely defined objective for choice than the mere signing of net wealth as a positive argument in the revolutionary's utility function. And, perhaps properly, the critics charge that such an extreme economistic model of behavior in such applications becomes caricature.

Extension of the economist's model to criminal behavior is perhaps somewhat less vulnerable to such criticism than the extension of the behavior of revolutionaries. Individuals who commit crimes can be predicted, especially in the more limited usage of the model, to respond to penalties measured in terms of their measured self-interest, for example, longer prison sentences and increased probabilities of capture and conviction. Such changes in the law enforcement structure can safely be predicted to reduce, say, the rate of burglary. This application of the model may be accepted without, at the same time, hypothesizing that individuals become burglars only if their expected "earnings" in this "occupation" equal or exceed those in legal employment (or receipt of welfare benefits). Or, to put the same proposition in the inverse, increases in the rewards to criminal activity can be predicted to lead to increased levels of crime (a simple application of elementary economics), without implying that relative rewards in criminal and legal activities are the primary determinants of the overall level of criminality.

2.5   Charity, Cost, and Redistribution

The proclivities of the "natural economist", again exemplified in the work of
Gordon Tullock, emerge clearly in analyses of interpersonal transfers of
values that remain outside the market exchange nexus. To the extent that
one person voluntarily gives a valuable item (money, claims, goods, services)
to another, the *homo economicus* model of behavior seems, on the surface, to
be inoperative. The natural economist is prompted to search for ways and
means of bringing such behavior within his inclusive explanatory model by
looking, for example, at the privately-enjoyed benefits stemming from the act
of giving *per se*, rather than at the prospects for the existence of genuine
altruism beyond minimal limits. He will also tend to look for sources of
institutional coercion that penalize the individual who does not voluntarily
"join" the charity drive by his firm, community, or church.

It is, however, at the level of collective or governmental rather than private
transfer that the natural economist's proclivity has led to genuine contributions to our understanding and interpretation of widely observed patterns
of behavior. One of Gordon Tullock's most imaginative papers, "The
Charity of the Uncharitable" (1971), was based on the simple cost-benefit
calculus of the person who might vote in support for or opposition to
collectively-organized transfer programs. The hypothesis is that charitable
giving, like all other economic activities, obeys the laws of economics.
Individuals are likely to be "charitable" when the costs to them, personally
and privately, are non-existent or very low. They become "uncharitable"
quickly as these private costs increase. This straightforward cost-benefit
calculus on the part of voters, along with the recognition of the publicness of
some transfers, and the minimal altruism that persons exhibit, satisfactorily
explains those elements of genuine transfers from rich to poor that we
observe to take place through our political institutions.

In the modern polity, we observe large government budgets that include
ever-increasing shares devoted to transfer payments. Given this budgetary
record as fact, there must be some explanation over and beyond that which
was noted above. The natural economist is led to explain what we see by
hypothesizing that much of the transfer system now in place is not at all
motivated by demands for vertical income redistribution, but is driven by the
political profit-seeking of competing interest groups. The transfer system
inclusively considered, is not primarily an altruistically driven welfare
system. It is, by contrast, best characterized as a complex structure of
inter-interest group payments, often with little or no relationship to those
ideals for redistribution policy that might be laid out by the philosopher of
altruism.

Gordon Tullock (1983), along with Aaron Director and George Stigler,
has been a leading figure among those economists who view the transfer

structure in this skeptical fashion, a view that is coming to be increasingly accepted by those who do not qualify as natural economists.

2.6 Rent-seeking

Many of his peers consider Gordon Tullock's most important single contribution to economics to be the theory of rent-seeking. Tullock's seminal paper was published in 1967 (Tullock, 1967), but he did not introduce the now-familiar term which was itself used first by Ann Krueger (Krueger, 1974). Analysis is far from closed in this area of inquiry, but, by 1985, rent-seeking was well on its way toward becoming an integral part of economics.

As with the several other extensions, already briefly discussed in this paper, the whole notion of rent-seeking, once introduced, seems to be a self-evident consequence of carrying through the economist's model of rational choice. There is an important difference, however, between this and the other extensions discussed, and one that warrants notice. The applications of the natural economist's model to political, criminal, revolutionary, and charitable behavior are straightforward efforts to widen the explanatory limits of the basic tool kit. The theory of rent-seeking becomes quite different in this respect. Consider Tullock's linking of monopoly, tariffs, and theft in his pioneering paper. The economist's model of behavior had traditionally been applied to the monopolist, and other extensions had already included the behavior of groups seeking tariff protection, and also the behavior of potential and actual thieves. Persons in each of these capacities had previously been analyzed as economic actors. What the theory of rent-seeking does is to extend the analysis one stage further back, so to speak, to bring in the behavior of persons before they become successful monopolists, recipients of tariff-cushioned rents, or thieves.

Rent-seeking analysis draws attention to the *process* within which the activity of many persons takes place, a *competitive process*, with a "profit and loss" structure, akin to, but quite different from, the market process in its implications for overall efficiency in resource allocation. As I noted in my introductory essay in the volume that collected the seminal works on rent-seeking (Buchanan, Tollinson, and Tullock, 1980), rent-seeking behavior is not different in motivation from the ordinary profit-seeking which characterizes the competitive market process. The critical difference lies in the sources of that which motivates the behavior in the two cases. In markets, potential profits emerge from the *increments* to value that are *created* by entrepreneurs who put together new resource combinations, or who meet new demands. In the non-market settings where rent-seeking takes place, there are no increments to value created. Instead, the value that potential rent-seekers attempt to secure is artificially created through interferences with resource adjustment.

2.7 Conclusions

I have discussed the qualities of the natural economist, with particular reference to the works of Gordon Tullock, in terms of several extensions of the basic model to unorthodox areas of interaction. My purpose here has not been that of examining any one of these extensions in critical detail, in part because I recognize that other contributors to this volume will take on such assignments. My aim has been the more limited one of utilizing these extensions or applications to indicate, at least indirectly, their potential usefulness to those of us who venture to engage in "political economy" or "constitutional economics", inquiries that focus attention on the evaluation of the working properties of alternative institutional – constitutional structures.

The man that is modelled by the natural economist may fail to attain desired levels of descriptive accuracy in many applications, and especially those interactions that are most removed from the ordinary exchange relationships of the market. However, any evaluation of proposals to change or to reform social institutions that ignores the economic content of human behavior is flawed from its inception. The natural economist provides a necessary input to any such exercise. *Homunculus* (the little man) he may sometimes be, but *homo economicus* is a part of the reality that is.

References

Brennan, Geoffrey, and Buchanan, James (1984) "Voter Choice: evaluating political alternatives", *American Behavioral Scientist*, 29 November/December, pp. 185–201.

Breton, Albert, and Wintrobe, Ronald (1982) *The Logic of Bureaucratic Conduct*. Cambridge: Cambridge University Press.

Buchanan, James M. (1954) "Individual choice in voting and the market", *Journal of Political Economy* LXII August, pp. 334–343.

Buchanan, James M. (1977) *Freedom in Constitutional Contract*. College Station: Texas A & M University Press.

Buchanan, James, Tollison, Robert, and Tullock, Gordon (eds) (1980) *Toward a Theory of the Rent Seeking Society*. College Station: Texas A & M University Press.

Buchanan, James and Tullock, Gordon (1962) *The Calculus of Consent*. Ann Arbor: University of Michigan Press.

Downs, Anthony (1957) *An Economic Theory of Democracy*. New York: Harper.

Downs, Anthony (1957) *Inside Bureaucracy*. Boston: Little Brown.

Krueger, Ann (1974) "The political economy of the rent seeking society", *American Economic Review*, 64, June, pp. 291–302.

Niskanen, William (1971) *Bureaucracy and Representative Government*. Chicago: Aldine-Atherton.

Schumpeter, Joseph (1942) *Capitalism, Socialism and Democracy*. New York: Harper.

Tullock, Gordon (1965) *The Politics of Bureaucracy*. Washington: Public Affairs Press.

Tullock, Gordon (1967) *Towards a Mathematics of Politics*. Ann Arbor: University of Michigan Press, 1967.

Tullock, Gordon (1967) "The welfare economics of tariffs, monopoly, and theft", *Western Economic Journal*, 5 June, pp. 224–32.

Tullock, Gordon (1971) "The charity of the uncharitable", *Western Economic Journal*, 9 December, pp. 379–92.

Tullock, Gordon (1973) "The Edge of the Jungle", *Explorations in the Theory of Anarchy*, Gordon Tullock (ed.). Blacksburg: Center for Study of Public Choice.

Tullock, Gordon (1974) *The Social Dilemma*. Blacksburg: Center for Study of Public Choice.

Tullock, Gordon (1974) "Does Punishment Deter Crime?", *The Public Interest*, 36 Summer, pp. 103–11.

Tullock, Gordon (1983) *The Economics of Income Redistribution*. Boston: Kluwer-Nijhoff.

3

Natural Economist or Popperian Logician?

CHARLES K. ROWLEY

3.1 Introduction

James Buchanan (1987) has characterized Gordon Tullock as a natural economist, defined as an economist with "intrinsic talents that emerge independently of professional training, education, and experience". Such a person, he suggests, views human beings as self-interested, utility-maximizing agents, basically independent from one another, and for whom social interchange is initiated and exists simply as a preferred alternative to isolated action. In short, individuals exist as isolated islands in an ocean of exchange, solipsist in vision, poised irreversibly on the edge of the jungle. In Buchanan's perception, the natural economist is comprehensively imbued with a Hobbesian vision of the world, indeed perhaps is incapable of comprehending the contractarian promise expounded by Hume, Locke and the young John Stuart Mill.[1]

Although Buchanan does not say so explicitly, there is more than a suggestion in his paper that the natural economist collapses the utility function of the individuals whose behavior he studies into the single argument of expected wealth. Such utility functions are deemed to be maximized consistently, subject to the institutional and budgetary constraints that condition behavior. This view of mankind comes instintively to the mind of the natural economist, quite independently of any training in economics. With it is associated closure against moral precepts, an almost philistine preoccupation with the narrow wealth-maximizing calculus in every aspect of natural economist's perception.

Buchanan is entitled to this definition of the natural economist, and indeed, may well be able to identify examples of this categorization. I shall

---

[1] Of course, a kind of contract may emerge as a retreat from the Hobbesian jungle. Whether or not such a contract is to be regarded as freely negotiated is very debatable. Even citizens of the Soviet Empire in "a sense" contract to remain. The opportunity cost of that decision, however, approaches infinity.

suggest in this chapter, however, that Gordon Tullock does not satisfy the necessary conditions for membership; indeed that he is the antithesis of the concept as above defined. First, however, it is important to address the question, must a natural economist be *homo oeconomicus*.

3.2 Must a Natural Economist be *Homo Oeconomicus?*

The natural economist, as defined by Buchanan, views all individuals in society as endlessly self-seeking in the normal wealth-maximizing sense of that term. Must such a person behave in full accordance with his perception of the world? In my view, such an automatic association, which Buchanan does not make, would be predicated upon a false notion of science.

Good science is concerned with understanding and/or predicting the behavior of a relevant system as economically as possible – obtaining a lot from a little. To this end, strong generating assumptions become essential as activating agents for theory. Such generating assumptions need have no relationship to reality, indeed may not even be observable in the real world.[2] They are as relevant as the predictions, derived from the theory woven around them, when tested in the real world. This is the essence of scientific theory in the post-inductive era. There is no reason why those who utilize self-seeking assumptions as the basis for theoretical advancement should be seduced by the assumptions that they employ into adopting an entirely solipsist mode of personal behavior.

Whether or not Gordon Tullock can be classified as a natural economist in his scientific endeavors, he evidently does not qualify as *homo oeconomicus* in the private sphere. In a very real sense, Tullock is a rent recipient in his beloved hobby of public choice.[3] It is a characteristic of true rent recipients that they are free from the compulsive marginal calculus of monetary reward. If necessary, they would work at their discipline in the absence of any economic inducement, consuming scholarship as a sufficient utility reward. As such, they are not susceptible to the discipline of any market in selecting the direction and the pace of their research. This is not a conventional characteristic of *homo oeconomicus*.

Nor is the narrow argument of wealth maximization much evident elsewhere in Tullock's life. How many scholars in public choice have dined – and dined well – at Tullock's table, even if he does ensure that the tax

[2] Certainly, this is the view of Popper, with whom Tullock worked for a period of six months, and who greatly influenced his approach to inquiry (Tullock, 1966).

[3] Interestingly, his personal wealth is a direct result of an act of altruism. Tullock bailed out an ailing company to assist his family, taking stock in the corporation. The corporation survived and became unexpectedly successful.

receipts of government are not too generously high. How many visitors to The Center for Study of Public Choice have diverted Tullock from his writings, drawing unashamedly from his intellect and his wit, revelling in his kindness and almost unfailing good cheer. These are not qualities in general that manifest themselves in *homo oeconomicus* operating at the edge of the jungle. If "Tullock's Law" is indeed correct, the maestro himself gives a very sizeable 5 per cent contribution to altruism out of his immense total contribution to public choice.

3.3 Should the *Homo Oeconomicus* Assumption be Limitlessly Employed?

George Stigler once suggested that a major difference between his own scholarship and the scholarship of Friedman was that whereas Friedman sought to change the world, he (Stigler) sought merely to understand it. Stigler's judgment of himself is also completely true of Tullock, though, like Stigler, this does not imply that Tullock himself, or indeed his scholarship, is policy-neutral. Because a scholar chooses to dedicate his scientific efforts to positive analysis, this does not imply that he is careless concerning the nature of the world in which he lives. He is not a policy-eunuch, just because he explores rather than seeks explicitly to shift or to consolidate the nature of his universe.[4]

Precisely because Tullock seeks to understand – even when what he learns is deeply unappetizing – he adopts no subterfuge in his analytical approach. Not for him the artifact of the veil of ignorance; or the allegory of the jungle as a forcer of consent; or reliance upon worst-case scenarios as a justification for institutional reform. If consent exists, it is noted and its rationale is explored. If conflict is manifest, the social dilemma is investigated to the extent possible with the tools of neoclassical economics. Dictatorships as well as democracies are evaluated from the same perspectives of positive public choice.[5] No judgment is passed, no policy recommendations proffered. It is all part of the pattern of a diverse universe that Tullock is eager to explore.

If *homo oeconomicus* assumptions help to explain reality, Tullock will employ them, be it in the field of public choice, or more widely on such topics as the economics of sex and marriage, or even of death (the "right way to go" implying equal marginal damage to all organs of the body).[6]

---

[4] The tendency to identify scholars' attitudes to life by their approach to scholarship is in large part the consequence of immaturity within the academy. In no other walk of life is such an association so quickly made.

[5] See Tullock (1987).

[6] See McKenzie and Tullock 1975, chapter 10.

Self-interest is not obnoxious, nor is it desirable, in Tullock's view. It is just an interesting and prevalent facet of the world in which he lives. In allowing 5 per cent altruism in "Tullock's Law", Tullock is not passing any moral judgment on individuals in society. He has simply observed the success and failure of private charity, has watched the offerings tray make its way down the aisles at Sunday Church.

Should arguments other than *homo oeconomicus* offer a useful mirror on the world – as for instance he suggests may be the case in analyzing wealth distribution – Tullock employs them, publishes articles in Public Choice pursuing such alternative generating assumptions. Who knows, he might even feel comfortable to discover that there are like-minded rent recipients in his world.

3.4 Has *Homo Oeconomicus* Led Tullock Far Astray?

Tullock is a pioneer, as his curriculum vitae (Appendix) clearly indicates. He works almost exclusively at the frontiers rather than within the civilized terrain of extant knowledge. Frontiers tend to be dangerous places to inhabit, which explains why the faint-hearted are there, if at all, only by chance. Has Tullock's systematic application of the self-seeking axiom led him far astray in this most decisive test? It is my view that he has been remarkably sure-footed in his journeys into the unknown, and that his forays have opened up new and fruitful avenues of research to a less adventurous public choice profession.

Tullock's first application of the *homo oeconomicus* axiom was to the politics of bureaucracy (Tullock, 1965), where he turned the existing literature on its head, exploring the internal organization of a bureaucracy via the assumption that all individuals pursued self-seeking objectives. Tullock, like Downs (1967) ignored the interaction between a bureau and its outside environment, thus missing a crucial link between bureaucracy and representative government. This gap was filled by Tullock's student, Niskanen (1971) and the modern theory of bureaucracy thus was born.

His second initiative, arguably his most important, came with the application of *homo oeconomicus* to the political market place, both at the constitutional and at the sub-constitutional levels. From the self-seeking axiom came chapter 6 of *The Calculus of Consent* (1969), arguably the most optimistic contribution so far to the science of public choice (see chapter 5). From the same axiom came the insights into logrolling, and the ability of a polity to reflect preference intensities, which was to spawn such a vast literature in positive public choice.

Later contributions were to flood into a torrent as the application of the self-seeking postulate to wealth redistribution (1983), to rent-seeking

(1967), to the vote motive (1962), to the law and legal institutions (1971), to the social dilemma (1974), to dictatorships and monarchies (1987), to inheritance (1974) and to theft (1974), opened up new areas of fertile research.

Yet in all these areas, Tullock failed to reap the full reward, found himself consistently outflanked by "fast seconds" who stole the glory of his rightful crown. To explain this paradox, it is necessary to reflect on the major methodological differences which simultaneously have set Tullock free and yet have encumbered him in his pursuit of original scholarship.

3.5 The Strengths and Weaknesses of a Training in the Law (Rowley, 1981)

Gordon Tullock graduated JD from the University of Chicago in 1947, long before his introduction to the economic analysis of politics. As Goetz argues in chapter 15, this initial training is deeply embedded in the Tullock psyche. It is no accident that he has never really carried over the public choice insight into his evaluations of the law. More centrally, the method of the law, which contrasts so sharply with Popperian logic in scientific analysis, has worked to impede Tullock in his attempts to consolidate upon major initial territorial advances.

Not all economists, by any means, subscribe to Popper's logic of scientific investigation. Many dislike the reliance of this method upon universal statements which may not be observable empirically. Many reject the entire "as-if" approach on the ground that it offers no real explanation of observed events. Some even reject the notion that positive science is concerned about predicting at all, and seek refuge instead in such criteria as realism of assumptions, elegance, generality or even mathematical complexity. At least, however, all of them have been trained in the Popperian tradition, and are aware of its widespread appeal not just in economics but in science writ large. How much more bewildering, therefore, is the logic of this approach for lawyers without any training in science as part of their program of professional studies.

In several important respects, the analytical approach of lawyers is sharply at odds with that of Popper.[7] Firstly, and most important, much of the analytical, positive study of the law is inductive rather than deductive in nature.[8] Lawyers search for the universal "truth" of the law by a careful selection of a number of singular statements encompassed in the judgments

---

[7] On this difference, see Rowley (1981).

[8] In a telling chapter on the problem of induction, Tullock (1966) skirts around the issue, viz. p. 107: "scientists go happily along engaging in what they call induction in spite of Hume's destruction of the possibility of logical progression from the particular to the general."

of the courts. Such is the thrust of precedent in the common law. But this movement from singular to universal statements is anathema to the deductive tradition which almost all economists employ. Secondly, in pursuit of the inductive approach, most lawyers move from observation of the facts to the derivation of theory, once again directly breaching the approach of Popper.[9] Thirdly, lawyers for the most part are not enamoured of the formal model-building approach of economics, and especially with the generalizations that economists derive from such models. Concerned as they are with the detailed facts surrounding a particular case, and with the precise formal arguments that encapsulate specific judgments, they see precious little scope for general theory. Finally, lawyers are not accustomed to evaluating partial relationships on *ceteris paribus* terms, since for the most part each case requires a total judgment in which all aspects of the relevant environment are sifted and evaluated. By training, they become suspicious when confronted with the *ceteris paribus* conditioning clauses of the typical economic model.

The methods of the law have not worked entirely to the disadvantage of Tullock. In a sense they have cut him loose from rigid rules which have canalized so many economists into normal research.[10] Tullock has a keen eye trained to observe the unusual in political markets and an imagination capable of welding such observations into theory. Until recently he has shown little stomach for detailed empirical work. Poor science his approach may be, but it is well fitted for entrepreneurship. No strict Popperian could ever have opened up so many original insights in a single lifetime, have so stimulated the development of an important new discipline.

Even for Tullock, however, free lunches do not exist. The price of such entrepreneurship has been a systematic loss of title to his own ideas. Followers have tracked his footsteps, have filled in the missing pieces in the logic of scientific discovery.[11] For the most part, they have seized his titles, each in a specific area, denying Tullock the full return on his initiatives. Yet, without Tullock, they would have been lost, without ideas and devoid of insight.

3.6 Conclusions

James Buchanan concludes that Tullock is a natural economist aware

---

[9] Again, read Tullock (1966, p. 120): "that we do put at least some reliance on directly perceived patterns, in the absence of contrary evidence, is obvious to anyone who takes the trouble to examine carefully his own thought patterns."

[10] Not surprisingly, many economists identify early in their careers with Adam Smith's pin factory. We can all recognize the economist now working on his fiftieth contribution to the economic valuation of human life; or on his centenary contribution to the new classical economics; even on his bicentennial team production paper. Tullock is not of that kind, as his scholarship indicates. Conversation at his dinner table does not die after fifteen minutes.

[11] Perhaps the best such example is the rent-seeking insight, discovered by Tullock in 1967, rediscovered and claimed by Krueger (1974) and Posner (1975).

without formal training of the power of the self-interest axiom in offering insights into human behavior. Certainly, he is correct concerning the limits on Tullock's formal training in economics, which comprises little more than a one-semester course at the feet of Henry Simons. However, for a mind as razor keen as Tullock's, operative almost on a 24 hour time-clock, formal training is unimportant, a minor facet of the self-education process.[12]

In my view, Tullock's mind has embraced the methodology of Popper, with the self-interest axiom an essential generating assumption. His heart still retains the method of the law with consequences above-outlined. The tension between the two methods has been highly productive for public choice, if not for Tullock's own reward. Of one thing, I am quite clear. Homunculus, (little man) Tullock could never be. His rightful claim is much closer to that of one of two jewels in the crown of public choice.[13]

References

Buchanan, J.M. (1987) "The qualities of a natural economist", cha. 2 of this book.

Buchanan, J.M. and Tullock, G. (1962) *The Calculus of Consent: Logical Foundations of a Constitutional Democracy*. Ann Arbor: University of Michigan Press.

Downs, A. (1967) *Inside Bureaucracy*. Boston: Little, Brown.

Niskanen, W.A. (1971) *Bureaucracy and Representative Government*. Chicago: Aldine-Atherton.

Popper, K. (1959) *The Logic of Scientific Discovery*. New York.

Rowley, C.K. (1981) "Social sciences and law: the relevance of economic theories", *Oxford Journal of Legal Studies*, I, 3, pp. 391–405.

Tullock, G. (1965) *The Politics of Bureaucracy*. Washington, DC.: Public Affairs Press.

Tullock, G. (1967) "The welfare economics of tariffs, monopoly and theft", *Western Economic Journal*, 5 June, pp. 224–32.

Tullock, G. (1971) *The Logic of the Law*. New York: Basic Books.

Tullock, G. (1974) *The Social Dilemma: The Economics of War and Revolution*. Blacksburg,: VA Center for Study of Public Choice.

Tullock, G. (1974) "Does punishment deter crime?", *The Public Interest*, 36, Summer, pp. 103–11.

Tullock, G. (1975) *The New World of Economics: Explorations into the Human Experience* (with R. McKenzie), Homewood, Illi. Irwin.

Tullock, G. (1983) *The Economics of Income Redistribution*. Hingham, Mass.; Kluwer-Nijhoff.

Tullock, G. (1987) *Autocracy*. Boston: Martinus Nijhoff.

Tullock, G. (1987) "The organization of inquiry", *University Press of America*, (2nd ed).

---

[12] Again, it is a fallacy of the academy that formal training and certificates are necessary testaments to knowledge. In this case, perhaps rent-seeking rather than naivety drive the fallacy.

[13] Buchanan, of course, is the other jewel.

4

Gordon Tullock as Rhetorical Economist

RICHARD E. WAGNER

4.1 Introduction

My first reaction when I was asked to write a brief essay about methodology and Gordon Tullock was to submit one blank page. So far as I know, Tullock has not written anything about economic method, nor has he shown any interest in questions of method. And had Tullock ever been inclined to enter into methodological discourse, I think it is likely he would have done so on the side of anti-methodology, as illustrated by Paul Feyerabend's *Against Method*, and for reasons quite similar to those that inform Feyerabend's work.

I suspect discussions about method seem at their best to be a waste of time to Tullock, because they divert people's energies away from working on the vast range of substantive questions that interest him and channel those energies into the unproductive labor of thinking about doing research rather than actually doing it. Tullock, I am sure, would much rather engage in economic scholarship than simply to talk about doing so. Moreover, I also suspect Tullock would recognize that there is a tyranny in methodological pronouncement, with its pretention to lay down rules for the conduct of scholary inquiry and discourse, that conflicts with his own willingness to leave open the processes of discovery. Tullock is always eager to engage in examination of a vast range of substantive questions, and would doubtless think that efforts to limit via methodological fiat the forms that inquiry takes represents, like central economic planning, an inefficient approach to inquiry.

The only hesitation I would have in classifying Tullock as an anti-methodologist is that I think his reluctance to engage in laying down rules for the conduct of scholarly inquiry would extend to methodological discourse as well. The Japanese saying that "many paths lead to the top of Mt Fuji", would, I think, capture Tullock's reluctance to ban any approach to inquiry. Tullock is surely the very epitomie of what Donald McCloskey (1983, 1985) describes as a rhetorical economist, where rhetorical is taken in its classical sense of meaning the art of persuasive argument, and not in the contemporary sense of bombast or flourish. While McCloskey argues that economists generally operate rhetorically, despite their official methodological strictures to the contrary, Tullock's vision of his work has never been clouded by such official methodology. Perhaps this is due to his initial training in the law, where the approach to inquiry is avowedly rhetorical. Tullock is an incisive, imaginative scholar with catholic interests, who is always eager to engage in a disciplined conversation with all willing participants. Tullock's view of appropriate method for economics (and for science in general) is, in my judgment, one of anarchical or polycentric rhetoric, with rhetoric understood as disciplined conversation and not as the airy cuteness captured by the phrase "mere rhetoric".

4.2   Methodology: between Tyranny and Futility?

To my knowledge, the closest Tullock has come to writing on matters methodological is in his book *The Organization of Inquiry* (1966), particularly chapter 3, entitled "The Subject and Methods of Inquiry". But even this chapter, which is devoted mainly to trying to distinguish between science and other types of inquiry, discusses method only in the concluding three paragraphs. And those three paragraphs merely note that "the relationship between the facts and the theories is a complex one" (1966, p. 65), and that "the method by which we reach our hypothesis is less important than the question of whether the hypothesis is true" (1966, p. 66). Earlier, Tullock seems almost to deny any sense to excursions into questions of method when he notes:

In practice, scientists do not have any great difficulty in differentiating between scientific and non-scientific methods, but the use of this fact to differentiate science from non-science would introduce a hopeless circularity. Scientific methods are simply those methods thought suitable by members of the scientific community (1966, pp. 10–11).

Tullock clearly acknowledges the value of what are commonly called "research tools": theoretical models, statistical methods, logical principles, historical awareness, and the like. But those tools do not constitute a method of inquiry, they are only instruments for inquiry. The methodological enterprise purports to lay down rules as to how those instruments must or must not be used in the conduct of inquiry, and Tullock, to his credit, has not tried to participate as a methodological legislator. Indeed, he has even argued in chapter 3 of *The Organization of Inquiry* that science cannot on methodological grounds be distinguished from such other activities as deciding where to locate a store, constructing an advertisement for toothpaste, or preparing a brief for a client. In each of these cases someone is trying to gather knowledge about a pertinent reality. There is no difference of method across types of inquiry; what distinguishes science from other types of inquiry, all of which use the same methods, is the existence of a scientific community, the social organization of which is the focal point of *The Organization of Inquiry*.

Tullock's silence on matters of methodology, in the light of his unbridled exuberance inquiring into a massive array of substantive questions, is consistent with the thesis that he sees no value to methodological self-consciousness and the legislative attitude that such self-consciousness breeds. People will engage in disciplined conversation by the methods they deem appropriate, regardless of whatever strictures or exhortations some self-appointed methodological guardian might postulate. But rules postulated *ex cathedra* by a cadre of methodologists are worse than futile, for they would, to the extent people try to adhere to such rules, also impose a centrally-directed tyranny upon what should, for the sake of efficient inquiry, be a polycentric process of inquiry. Tullock does not care to tell people how they should go about deciding they have learned something, nor does he want anyone to tell him how he should reach such decisions. Such tyranny reduces the efficiency of inquiry.

Moreover, once it is recognized that much knowledge is tacit and not explicit, as explained by Polanyi (1962), it is impossible for someone to make fully explicit a procedure for acquiring knowledge. As Polayni explains, we know much more than we can make explicit and, hence, convey to someone else. Moreover, even in conveying explicit knowledge we make use of tacit knowledge, which means that the explicit knowledge we do convey is necessarily incomplete. It is impossible to explain fully how we come to decide we know something, and any effort to legislate rules for acquiring knowledge will be incomplete and misleading. Tullock's *Organization of Inquiry* and Polanyi's *Logic of Liberty* clearly reveal kindred spirits at work, and with respect to the conduct of scholarly inquiry, the central thrust is that the necessity to gain an audience, which can only be done voluntarily within a polycentric system of inquiry, is the most efficient discipline on the construction of reasoned argumentation.

4.3 Glimpses of Tullock's Economic Conversation

Scientific inquiry is a social process of conversation, in which people are participating in a process of persuasive reasoning in which they are trying to communicate what they believe to be true to others who are interested in the same subject. There are many ways this process of communication might proceed, but in any event it will involve a conversational process of exchanging ideas and arguments. Tullock's own argumentation makes use of nearly the full gamut of rhetorical instruments that McCloskey describes in his examination of the essentially rhetorical character of economic inquiry. In particular, Tullock makes much use of analogy, metaphor, thought-experiment, introspection, and historical precedent. His efforts at persuasive argumentation revolve around efforts to show that by virtue of the reader's prior belief, what Tullock has found out fits comfortably within that structure of belief. It is perhaps noteworthy for Tullock's rhetoric that he was not trained as an economist, and so was not exposed to the contamination of methodological postulation, but rather was trained in the law, where the full emphasis, as Edward Levi (1974) notes, is upon the construction of persuasive argument.

In the rest of this section I shall describe a few illustrations of Tullock's economic conversation, following McCloskey's analytical framework. McCloskey, quoting Wayne Booth, notes that rhetoric is the "art of probing what men believe they ought to believe, rather than proving what is true according to abstract methods" (1983, p. 482). Tullock is fully engaged in probing such probable arguments; he sensibly recognizes the impossibility of demonstrating indubitable knowledge. He is engaged in bringing such research tools as theoretical models, statistical evidence, and historical awareness to bear upon the construction of persuasive reasoning, and without letting that reasoning process be limited or contaminated by methodological postulation. My objective in setting forth the following illustrations is not to argue that Tullock is always correct – though I happen to think he is in all but one of them, and with respect to the exception, I do not so much think he is wrong, but find the case which he presents unconvincing. Rather my point is only to illustrate that Tullock's approach to economic inquiry fits comfortably within McCloskey's portrait of the economist as rhetorician.

Introspection or *verstehen* is central to Tullock's economic conversation. In his 1965 book *The Politics of Bureaucracy*, he closes his opening chapter with a four-paragraph section labeled "Methodology". These paragraphs most certainly do not lay down rules that should be followed, but instead note that "instead of presenting concrete evidence" Tullock will in many cases "try to convince the skeptical reader by appealing to his own intuition and experience" (1965, p. 15). The array of arguments Tullock subsequently develops are largely crafted in a form to be sensible to people who have had experience in bureaucratic organizations. The maneuvering, the back-biting, and the politicking that are common conversational topics to people who have worked in bureaucratic organizations are used by Tullock to support such arguments as the presence of an organizational bias against morality (p.

23), the strong thrust toward conformity (p. 41), and the upward rise of dull people (p. 75).

Tullock argues in *The Politics of Bureaucracy*, that "department store managers are on the whole much more honest in dealing with their customers than are politicians" (1965, p. 93). The argument proceeds metaphorically by comparing a politician to the manager of a department store: "A politician who considers entering an election is in somewhat the same position as a manager of a department store. He seeks to attract a very large clientele and hence must have a diversified stock in trade" (1965, p. 92). Tullock qualifies the comparison with "somewhat", but the subsequent thrust of his argument is to de-emphasize the differentia the qualifier implies, thereby leading to the argument, grounded largely in introspection and personal, historical observation, that politicians stick to their promises less fully than department store managers, because both legal liability and the need continually to attract patronage places a stronger penalty upon department store managers who violate their promises than it places upon politicians.

The argument in one of Tullock's (1967) most successful papers that initiated what has since swelled into the literature on rent-seeking was predominately an exercise in the use of metaphor. That paper challenged the thesis inspired by Arnold Harberger (1959) that the welfare losses from monopolies and tariffs were quite small, and it did so through the cultivation of telling metaphors and analogies. The predominant effect of monopolies and tariffs in the analysis that Tullock was challenging was a transfer of income away from consumers toward resource owners. In constructing his argument, Tullock first compared a tariff to an excise tax of the same magnitude. In this case the triangular measure of welfare loss would be unaffected, and would be presumptively small. Next, the tariff was regarded as equivalent to an excise tax, in which case the predominant effect would once again be the transfer of income from taxpayers to the Government.

But, Tullock then asked, what if the Government wasted its revenues, as in "building tunnels which go nowhere" (1967, p. 225)? The obvious and inescapable response is that the transfer rectangle also becomes a component of welfare loss. And in further exploring the analogies between this form of wasteful tax with tariffs, with governmental requirements that a domestic industry substitute inefficient for efficient methods of production, and with theft, Tullock engaged in persuasive argument with his colleagues that previous concepts of inefficiency were not adequate for their subject, and the theory of rent-seeking was born.

The loss of information in hierarchical organizations and the problems of designing incentives to provide control, was developed by Tullock through analogical reasoning in *The Politics of Bureaucracy*. Tullock began in chapter 14 by developing an analogy between the loss of information in hierarchical organizations and a simple exercise once upon a time performed in the American Army – an exercise that even those who had not done it could relate to. The exercise involved placing a group of soldiers in the middle of a circle of soldiers, with the soldiers on the perimeter being out of earshot of one another. The message was read to the soldiers in the middle, one of whom then delivered it to a soldier on the perimeter, who in turn passed it on to the next soldier on the perimeter, with the process continuing until the last soldier on the perimeter returned to the center of the circle to relay the message to the soldiers standing there. "There was normally little resemblance between the message after it had completed its circuit and the original text (1965, p. 137), Tullock declared. No statistics were given to support his declaration, but rare would be the readers who had had no related experience with rumors later proven to be wildly inaccurate, and the thought-experiment combined with introspection surely made the story highly credible.

In the remainder of chapter 14 Tullock explored the analogy between the passage of information around the circle of soldiers and the passage of information up and down an organizational hierarchy. In conducting this exploration, Tullock notes that there are differences between the army experiment and ordinary organizations. For instance, had the message been written and passed from soldier to soldier, it would have arrived at its destination in the same form it had left. But even if organizations pass only written information, the distortion illustrated by the army experiment will arise because messages must be condensed and rewritten as they move up the hierarchy. This condensing and rewriting of messages in organizations generates the same problem of information loss that the army experiment illustrates.

From this analogy between two processes of information loss, Tullock developed the inference that it would be impossible for organizations to function in this hierarchical manner. To be able to function, such organizations would have to have decisions being made at various levels in the organization and not just at the top. Such a conclusion would surely seem inescapable, as well as congruent with experience, to those who had followed Tullock's preceding analogy. But once this conclusion is accepted, it is necessary to admit that the quality of organizational decisions will depend on the character of the decisions made by people throughout the organization – an admission that in turn leads one, willing or not, into the examination of incentives within organizations. As Tullock notes: "The head of a hierarchy has as his principal problem in organizational efficiency, arranging the structure so that his inferiors reach decisions which he would have reached if he should have possessed as much information about the particular situation requiring decision as they do" (1965, p. 141).

Chapters 15–17 extend this basic conclusion about organizational performance to a further consideration of the loss of information in organizations and of different ways of dealing with that. Tullock is always engaged in probable argument about reality, and runs no danger of the reification of models that is so common in economics. Historical illustration abounds in his work. For instance, in his consideration of ways of combatting information loss in organizations, Tullock explains that the use of an executive office actually worsens the problem of hierarchical control by adding one more level to the process of filtering information, thereby distorting information still further (1965, pp. 144–6). An organization that pursues efficiency will not have an executive officer, but an executive officer can be valuable to an organization where the head wishes to substitute leisure for work. Hence Tullock notes that "Louis XIV ruled successfully without a Prime Minister. When his less energetic and talented successor tried the same method, the result was administrative chaos. Louis XV was neither willing nor able to give his cabinet adequate supervision" (1965, p. 145).

Tullock (1975) argues that the court system employed on the European continent, the inquisitorial system, is more efficient than the court system employed in the Anglo-Saxon nations, the adversary system. An important aspect of his argument is that he develops the idea that the adversary system is analogous to an arms race. He fortifies this analogy by pointing out that the adversary system "descends from trial by battle in which the government official present at the trial simply refereed the contest" (1975, p. 746). Each party to a suit can increase its likelihood of success by increasing its investment in litigation, given the investment by the other party, just as each party to a potential conflict can increase its security by increasing its arms expenditure. In the case of the arms race, the same degree of security could be secured by a lower expenditure on arms, if only the parties could reach such an agreement and feel confident about its maintenance. In similar fashion, the parties to a suit could achieve the same outcome, defined in terms of their comparative likelihoods of success, with less expenditure, if only they could conclude the judicial equivalent of an arms-limitation treaty. The inquisitorial system, Tullock argued, offers a means of concluding such a treaty.

4.4 Realism, Nominalism, and Economic Imperialism

Tullock (1972) presents a defense of economic imperialism, or the tendency of economists to apply their modes of reasoning to a wide variety of phenomena not customarily considered to be economic in nature. Tullock himself is one of the premier economic imperialists of our time. In terms of the organization of universities, his publications relate to matters treated by departments of political science, public administration, biology, philosophy, sociology, history, and military science. His publications also contribute to matters of interest to faculties in schools of law and criminology, as well as to faculties associated with interdisciplinary programs in international relations and Asiatic studies. All of this is in addition to his contributions to fields more narrowly economic. Someone writing a survey of Tullock's works would surely think he was surveying the work of the faculty of a small university.

It is an understatement to note that this economic imperialism has been greeted with less than universal glee. And Tullock himself is doubtless sometimes to blame, as when he becomes so enraptured with the charm of symmetrical argumentation that he (McKenzie and Tullock, 1978 chapter 10) makes such observations as: the person who dies of a heart attack but has a sound liver has not lived right, and perhaps should have drank more, because an efficient style of living would have all organs giving out at the same time. As a matter of the logic of the efficient allocation of maintenance expenditures to the capital equipment that the human organism represents, Tullock is right, but in this, and a few other instances he seems to be perhaps not so much a rhetorical economist as an economist engaged in mere rhetoric. To many economists such writings perhaps seem, correctly in my judgment, as expressions of whimsy and playfulness. But I also suspect that to the many non-economists to whom Tullock has much to offer, but who are often reluctant to listen, such efforts are seen as further evidence of the menace presented by their disciplinary neighbour.

Much of the opposition to economic imperialism reflects the argument that the economic model of human conduct is insufficiently rich to accommodate the range of that conduct that such imperialists as Tullock seek to examine. Tullock's writings on politics, crime, and revolution, for instance, have the same cast of people found in his writings on more conventional economic topics. Politics is a business, crime is a labor-supply choice, and revolution is an investment. With respect to understanding the structure of individual choice in activities such as these, a cost-and-gain calculus of rational conduct is fully appropriate, for to deny this would be to consign such conduct to the realm of inexplicability. Murder and rape, for instance, are often referred to as "crimes of passion", to imply the inadequacy of reasoning grounded in rationality. Yet murder and rape do not occur on Fifth Avenue in the middle of Macey's Thanksgiving parade. That they occur instead on side streets, at night, and under general conditions of stealth is fully consistent with the premise that murders and rapists seek to be effective in what they are doing.

To someone who professes to be a nominalist, this aversion to economic imperialism is perhaps necessary. If all that exists are particulars, there is no universal quality that links business, politics, crime, and revolution. But Tullock is a realist in the Platonic sense that reality represents the form to which existence or actuality conforms. Hence the desire to substitute more desirable for less desirable states is a universal quality of humanity, a quality that finds particular expression in an enormous variety of settings. The revolutionary, the criminal, the politician, and the businessman are all seeking to give up what they value less to get what they value more, and their various concrete activities are understandable as particular manifestations of this universal reality.

Indeed, in his essay on economic imperialism, Tullock proposed to redraw the disciplinary boundaries of the social sciences, with one discipline treating choices and social relationships that thus result, and the other discipline treating the formation of preferences (Tullock, 1972, pp. 321–9). Or as Tullock put the point elsewhere (1965, pp. 27–8), rationality applies to instrumental actions but not to ultimate motivation. People seek to be effective in action, but to say this is to imply nothing about the actual object of action.

One person may paticipate in a revolution or *coup d'etat* because of the upward jump in standard of living it offers: another may do so because of a desire to remove a source of despotic control over people's lives: yet another joins in because it seems like an interesting adventure. Regardless of the reasons that ultimately motivate people, the substitution of more desired for less desired states will be recognizable in all such people. The revolutionary who is interested in adventure will, for instance, be less likely to participate in the revolution as the price of such an alternative adventure as an expedition to climb Mt. Everest declines. The revolutionary who is interested in freeing people from despotic control will be less likely to participate, the greater the ability of the government to monitor his movements and activities. The revolutionary who is interested in increasing his standard of living will be less likely to participate, should his alternative income prospects jump, as perhaps in being granted an exclusive dealership for the sale of certain imported goods.

4.5   Some Final Words

James Buchanan in chapter 2 of this book argues that Gordon Tullock is a "natural economist". Buchanan notes that Tullock has a natural or intuitive understanding of economic reasoning, but laments that Tullock has made little conscious effort to construct his arguments in a manner that conforms to a style that might be called Standard Economic. Tullock's approach to the presentation of economic argument seems generally to lack some of the trappings that characterize Standard Economic writing, as well as being short on obscurity. Tullock's works clearly have a less scholarly appearance than is common for academic works, though it is easy to confound the appearance of scholarship with the substance.

While Tullock's approach to economic argumentation fits fully within the rhetorical mode set out by McCloskey, it is perhaps not surprising that his style of presentation is not a model of Standard Economic. After all, Tullock was not trained in economics – a point that he has often noted. Being trained instead in the law, he undoubtedly saw, right from the start, the importance of engaging in persuasive reasoning through use of the appropriate tools. And having never become involved with the superstition of constructing *indubitable* argument, but being content always to engage in *probable* argument, his scholarship has always had a grounding in reality that in many reaches of economic discourse is viewed as a lack of sophistication through his failure to try to demonstrate what must be or what cannot be.

On several occasions I have used books by Tullock as texts, with the general result that students find his books more interesting than typical texts. His tone is conversational; reading Tullock is much like having him sit across from you. Students seem generally to like Tullock's conversational tone and his extensive use of personal experience as a vehicle for illustrating arguments. Perhaps Tullock's appeal is that he writes as an amateur: he makes no effort to bury his effort at persuasive argument beneath mounds of formal argumentation. And writing as an amateur with substantative interests, he simply seeks to explain why he thinks an inquisitorial system is better than an adversarial system, why the managers of department stores are more honest than politicians, or why organizations with executive officers are not promoting efficiency but are providing for the leisure of the chief executive.

Tullock is also a natural economist in the sense that he pursues his work according to his "natural" interests, without regard to the ordinary incentives that so often guide work within a discipline that has become professionalized. He is less engaged in specialization and is less prone to revert to Standard Economic in the presentation of his arguments. This may well diminish his standing in the profession, though I have no evidence on this point. He is, though, a curious and not an induced scholar, a distinction he explains in *The Organization of Inquiry*, and a distinction that corresponds to Ludwig von Mises" distinction between introversive and extroversive labor (Mises, 1963, pp. 587–8): introversive labor or curious scholarship is undertaken largely for the fun of it, while extroversive labor or induced scholarship is undertaken largely because someone else is willing to offer something else in exchange for it.

With the increasing professionalization of economics, or of any discipline, the practitioners are ever more likely to be induced scholars or extroverted laborers. Tullock, however, is in this regard an amateur or curious scholar who likes to exercise his inquiring mind without regard for professional mores. He is much like a child playing with toys. A child who would specialize in one or even a few toys, and who would meekly follow the manufacturer's suggested instructions regarding usage, is surely a rarity – to say nothing of being a source of parental concern. A child will normally play with one toy until his interest declines sufficiently to make another toy seem more interesting. In the normal course of play a child will play with a wide variety of toys, and in a manner that a realist such as Tullock could offer a formal economic explanation of – though it would be an explanation that would never be confounded with any substantive statement about the content of the child's efforts.

The range of Tullock's curiosity is enormous. Yet he has not turned his curiosity to questions of method. He is willing to listen to all kinds of arguments by people to profess to know something that he would like to know about. Tullock is an exceedingly active participant in the disciplined conversations out of which persuasive argument arises. These conversations make use of the principles of logic, have recourse to statistical and historical evidence, and call upon theoretical models. But they are not encumbered by a methodological baggage that advances falsification over verification, that calls for operationalism, that interposes a radical disjuncture between theory and history, or that engages in any of many other efforts to legislate the boundaries of economic conversation beyond those implied by the principles of logic, statistics, and the like. Gordon Tullock falls fully within the category of rhetorician that McCloskey has described so clearly, and it should be added that he is an extraordinary conversationalist, whose variety of interesting conversations would certainly put to shame many of the occupants of faculty dining rooms throughout the land.

References

Feyerabend, Paul (1978) *Against Method: Outline of an Anarchistic Theory of Knowledge*. London: Verso.

Harberger, Arnold C. (1959). "Using the resources at hand more effectively", *American Economic Review*, Proceedings **49**, May, pp. 134–46.

Levi, Edward (1948) *An Introduction to Legal Reasoning*. Chicago: University of Chicago Press.

McCloskey, Donald N. (1983) "The rhetoric of economics", *Journal of Economic Literature*, **21**, June, pp. 481–517.

McCloskey, Donald N. (1985) *The Rhetoric of Economics*. Madison: University of Wisconsin Press.

McKenzie, Richard B. and Tullock, Gordon. (1968) *The New World of Economics*. Homewood, IU: Irwin.

Mises, Ludwig von (1963) *Human Action* (3rd ed) Chicago: Henry Regnery.

Polanyi, Michael (1951) *The Logic of Liberty*. London: Routledge & Kegan Paul.

Polanyi, Michael (1962) *Personal Knowledge* (rev. edn) London: Routledge & Kegan Paul.

Tullock, Gordon (1965) *The Politics of Bureaucracy*. Washington: Public Affairs Press.

Tullock, Gordon (1966) *The Organization of Inquiry*. Durham, NC: Duke University Press.

Tullock, Gordon (1967) "The welfare costs of tariffs, monopolies, and theft", *Western Economic Journal*, 5 June, pp. 224–32.

Tullock, Gordon (1972) "Economic imperialism", In *Theory of Public Choice*, James M. Buchanan and Robert D. Tollison (eds). Ann Arbor: University of Michigan Press, pp. 317–29.

Tullock, Gordon. (1975) On the efficient organization of trials, *Kyklos*, 28 4, pp. 745–62.

II

The Original Insight

II

The Original Insight

5

The Calculus of Consent
CHARLES K. ROWLEY

5.1 Introduction

The Calculus of Consent (1962) is the jewel in the crown of Virginian Political Economy, its most frequently cited and its best known contribution.[1] More, it is the seminal work in constitutional economics, presenting, as its subtitle presciently suggests, the logical foundations of constitutional democracy. It has also served as a methodological basis for the wider discipline of public choice, delineating contractarianism in individual political exchange as the fulcrum for normative analysis, together with *homo oeconomicus* as a self-seeking generative assumption for the positive analysis of political markets.

The book thus offers an inevitable tension, in a sense between good and evil; between the gains-from-trade available to all participants in a well-functioning constitutional order on the one hand, and the prisoner's dilemma utility losses imposed upon all participants in the unregulated jungle of in-period politics on the other.[2] Man is endlessly and myopically self-seeking in the adverse institutional environment; but is capable of rules selection at a constitutional level on the basis of a much more far-sighted, if yet still solipsist, vision.[3] To read *The Calculus* is, almost inescapably, to become inbued with the earth-moving constitutional perspective which is so skillfully imposed on the conventional approach of analysing the behavior of

---

[1] *The Calculus of Consent* was cited as the most important single contribution by the Alfred Nobel Committee when announcing the award of The Nobel Prize in Economic Science to James M. Buchanan in October 1986.

[2] As I shall suggest later in this chapter, the trade-off relationship changes markedly once Tullock's rent-seeking insight is introduced into the process of constitutional decision-making. For further work on this subject see Rowley (1987).

[3] Buchanan and Tullock do not rule out altruism. However, they do not rely upon it to generate constitutional equilibria. Their emphasis is much more on the reduction in myopia evident in solipsist decision-making in the uncertain environment of constitutional decision-making.

the in-period legislature.[4] Of course there are other books, extremely important and full of insight, that contributed significantly to the early development of the public choice research program. *An Economic Theory of Democracy*, by Anthony Downs (1957), preceded *The Calculus* into print by some five years.[5] *The Logic of Collective Action*, by Mancur Olson (1965) followed hard on the heels of *The Calculus*, again applying economic analysis to the understanding of political market behavior.[6] These texts have earned their places on the roll of honour of public choice. Yet both of these are trapped by an over-emphasis upon in-period politics, like the swan iced into the lake, unable to wing skywards to the constitutional perspective.

This difference is extremely important. The public choice of spatial politics, in the sense of Downs (1959) of interest groups in the sense of Olson (1965), of bureaucracy in the sense of Tullock (1965), Downs (1967), and Niskanen (1971), of rent-seekers, in the sense of Tullock (1967) and Tollison, (1983), of congressional brokering of policies, in the sense of Crain, Tollison and others (1979), in a sense the public choice surveyed by Mueller, so impressively in 1979, is the public choice of the twilight zone. Powerful though the insights of this burgeoning literature undoubtedly are, they are driven by the most pessimistic vision of mankind.[7] So pervasive is the emphasis in this literature on the utility and wealth destruction imposed by self-seeking agents, that few scholars of public choice escape completely untainted by cynicism, if not despair, concerning the prognosis for democracy through the remaining years of the twentieth century.[8]

Of course, the truth must be told, and theories of public choice are only as good as the evidence allows them to be. At the relevant margin, each such theory holds its own. The destructive potential of self-seeking individuals at each margin of the political process is now denied only by the ignorant or by

[4] This was much my own experience. I read *The Calculus of Consent*, belatedly in 1967, on one hot, humid night in a New York apartment, having been thrown to the ground by troubled blacks whilst packing my bag in a take-away restaurant, and following television scenes of Newark in flames as race riots exposed the fallacy of The Great Society Program. At that time, the notion of any calculus of consent in a US seemingly close to political disintegration, seemed an ocean away. I read *The Calculus* and longed for my return to Canterbury, England. It was a fortuitous read.

[5] *An Economic Theory of Democracy* by Downs (1957) was (is) much more popular in England, partly because its emphasis upon parliamentary party competition is much closer to the English, continental Europe experience.

[6] Olson's book, though written by a person of more liberal persuasion, arguably is one of the most conservative contributions in the post-middle years of the twentieth century.

[7] This pessimism is not a consequence of individual's motivation. Solipsism is not necessarily an inefficient motivation, as the invisible hand literature clearly shows. Rather, it is self-seeking in an adverse institutional environment that destroys wealth.

[8] Buchanan (1986) raised a clarion call for scholars to reject dystopia and to pursue avenues toward a constrained utopia. For the most part, pre-occupation with the extant forces of evil persists in the public choice academy.

the fools. Yet, in aggregate, what appears when all the relevant margins are combined, by the thoughtful convert to the public choice approach, is little less than the mathematics of unmitigated misery. Worse still, the cynicism encouraged by this mounting evidence of self-mutilation undoubtedly has imposed generalized Heisenberg principle costs upon society, as political agents eagerly ape the behavior ascribed to them by scholarship. (Gramm, Miller, Johnson, 1986)[9] Small wonder then that Richard Musgrave and others wish to stamp out public choice, rather in the way that Martin Luther desired to burn Papal Bulls and decretals.

Yet, in this developing environment of despair, there remains hope for those who desire to combine wealth-achievement with a political system compatible with liberty. More than hope, there exists evidence that self-mutilation is bounded by the institutions of a free society.[10] Rent-seeking is more pervasive than neoclassical economists earlier conceived. The cost of monopoly and regulation may be some hundred times greater as a percentage of gross national product than Harberger believed, as Cowling and Mueller now suggest.[11] But it has not risen yet by that additional crucial factor of ten. Individuals in the USA save by choice, do not live in caves, painted in wode, feasting on wild berries. There are constraints; and these constraints are man-made. For the most part, they are imposed in constitutional form. The story of how such constraints emerge constitutes the essential message of *The Calculus of Consent*, and it is to a more detailed evaluation of that work which I shall now turn.

5.2 The Calculus of Consent as Team Production

The academic year 1958/9 was a momentous year for political economy, marking the watershed between a "new" welfare economics, in which government was perceived to be the omniscient and impartial servant of the public good, and the more realistic world of "public choice", in which governments as well as markets were perceived to fall short of the demanding standards of Paretian welfare economics. For the year 1958/9

[9] *The Washington Post*, January 1986; in this article, Gramm, Miller and Johnson join in praise of public choice, not because of its scholarly insights, but because of the rent-seeking opportunities that it provided for them respectively in the US Senate, in The Office of Management and Budget and in the Federal Reserve Board. How far distant is this manipulation from the vision of a consent calculus presented a quarter century before. The depiction of these three individuals surrounding a bemused Buchanan and Tullock framed against Capitol Hill somehow perfectly defined the problem of the generalized Heisenberg Principle of which these actors are the living embodiment.

[10] On this, see Buchanan (1986).

[11] See Cowling and Mueller (1978). They claim upper-bound estimates of 13 percent of GNP for the US and of 3 percent for the UK. Their calculations ignore losses due to regulation.

was the year when *The Calculus of Consent* first became a gleam in the eyes of its co-authors, James M. Buchanan and Gordon Tullock.

Gordon Tullock entered the Thomas Jefferson Center for Studies in Political Economy at the University of Virginia in Fall 1958, joining James Buchanan and Warren Nutter who then directed the Center. Buchanan was already distinguished as a reflective and original scholar of public finance, and welfare economics, with four books and many important articles to his credit. Tullock, in contrast, was at thirty-six, more or less unknown to the academy. Despite his anonymity, he brought two important assets to the Center: a brilliant intellect, trained in the law and honed down by real-politik; and an unbounded energy and enthusiasm for his adopted discipline of political economy.

The interaction between the two scholars, the one deep-thinking, reflective, academically mature, and the other quicksilver, discursive, unsure, and yet full of original insight, was dynamite,. Surely one of the more fruitful links in science to be forged at that time. Yet, the intellectual encounter was brief, lasting only through the period 1958–62, from conception to birth of *The Calculus of Consent*. Even this time was to witness lengthy periods of locational separation, since Tullock's fellowship lasted only one year, to be followed by two years of professorships at the University of South Carolina. Buchanan was to spend the academic year 1961/2 as a Fulbright Visiting Professor at Cambridge, England. Moreover, the intellectual relationship was not to renew itself, even when physical separation ceased, in the post-*Calculus* new world. The two scholars were only rarely to engage in team production thereafter; more rarely still in the field of constitutional economics which *The Calculus* had made their own.

In any event, however brief, the link *was* made. The prize, was to be the development of constitutional economics in its unique Virginian perspective; and, eventually, the birth of an important new program of public choice research. Discussions between Buchanan and Tullock took place through the academic year 1958/9, on issues at the interface of economics and politics, and were the basis for many of the specific parts of the final publication. By the year's end, however, plans for any collaborative venture had not emerged.

Tullock, meanwhile, continued his research, completing, in June 1959, a study of logrolling in democratic government which, as chapter 10, was to constitute the first organic component of *The Calculus of Consent*. This paper, with a speed unrecognizable in the 1980s, was published in December 1959 by *The Journal of Political Economy*. In the summer of 1959, Buchanan also prepared an exploratory survey of the field encompassing their joint discussions, entitled "Economic Policy Free Institutions and Democratic Process". This survey paper was presented in 1959 at the meeting in Oxford of the Mont Pelerin Society, and was later published, in 1960, in the Italian journal, Il *Politico*. The first fruits of collaboration had now been garnered.

Thus encouraged, Tullock shifted the research emphasis to the heartland of constitutional economics. The final months of his fellowship were devoted to fundamental research, which he completed following his relocation in South Carolina. The results of this were presented in an unpublished paper, entitled "A Preliminary Investigation of the Theory of Constitutions". In all essentials, this paper outlined the basic model of constitutional economics, and in revised form, became chaper 6 of *The Calculus of Consent*. It is widely regarded as the most important chapter of that book, etching out the trade-off diagram between external cost and cost of decision-making in rules selection which forms the contract basis for constitutions.

The final decision to collaborate in a joint project was made in September 1959; and the book was written for the most part, during the academic year 1959–60. Insofar as separation of marginal products is possible, Tullock was primarily responsible for: chapter 6, which introduces the constitutional model, which evaluates the nature and magnitude of decision-making costs in constitutional choice; for chapter 10, which evaluates the nature of logrolling and its implications for the operation of the simple majority vote rule; and for chapter 16, which applies the central constitutional model to the bicameral legislature and, briefly, to the separation of powers.

Buchanan was primarily responsible for: chapter 5, which defines a methodological individualist approach to the issue of constitutional design; for chapter 7, which emphasizes the unique position occupied by the Wicksellian unanimity rule in democratic theory; for chapter 11, which analyzes simple majority voting within a game-theoretic framework; and for chapters 12 and 13 which evaluate constitutional choice and specific voting rules from the demanding perspective of theoretical welfare economics.

Fundamentally, however, even this limited separation of marginal products is misleading in the evaluation of a scholarship which is quin-tessentially the outcome of team production. "Team production" is defined by Alchian and Demsetz (1972) as production in which several types of resources are used, the product is not a sum of separable outputs of each cooperating resource and where not all the resources utilized belong to one person. Team production, if such indeed was the case with *The Calculus* (*C*), requires a cross partial derivative of output in relation to the two inputs, X_B and X_T of the form

$$\frac{\partial^2 C}{\partial X_B \partial X_T} > 0$$

in which case, the marginal products of Buchanan and of Tullock are not susceptible of a separate evaluation.

The non-separable nature of the production function that gave birth to *The Calculus of Consent* is strong rather than weak in form, as the following evidence undeniably confirms. First, let us look at the work of the collaborators, prior to the publication of the book. Buchanan's extensive publications offer little sign of what was about to emerge. His books, revolutionary though they were in that era of Keynesian constructivist rationalist excess, nevertheless, were orthodox in their radicalism, reflective of welfare economics in its unreconstructed form, rather than of any serious latent notions of public choice.[12]

His work on federalism and fiscal equity (1950) was a good decade before its time, and indeed touched on the political viability of specific transfer systems; but for the most part it was well within the conventional public finance tradition. His work on marginal cost-pricing was reflective of Wicksell's unanimity principle (1951); but devoid of any interest in the distinction between constitutional and sub-constitutional decision-making. His work on individual choice in voting and in the market (1954) was closer, but still locked in to the conventional political market approach. His important paper on positive economics, welfare economics and political economy (1959) was reflective of an universal consent imperative in specific in-period collective actions. Throughout, both the constitutional economics and the public choice sparks are absent. From 1960 onwards, his work demonstrates a categorical shift of thrust. A "Weltanschaaung" evidently had taken place, and the constitutional economics perspective, thereafter, haunts his many important contributions to the Virginia Political Economy research program.

Tullock's academic life had, of course, been much shorter than Buchanan's and thus is easier to evaluate. He came to Charlottesville with just four papers published, all of them connected with his experiences of paper money, inflation and hyper-inflation whilst employed in the Foreign Service in China and Korea. Remarkably, for a non-economist, two of those papers were in the *American Economic Review* and one in the *Journal of Political Economy*. The only real sign of Tullock's interest in political economy was a typescript on bureaucracy which was not to hit the printing press for another seven years.

His work on constitutional economics in *The Calculus of Consent* – and he was primarily responsible for the basic constitutional model – in retrospect seems to have been something of an aberration in the Tullock approach to public choice. His later contributions are directed much more frequently to issues in majority voting, logrolling, stability in political markets, and the pursuit of *homo oeconomicus* in all his political market activities. When Tullock lifts his eyes to the constitutional level, he does not always see

---

[12] See, for example, Buchanan, 1958.

contract curves etched across the Edgworth – Bowley box; upon occasion, he sees a Brennan box[13] where the contract curve runs the other way as the actors seek utility via wealth destruction motivated by mutual envy and malevolence. Buchanan's vision is that of contractarian solutions to problems of government failure; his world is that of Hume and Locke and the young John Stuart Mill. Tullock's vision is that of tanks and guns; his natural world is that of Thomas Hobbes; of dictatorship and *coup d'etat*, rather than of constitutional contract in democracy.

The conjunction of the two minds with their different experiences and ideas was fortuitous, and the evidence is powerful in its support of the joint-product hypothesis. Neither author, before or after *The Calculus*, was able to bridge so effectively the apparent abyss that separates the catallactics of exchange from *homo oeconomicus* in political market analysis. Indeed, it is a remarkable testament to the strength of the authors' relationship that the basic constitutional model was drafted not by Buchanan, for all his normative, contractarian thrust, but by Tullock, who is much better known for his fascination with *homo oeconomicus* as a generating assumption in positive analysis.

Hermeneutical evidence futher supports the team production hypothesis, both at the time of writing the book and in a later perspective. Thus, in the preface to the book, the authors write:

In the most fundamental sense, the whole book is a genuinely joint product. The chapters have been jointly, not severally, written. We believe that the argument is co-ordinated and consistent, one part with the other. We hope that readers will agree. To some extent this co-ordination results from the rather fortunate compatibility of ideas that have been separately developed, at least in their initial, preliminary stages.

Some 21 years later, Buchanan was to reaffirm this judgment in his important paper: "The Public Choice Perspective" (1986):

I look on *The Calculus of Consent* as the first contribution in modern public choice theory that combined and balanced the two critical elements or aspects of the inclusive perspective. This combination might well not have occurred but for the somewhat differing weights that Gordon Tullock and I brought to our joint venture in that book. I think it is accurate to say that my own emphasis was on modelling politics-as-exchange, under the acknowledged major influence of Knut Wicksell's great work in public finance. By comparison (and interestingly because he was not initially trained as an economist), Gordon Tullock's emphasis (stemming from his own experience in, and his reflections about, the bureaucracy) was on modelling all public choosers voters, politicians, bureaucrats) in strict self-interest terms. There

---

[13] See Brennan (1973) for a forceful representation of potential wealth destruction in an economy characterized by widespread malevolence and envy.

was a tension present as we worked through the analysis of that book, but a tension that has indeed served us well over the two decades since initial publication.

5.3 The Environment and its Reactions

The Calculus of Consent was written during the dying years of the second Eisenhower administration. The world, more or less, was at peace, with Europe by then inevitably divided, the Korean War forgotten, and Vietnam an unknown dot on the map of Indo-China. The late 1950s was a period of optimism concerning Western political systems. Eisenhower himself was a popular president, his relationships with Congress cordial. Budgets balanced and continuing economic growth oiled the edges of redistributive politics. In France, the chaos of the Fourth Republic was over, with de Gaulle a popular President of an essential autocracy. In Britain, post-Suez consensus government had emerged under the non-divisive leadership of Harold Macmillan. The Common Market augured well for the integration of Western Europe. It was not hard, in such an environment, to be inspired by a contractarian vision of democratic politics.

The Calculus of Consent was published in 1962, when this image of Arcadia was still widespread in the Western World. Kennedy was president; indeed, was all but king. Keynesian demand management had reached its zenith,[14] but its costly aftermath was not yet perceived. The democrats in the academy and in government believed that Camelot had come; that constructivist rationalism would rule under a Rousseau-type social contract. Surely *The Calculus of Consent* would be welcomed, its message endorsed and implemented, in this apparently favorable environment?

Such a judgment could be recorded only by a profound misinterpretation of the essential message of that book, as later analysis will confirm. For the *Calculus* was grounded on methodological individualism;[15] its social contract was the catallactics of exchange.[16] Its emphasis on *homo oeconomicus* active in in-period political markets could not be squared with the concept of Platonic politics then widespread in the social sciences.[17] The message of the *Calculus* was death to constructivist rationalism and destructive of the Rousseau social contract vision. It is remarkable, therefore, that potential

---

[14] As evidenced by the pressure in favor of tax cuts to counteract a limited recession despite adverse budgetary implications. Samuelson acted as Merlin to King Arthur's Court in this regard, with little attention to the rise of Mordred, in the guise of congressional discretionary power as Victorian budget constraints were cut by Excaliber.

[15] The notion that only individuals count, that there is no organic state or independent notion of the social good or bad other than that contemplated in the individual psyche.

[16] Catallaxy, which has its origins in early Austrian economics, emphasizes the origins, properties and institutions of an exchange economy.

[17] Or with rising emphasis upon redistributive politics evident in the late 1950 democracies.

reviewers did not emerge to destroy the book that threatened so much of their human capital. Perhaps they did not perceive the threat; or perhaps they underestimated the danger; or, more likely, they were honest men operating on that 5 per cent of altruism that Tullock allows at the margin of self-interest. In any event, Buchanan and Tullock were fortunate that their reviewers, for the most part, were well-disposed to their approach.

Let us remind ourselves of the intellectual climate in 1962 by referencing contemporary writings on the social contract and on the role of government in economics pervaded by "market failure". For this was the era of "impartial social decision-makers" and "social welfare functions", of "good government" and "bad markets", of "private vice" and "public virtue". Economics, at that time, was dominated by Arrow, Samuelson, Solow, Tobin, et al., and not by Hayek, Friedman, Stigler, et al., who were all in exile from Camelot.

First let us look at Arrow, then riding high on the social welfare function as a welfare maximizing paradigm of government.[18] What were his views on the catallactics of exchange? As you may suspect, they were not exactly inspired by the spirit of methodological individualism. Arrow's article entitled "A Difficulty in the Concept of Social Welfare" published in 1950, had identified a problem in social welfare maximization via the new welfare economics, on the basis of individualistic assumptions. One might have thought that the impossibility theorem itself would have alerted Arrow to the dangers of collective decision-making. Not so. Let us restrict the preferences (which he used to define human beings) was the essential conclusion of his Nobel winning essay:

The failure of purely individualistic assumptions to lead to a well-defined social welfare function means, in effect, that there must be a divergence between social and private benefits if we are to be able to discuss a social optimum. Part of each individuals' value system must be a scheme of socioethical norms, the realization of which cannot, by their nature, be achieved through atomistic market behavior. These norms, further, must be sufficiently similar among the members of the society to avoid the difficulties outlined above. (Arrow, 1983, p. 25)

Bergson had worried in his article "On the Concept of Social Welfare" 1954) lest the judgments on social welfare might not be those of the individuals involved. Such worries were swept aside, however, during the decade and more that followed, by the flood of articles which engulfed the journals, written by mathematicians who were conditioned to work with symbols, rather than with individuals in society, and who specified general preference orderings that could be massaged, rather than the irritatingly

---

[18] It is amazing that a scholar who presented the impossibility theorem to economics nevertheless placed continuing faith in the constructivist social welfare function. As will be demonstrated, Arrow's preferred solution essentially was that of dictatorship.

independent values that human beings might hold. Arrow, as their acknowledged leader, was to sweep away Bergson's worries in 1964 and to endorse
dictatorship in the social decision-maker:

A welfare judgment requires that some one person be judge; a rule for arriving at
social decisions may be agreed upon for reasons of convenience and necessity
without its outcomes being treated as evaluations by anyone in particular. Indeed, I
would go further and argue that the appropriate standpoint for analyzing social
decision processes is precisely that they not be welfare judgments of any particular
individuals. In my view, the location of welfare judgments in any individual, while
logically possible, does not appear to be very interesting. "Social welfare" is related to
social policy in any sensible interpretation; the welfare judgments of any single
individual are unconnected with action and therefore sterile. (Arrow, 1983, pp.
68–9).

It is small wonder that Buchanan was later to comment on the relationship
between *The Calculus* and Arrow's methodology in the following cryptic vein:
"The maximizer of social welfare functions could never have written such a
book and indeed, even today, the maximizer of such functions cannot
understand what the book is all about. (Buchanan, 1986, p. 23).

Next, let us turn to Samuelson whose three papers on the pure theory of
public expenditure, which were published between 1954 and 1958, offered a
convincing rationalization for the public provision of certain kinds of goods
and services. Emphasizing the zero opportunity cost in individual consumption characteristic of such commodities.[19] Samuelson proved that private
markets must fail to satisfy the necessary conditions for Pareto optimality in
an economy in which such commodities exist. In the spirit of constructivist
rationalism, Samuelson put forward the following proposition:

The failure of market catallactics in no way denies the following truth: given,
sufficient knowledge the optimal decisions can always be found by scanning over all
the attainable states of the world and selecting the one which according to the
postulated ethical welfare function is best. The solution "exists"; the problem is how
to "find" it. (Samuelson, 1954, p. 389).

Whilst recognizing the major problem of obtaining an honest revelation of
preferences concerning the requisite rate of public good provision – a
problem resolved at least in theory by the seminal 1976 contribution of
Tideman and Tullock – Samuelson proferred a constructivist rationalist
solution (not dissimilar to the approach of Arrow outlined above:

---

[19] Has anyone yet discovered a true public good in the polar sense of Samuelson? A negative
answer surely does not constrain interventionist scholars from analyzing government as if such
theoretical curiosa actually exist.

One could imagine every person in the community being indoctrinated to behave like a "parametric decentralized bureaucrat" who *reveals* his preferences by signalling in response to price parameters or Lagrangian multipliers, to questionnaires, or to other devices. (Samuelson, 1954)

In an America so heavily indoctrinated in Lange – Lerner socialist methodology,[20] so ignorant of the problems of socialist calculation that had concerned the Austrian economists, and so careless of the individuals supposedly represented by the preference orderings that had suborned them, what a strange, unworldly and irrelevant creature *The Calculus of Consent* must have appeared to be. Yet, the reviews for the most part were generous indeed in some cases, were glowing, as the following short but representative selection of contributions clearly indicates.

Mancur Olson reviewed *The Calculus* for the *American Economic Review* (1962) from a vantage point firmly at the interface between economics and politics. Praising the book as "a stimulating addition to this new literature", Olsen was ambivalent about the "ideological bias" that he detected in its contents:

Their work is, however, distinguished from most other theorizing about political problems by its implicit ideological emphasis. The somewhat eccentric ideological quality that characterizes their writing unfortunately narrows their appeal and perhaps obscures the objective importance of some of their theories. Their right-wing view is, on the other hand, also a blessing in that it gives them an unusual perspective that must account for many of their fresh insights. In scholarship it is not perhaps necessity, but prejudice, that is the mother of invention. (p. 1217)

Olson was convinced by the application of utilitarian, rational behavior analytics to the study of politics. He criticized the analysis of external cost, understandably given his own researches, for its failure to recognize the difficulties posed by the logic of collective action on large group organization. He further criticized the book's identification of potential profit as opportunity cost and opportunity cost as external diseconomy on the ground that:

to define these unexploited profit opportunities as externalities, and therefore to deny that government action will be needed to cure the misallocations of resources resulting from externalities, is merely to create confusion by giving words meanings that are the opposite of those they have had in the past. (p. 1218)

[20] To re-read Lerner's *The Economics of Control* in 1986 perspective is to experience first-hand the initial reactions of Dorothy when transported in her dreams to the yellow brick road and the Land of Oz. Unfortunately, social decision-makers are less benign than munchkins and senior politicians are less helpless than the Wizard of Oz.

This said, however, Olson recommended the book to economists and
social scientists generally as deserving of their "careful attention and
criticism" by nature of its "distinctly original" theoretical contribution. Not a
"rave review" perhaps. But infinitely more favorable than the judgment that
might have been passed upon it by Samuelson, Solow, Arrow, Tobin or
others within the New England establishment.

There followed in 1964 an extremely generous review by Anthony Downs,
whose own seminal contribution to the economics of politics had been
published in 1957. Designating the book as "a brilliant and significant
contribution to the literature", Downs grasped much more precisely than
Mancur Olson, the distinctive constitutional perspective that *The Calculus*
imposed on the analysis of political market behavior:

> By applying the decision-making logic developed in economic theory to a wide range
> of political questions, James Buchanan and Gordon Tullock have developed some
> extremely useful insights. These include why bicameral legislatures make sense, why
> men who disagree about concrete issues can rationally agree on constitutional rules,
> which types of activities should be "collectivized" under government control and
> which should not, why a federal governmental structure minimizes political bar-
> gaining costs, the nature of "logrolling", and when a requirement for a special
> majority is the most efficient decision-making rule. (p. 87)

Downs was, however, unconvinced by the book's attempt to bypass
Arrow's problem of social choice, on the grounds that there is "no reason
why we should expect these social choices to exhibit any sense of order".
Since the coordination of government's actions was an important problem,
such individualism in approach, for Downs, was an important limitation of
the book's methodology. (Subsequently, Tullock was to challenge Arrow's
problem as irrelevant, attacking the impossibility theorem within its own
methodology.)[21] Downs praised the analysis of logrolling in multi-issue
decision-making and the emphasis placed on unanimity as forcing
individuals to search for agreement rather than to remain in conflict.

Downs suggested that the book was not definitive, even of the problems
with which it dealt. It made no allowance for coalitions or for political
parties, nor did it pretend to offer a cohesive model of the democratic
process. He was unconvinced by the book's interpretation of the impact of
majority voting upon resource allocation, by the relationship posited between
compensation payments and external economies, and by the absence of
strategic behavior assumptions in individual utility calculations. In general,
however, Downs commended a book which applied rational choice analytics
to the important institutions of politics at a time when the public sector was
the fastest growing segment of the US economy.

[21] See Tullock (1967).

Finally, there was the 1963 review by James Meade, published in *The Economic Journal*. Of the three reviewers here discussed, Meade was potentially the most dangerous for the authors of *The Calculus of Consent*. A disciple of Keynes, responsible for some of the formal modelling of *The General Theory*, a member of the Cambridge economics faculty, though far-distanced from the crypto-Marxists organized by Richard Kahn and Joan Robinson, Meade was very much the social democrat constructivist rationalist. He was not specialized, as were Olson and Downs, in the economics of politics. How would he react to the strange incantations from Jefferson's Virginia?

Fine scholar that he is, Meade reacted favorably, displaying an unusual penchant for the appreciation of an essentially alien methodology. He complimented the book as providing "a most laudable attempt to close the gap by producing a first simple "model" of democratic political action based on the assumption that the individual citizen is wholly selfish in his behavior in the voting booth and in the market-place." He centered detailed attention, in his review, on the basic constitutional model, as outlined in chapter 6, emphasizing the unanimity aspect of the choice rule itself, suggesting that this "in its barest outline" was the basic argument of the book.

Meade detected two weaknesses which rendered the argument of *The Calculus* complete. The first was the too-easy assumption that the existence of gains-from-trade would induce unanimous agreement to effect such gains. Meade correctly noted that bargaining costs might obstruct such an outcome, especially where distribution as well as efficiency was at issue. This important criticism will be explored in section 5.4. Second, was the exclusive emphasis in the book on problems of externality which were amenable to long-term marginal adjustment. In Meade's view, *The Calculus* could not maintain its distinction between the unanimous constitutional and the subsequent day-to-day decisions by majority or qualified majority vote when issues of once-for-all structural change arise. In such cases, Meade argued for a fundamental democratic value to be attached to simple majority voting, given the certain failure of the Wicksell condition.[22]

5.4 The Calculus of Consent in 1986 Perspective

This is not the occasion to attempt a major revisitation of *The Calculus of*

---

[22] Meade was preoccupied at that time with issues surrounding Britain's possible entry into the European Economic Community. Not all reviewers praised all aspects of the book. For example, Benjamin Ward (*Southern Economic Journal*), April, 1963, p. 352) criticized the poor organization and loose reasoning of the writing. Even he, however, concluded that "this is a pioneering work", offering "a number of insights which should provide the inspiration for much future work!"

Consent from the public choice perspective of 1986 – though I shall argue that there is great need of such an exercise. Instead, I shall briefly survey three areas central to *The Calculus* and attempt to identify unfinished business worthy of continuing research.

The Catallactics of Exchange

The Calculus of Consent mounted a major attack on the maximizing paradigm which by 1962 had come to dominate political economy in the wake of the "new" welfare economics revolution, with its unremitting ends-related emphasis on efficiency in resource allocation. The normative message of *The Calculus* was that economists should concentrate instead upon the origins, properties and institutions of exchange; an approach referred to as "catallactics", the science of exchanges, by some nineteenth century proponents, and which is process-rather than ends-oriented. In this perspective, the authors of *The Calculus*, were able to analyze the political process in terms of the exchange paradigm, modelling collective actions with individual decision-makers as the basic units.

In this perspective, the distinction between economics and politics as research disciplines, at first sight, is defined as the borderline between voluntary and non-voluntary relationships among individuals. This, at least, is Buchanan's 1983 interpretation of the issue. In particular, as the analysis departs from the conceptual ideal of *The Calculus*, as rents, actual or potential, emerge in the relationships between and among individuals "elements of power and potential coercion arise, and behavior becomes amenable to analysis by something other than pure catallaxy" (Buchanan, 1983, p. 21).

In my view, however, this judgment is too sweeping, and indeed threatens to take away from the economics of politics, even in constitutional perspective, some of the most important, if intractable, research issues of our time. Meade's criticism of the lack of attention in *The Calculus* to bargaining cost impediments to voluntary exchange is highly relevant to this assertion. Equally relevant is the apparent shift in the evaluation of Western democracies in general, and of the US constitutional democracy in particular, in the quarter century since *The Calculus* was in the printing press.

Camelot was destroyed not long after *The Calculus* appeared; or rather it was recognized for the myth that it had always been. The assassination of Kennedy, the venality of Johnson, the treachery of Nixon and his pardoning by Ford, followed by the weakness and self-doubt of Carter, played out for much of the period against the back-cloth of Vietnam, which from 1964 was a spreading blot rather than a dot on the Indo-China map, weakened the catallactics, such as they were, of US constitutional exchange. With Congress predominant, the US Constitution threatened by legislative invasion supported by an interventionist Supreme Court, and with consequential riots and fire-hoses in The Mall, bargaining costs, rents and rent-seeking no longer could be ignored, *even in the process of rules formation itself.*

If the principle of unanimity is vulnerable to transaction costs, even at the level of constitutional choice, even when all possible layers of meta-level analysis have been explored and found to be wanting, does this imply the end of the calculus of consent in catallactic perspective?[23]

I would suggest that work is now necessary to take account of the following research findings since 1962:

1   The Tullock insight that rents induce rent-seeking behavior. Of what relevance is this for catallaxy? How is the external cost/bargaining cost diagram of the basic model affected if rent-seeking is evident at the highest available level of constitutional choice?
2   The literature on prisoners' dilemmas and their resolution. Can this literature be developed to encompass within the catallactics approach issues of rents and power that have been judged by Buchanan to lie without the field?
3   The literature on transaction costs, both Virginian and new institutional. The bargaining cost aspect of *The Calculus* was always weak. It now requires major reconsideration if the basic constitutional model is to retain credibility in a much more demanding profession.
4   The Sen paradox of the impossible Paretian liberal. In 1962, unanimity seemed to guarantee not just process efficiency but liberty itself. Such a judgment must be more muted in 1986. What happens if individuals do not value liberty sufficiently highly in their constitutional contract? Should they be forced to be free?

Homo Oeconomicus

The second major thrust of *The Calculus*, in this case borrowed from the 1957 work of Downs, was the modelling of individuals in the political process as pursuing utility maximization subject to the institutional and budgetary constraints that confront them. This important insight had escaped the attention of the classical political economists, despite their deep-rooted suspicion concerning the behavior of political markets. It was, of course, completely alien to the constructivist rationalists of the "new" welfare economics who saw government as an impartial agent in the maximization of social welfare.

---

[23] If there is a problem of non-existence, the absence of constitutional consent does not imply a prisoner's dilemma problem, as Buchanan and others have argued. One cannot conceivably attain what does not exist.

Since the early contributions by Downs in 1957 and by Buchanan and Tullock in 1962, the literature of public choice has become replete with the application of *homo oeconomicus* assumptions in the analysis of political market behavior. Economists may have been slow to make the initial link. They have not been slow to pick up the baton of the self-interest axiom. I have argued earlier that the normative legacy of this powerful positive thrust, in the absence of any constitutional perspective, is the politics of despair. That of course is not a criticism of an essentially scientific endeavor.

Nevertheless, a careful reconsideration is now necessary of the following issues, which could not have been perceived in 1962:

1 How essential is it to collapse utility maximization into the narrow perspective of expected wealth maximization? The latter emphasis is clearly viewed with distaste by many scholars. That is not a relevant criticism. I wonder, however, whether a greater explanatory power might be achieved by expanding the objective function. Of course, expected wealth is relevant, as the regression results usually indicate; but the regression equations do not always perform so well as to rule out additional assumptions about human motivation.
2 It is important that public choice should not overstep the limits of good science. The *homo oeconomicus* assumption may perform well. That does not imply its universality in the political process. Public choice analysts should beware swallowing as fact motivations that are employed to generate predictions. Both Popper and Friedman have warned about excessive reliance on the realism of assumptions.
3 Surely the time has come to look at the margins in political markets from a total as well as a subdivisioned perspective. On each margin, homo oeconomicus may take his toll. But what are the total as well as the marginal implications of such behavior?

Log-rolling and the Majority Vote Rule

By recognizing that the in-period political process embodies a continuing stream of separate decisions, Buchanan and Tullock were able to introduce vote-trading or logrolling, both explicitly and implicitly into their model of simple majority voting. This contribution was favourably received by those who reviewed the book. Their logrolling analytics, applied to political markets where collective action benefitted specific individuals, but was financed by general taxation, allowed preference intensities as well as preference orderings to make their mark on the political process. In the absence of compensation requirements, logrolling opportunities, which are most successful when applied to bare majority coalitions, implied *ex ante* that individual voters must anticipate external costs as a consequence of collective action.

Tullock subsequently applied the logrolling analytics of *The Calculus* to an explanation of why there is so much stability in political markets, despite the apparent instability of any vote rule, other than unanimity, that can be conceived. A lengthy literature in public choice has been generated by this initiative. The logrolling explanation, however, is currently under attack from those who argue instead that "coalitions of the whole" tend to emerge and to dominate the political market process. (Shepsle) Tullock is presently revisiting the field, to re-establish the pre-eminence of the logrolling model. This is an important area of research, more central now, than it was in 1962, to any reconstituted *Calculus of Consent*.

5.5 Towards 1987

Thus my story ends, with praise for a monumental contribution to the literature of public choice, with suggestions for future work and, yet, with a word of warning. There is a false notion at large in economics, taken from Satchley Paige, which is already penetrating public choice: "Do not look behind at your competitors, lest they take advantage of your hesitation to pass you by." Those who fail to look behind are not infrequently passed by anyway, without even noting the need to shift their pace.

The Calculus of Consent will be 25 years old in 1987, the bicentennial of the US Constitution. It has run a good race and has always led the field. But new competitors have now entered the race, from Texas, St. Louis, Chicago and Los Angeles. They are fresh, and youth is on their side. The old professionals who still lead the field might do well to glance behind them, to regalvanize their combined energies and to make a game-plan for the quarter century now to come.

My suggestion for 1987, to the two fine scholars concerned, is that they negotiate in free exchange, to reactivate that mighty cross-partial and to offer a *Calculus of Consent Mark 2* to an eagerly awaiting profession.

$$\frac{\partial^2 C_2}{\partial X_B \partial X_T} \qquad >> 0$$

It surely would be a winner!

References

Alchian, A. and Demsetz, H. (1972) "Production, information costs, and economic organization", *The American Economic Review*, December, pp. 777–95.

Arrow, K.J. (1983) "A difficulty in the concept of social welfare", in *Social Cost and Justice* Collected Papers of K.J. Arrow, Harvard University Press, pp. 1–29.

Arrow, K.J. (1983) "Values and collective decision making", in Collected Papers of K.J. Arrow, pp. 59–77.

Bergson, A. (1954) "On the concept of social welfare", *Quarterly Journal of Economics*, pp. 233–52.

Brennan, H.G. and Buchanan, J.M. (1986) The Reason of Rules. Cambridge: University Press.

Buchanan, J.M. (1960) "Economic policy, free institutions and democratic process", II *Politico*, XXV, pp. 265–77.

Buchanan, J.M. (1975) *The Limits of Liberty.* "Chicago: University of Chicago Press.

Buchanan, J.M. (1986) "The public choice perspective", in J.M. Buchanan *Liberty, Market and State.* Brighton: Harvester Press, pp. 19–27.

Buchanan, J.M. (1960) "Economic policy, free institutions and democratic process", *Politico.*

Cowling, K. and Mueller, D.C. (1978) "The social cost of monopoly power", *Economic Journal*, **88**, pp. 797–848.

Crain, W.M. and Tollison, R.D. (1979) "Constitutional change in an interest–group theory of government", *Journal of Legal Studies*, 8.

Downs, A. (1975) *An Economic Theory of Democracy.* New York: Harper and Row.

Downs, A. (1964) Review of "The calculus of consent", *Journal of Political Economy*, 72, February, pp. 87–8.

Meade, J.M. (1963) Review of "The calculus of consent", *Economic Journal*, 73, March, pp. 101–4.

Mueller, D. (1979) *Public Choice.* Cambridge: Cambridge University Press.

Niskanen, W.A. (1971) *Bureaucracy and Representative Government*, Chicago: Aldine.

Niskanen, W.A. (1971) *Bureaucracy and Representative Government.* Chicago: Aldine – Atherton.

Olson, M. (1965) *The Logic of Collective Action.* Cambridge, Mass.: Harvard University Press.

Olson, M. (1962) Review of "The calculus of consent", *American Economic Olson, M. (1965) The Logic of Collective Action.* Cambridge, Mass.: Harvard University Press.

Olson, M. (1965) *The Logic of Collective Action. Cambridge, Mass.: Harvard University Press.*

Rowley, C.K. (1978) *Liberalism and Collective choice: A Return to Reality?* The Manchester School, September, pp. 224–51.

Samuelson, P. (1954) "The pure theory of public expenditure", *Review of Economics and Statistics*, November, pp. 387–9.

Sen, A. (1970) "The impossibility of a Paretian liberal", *Journal of Political Economy*, January, pp. 152–7.

Tideman, N. and Tullock, G. (1976) "A new and superior process for making social choices", *Journal of Political Economy* October, pp. 1145–59.

Tollison, R.D. ( ) "Rent seeking: a survey", *Kyklos*, 35 (fasc. 4) pp. 575.

Tullock, G. (1959) "Problems of majority voting", *Journal of Political Economy*, 67, December, pp. 571–9.

Tullock, G. (1965) *The Politics of Bureaucracy.* Washington, DC: Public Affairs Press.

Tullock, G. (1967) "The general irrelevance of the general impossibility theorem", *Quarterly Journal of Economics*, 81, May, pp. 256–70.

Tullock, G. (1959) "Problems of majority voting", *Journal of Political Economy*, 67, December, pp. 571–9.

Tullock, G. (1967) "The welfare costs of tariffs, monopolies and theft", *Western Economic Journal*, 5, June, pp. 224–32.

Tullock, G. (1974) *The Social Dilemma*, Blacksburg VA.: Center for Study of Public Choice.

Tullock, G. (1987) *Autocracy*, Boston: Martinus Nijhoff.

6

Calculus and Consent

PETER H. ARANSON

6.1 Introduction

The Calculus of Consent (1962) has been one of the most influential works in public choice since that field achieved a separate identity in political science and economics. Scholars in both disciplines had always recognized that a hierarchy of rules defined every human institution. And indeed, economists had known for a long time that these rules had consequences for costs in private-sector organizations – and therefore for the prices and other attributes of final goods – and for the return to capital (see, for example, Coase, 1937, and Alchian and Demsetz, 1972). But few writers ever had grasped that we could analyze the constitutive rules, the organic laws, of political institutions in quite the same way.

Surely Aristotle, as revealed in the *Politics*, understood that these rules had consequences. But for him the occurrence of rules was more a matter of *force majeure* or an evolutionary process, and less the result of an implicit or explicit calculus of choice relying on a general theory of individual preferences, beyond those concerned with narrow and immediate self-interest. While political scientists since Aristotle had been aware of certain general consequences of electoral laws and the like (Duverger, 1963: Rae, 1967; Riker, 1982; and Grofman and Lijphart, 1986), they, too, did not grasp the full nature of the relationship between the choice of rules and the more nearly general character of human preference and choice, as these work in their revealed form through the intermediation of cost. Therefore, it is not hyperbole to say that *The Calculus of Consent* is the very greatest work on the theory of constitutions since Aristotle's Politics, and that it has seen no equal since its publication.

I shall argue here that a fundamental contradiction pervades this very great work. That contradiction concerns the problem of the alienability (or inalienability) of the liberal freedom to choose. I was not aware of this contradiction until my third reading of this work. But it has been brought home to me by studying other work by Buchanan (1969), as well as by a more recent reading of Leoni (1971). The presence of this contradiction in no way detracts from the fundamental importance of *The Calculus of Consent* or its place in the development of political and economic theories of the state. It "merely" calls for a revision in the way that we think about certain problems in the science of human government and in our research agenda.

6.2 The Structure of *The Calculus of Consent*

Before reflecting on the nature of this contradiction, it is useful to say what *The Calculus of Consent* is, and what it is not. First, except in a very narrow sense, and although the authors from time to time hint at claiming otherwise (pp. 299–300), it does not set out any palpable explanations or predictions that apply to real-world phenomena. It does develop the preferences of an individual human being when confronted with two general kinds of costs, whose sum he acts as if he tries to minimize by adjusting the basic constitutional decision rule: the number of persons, in a polity of N persons, required to change the status quo.

But this person is nested in a set of assumptions that go beyond those that we ordinarily impose on predictive, positive models of human choice, for the purpose of efficient deduction. He does not know his position in the post-constitutional order of things, nor, at the preconstitutional stage, does he belong to a discernible group. But most important, he shares in a (unanimous) consensus based on individual autonomy, of the sort that we once identified as "liberal freedom". More important, at least initially the decision to engage in collective action with respect to a particular human pursuit is taken as given, as is a system of rights, the legal means to defend those rights, and a consensus on their (present) relative inviolability. All that is at issue, again at least initially, is the decision rule that this person and others will use to adopt (or fail to adopt) a departure from the status quo concerning this particular subject of collective choice.

Even in contemplating these strictures, which change the problem from one of collective choice to one of individual choice, the reader cannot resist the temptation to turn what is, in the best sense of the term, a philosophical exercise, into an explanatory one. Thus, we think about the unanimity or near-unanimity rule of criminal law, deciding cases on a standard of "beyond a reasonable doubt", and on the majority rule of civil law juries, deciding cases on the basis of the "preponderance of the evidence"; we consider the extraordinary majorities required to amend the Constitution, to shut off a filibuster, or to ratify a treaty; and we reflect on the observation that one bothersome spoiled child alone can expend public funds (for electricity) by riding the elevator in city hall for an entire afternoon.

6.3   Constitutional Choosers and Post-Constitutional Choice

The problem with this construct begins when we recognize, with the authors, that the person who chooses the decision rule and the person who then chooses a public policy by using that rule are not the same persons. The constitutional decision reflects one set of costs and the most general kinds of interests imaginable, all within a consensus about certain rights guaranteed by the constitution-forming requirement of unanimous consent. The public-policy decision, by contrast, concerns a "venal" person who knows his position exactly and pursues his particular self-interest within the previously established constitutional rules. These two "persons", of course, merge their personalities at the constitutional stage, but they go their separate ways thereafter. Indeed, everything that we have learned about political entre-preneurship and rent-seeking in the post-constitutional stage of decision-making reinforces the view that these two persons are not the same human being (see, for example, Buchanan, Tollison, and Tullock, 1980, and Aranson and Ordeshook, 1985).

Now it is a simple matter to claim that in this division of persons lies the central genius of the work. And that argument, which the authors forcefully present (pp. 305–14), is persuasive. After all, the threat of external-cost imposed, as a consequence of rent-seeking, or the correlative threat of decision-cost absorbed, perhaps because of costly bargaining or sharp practices, finds a direct reflection in the external-cost and decision-cost functions that make up the intermediate arguments in the function expressing interdependence costs, even as expanded in later parts of the work to the analysis of logrolling. These costs the chooser must "know" to make decisions about the constitution's terms.

But that is just the problem. How would our hypothetical constitution-chooser, with all of the assumptions that apply to him and limit his knowledge of his own post-constitutional position, find himself able to reproduce these kinds of costs at the stage of constitutional decision-making? Plainly, these are cast as choice-influencing costs in both contexts of choice, to use Buchanan's (1969) very apt phrase, but they cannot seriously influence choice at *both* stages of decision-making.

To deflect the easy answer that "yes they can", let me press the matter a bit further. In an Austrian universe of discourse, both political and economic actions generate "spontaneous orders", which in large measure remain unpredictable – although the spontaneous order growing out of political entrepreneurship suppresses and constrains that growing out of the market relation, and ordinarily in wholly undesirable ways. The absence of predictability reflects the larger problem of the subjective, decentralized, and fragmentary character of knowledge, much of which has an importance that no one yet recognizes (Hayek, 1945). Translated into Buchanan's terms, we can measure choice-influenced costs, *ex post*, but we cannot measure choice-influencing costs, *ex ante*.

How, then, can our constitution chooser know what the levels of external and decision costs might be after the constitution is ratified? I do not believe that he could predict them. My confidence in this belief grows out of two different kinds of considerations. First, we need not "pierce" the preconstitutional "veil of ignorance" to speculate about just how complete it may become. Presumably, in discerning the levels of interdependence (and especially external) costs, the constitution chooser has before him two sets of political demands and strategies; elements of the first set he can anticipate, but elements of the second set he cannot. His estimates of external costs, perforce, will reflect only this first set, but not the second. The elements of this first set may even include notions of political ethics prevailing at the time of constitutional choice, but these may waste away at an unknowable rate, to be replaced by other political ethics that the chooser cannot anticipate. Second, because politics is profoundly a process of discovery and invention (Hayek, 1944), the kinds of collective actions that others may propose and eventually adopt, as well as the strategies of adoption themselves, may remain likewise unanticipated in the constitutional calculus. (Notice that neither information set contains knowledge about the chooser's post-constitutional position.)

6.4 Constitutional Construction in Historical Perspective

In my view, the Founding Fathers had done about all that could be done with their information at the constitutional stage of decision-making. With respect to the Federal Government, they set decision rules that overlapped constituencies and made very difficult the formation of successful coalitions in support of policy changes.[1] They also declared purposes for the public sector, thus constructing a government of "enumerated powers", not one of general capability.[2] And they provided restrictions on that government's ability to take life, liberty, or property without "due process of law".

With respect to the state governments, which, after all, were to be the principal agencies of collective action in the model that they had in mind, being very much aware of the larger problems of rent-seeking, the Founding

---

[1] See, e.g., Article I, on the process of law-making, and Articles I, II, and III on election and selection rules.

[2] See the "enumerated powers" of Congress in Article I, Section 8 and the tenth amendment to the Constitution. The powers of the federal government were largely confined to providing for a common market among the states; for national defense and the conduct of foreign relations; and for "guarantee[ing] to every State in this Union a Republican Form of Government".

Fathers placed very strong substantive prohibitions on the states. (See, for example, Sunstein, 1984; and Epstein, 1982.) The states could not "impair the obligation of contract", treat citizens of other states differently than they treated their own citizens, nor unduly burden interstate commerce with tariffs or other restrictions unfavorable to "foreign" corporations. The Constitution appeared to work well for some time, although it was not long before the Supreme Court, in its own form of rent-seeking, began to undermine constitutional foundations (Epstein, 1984; and Aranson, 1984). By 1937, however, the Constitution had lost most of its prohibitionary force.

The Founding Fathers, of course, were not merely constitution choosers of the sort that *The Calculus of Consent* had in mind. They were also students of practical politics, who understood the rent-seeking problems that we now model, who tried to overcome them, and who – at least in the long run – partly failed in that attempt. There is operating in all of this a kind of constitutional Coase Theorem, as I refer to it elsewhere (Aranson, 1986). It may be that constitutional rules actually do not work well to restrain political entrepreneurship and rent-seeking.

6.5 Calculus and Consent

The contradiction that I refer to in the beginning, then, is a possible conflict in the words of the volume's title: "calculus" and "consent". The immediate result of political action may be rent-seeking and the decline in human welfare that accompanies it. But the further consequence of rent-seeking reflects that its instrumentality is the restriction of liberal freedom, as Leoni (1971) and Hayek (1960) define it. This "freedom from constraint" is the first freedom to go as a consequence of rent-seeking. Therefore, consent within the framework of constitutional choice perforce implies today the alienation of liberal freedom, the freedom to choose, which falls before the pursuit of gains that the constitution writers themselves found wholly undesirable, and which we call today by the term "positive freedom", or worse.

With the rent-seeking derogation of liberal freedom, then, come the alienation of rights such as the Constitution sought to protect. Yet the Founding Fathers" inability to predict this outcome led them to alienate (for us) a far more limited (and, some would argue, preconstitutional) set of rights, which no longer have much force. Can such rights be alienated within the structure of *any* constitution that begins with unanimous consent? The practical matter is that, in ignorance of the consequences, we have done so. The challenge of the future is to devise their restoration. The lasting central virtue of *The Calculus of Consent*, then, may be not so much its discernment of the economic principles of constitutional choice (though that discernment is a necessary condition for understanding our present discontent and removing its cause) as much as it is its crystalizing for us the central importance of preserving liberty after constitutional choice.

References

Alchian, Armen A. and Demsetz, Harold (1972) "Production, information costs, and economic organization", *American Economic Review*, **62**, December, pp. 777–95.

Aranson, Peter H. (1986a) "Judicial control of the political branches: public purpose and public law", *Cato Journal*, **4** Winter, pp. 719–82.

Aranson, Peter H. and Ordeshook, Peter C. (1986b) "Public interest, private interest, and the Democratic polity", in Roger Benjamin and Stephen S. Elkin (eds), *The Democratic State*. Lawrence: The University Press of Kansas, 1985, chapter 4.

Aranson, Peter H. (1986) "Bruno Leoni in retrospect", essay prepared for a Liberty Fund, Inc. colloquium on "Bruno Leoni's *Freedom and the Law: a 25-Year Perspective*". Atlanta, Georgia, 2–4 May.

Buchanan, James M. (1969) *Cost and Choice*. Chicago: Markham.

Buchanan, James M. Tollison, Robert D. and Tullock, Gordon (1980) *The Theory of the Rent-Seeking Society*. College Station: Texas A and M University Press.

Buchanan, James M. (1962) *The Calculus of Consent: Logical Foundations of Constitutional Democracy*. Ann Arbor: University of Michigan Press.

Coase, Ronald H. (1937) "The nature of the firm", *Economica*, **4** pp. 386–405.

Duverger, Maurice (1963) *Political Parties: Their Organization and Activity in the Modern State* translated by B. North, and R. North, New York: Wiley.

Epstein, Richard A. (1982) "Taxation, regulation, and confiscation", *Osgood Hall Law Journal*, **20**, September, pp. 433–53.

Epstein, Richard A. (1984) "Toward a revitalization of the contract clause". *University of Chicago Law Review*, **51**, Summer, pp. 703-51.

Grofman, Bernard and Lijphart, Arendt (1986) *Electoral Laws and Their Political Consequences*. New York: Agathon.

Hayek, Friedrich A. (1960) The Constitution of Liberty. Chicago: Regnery.

Hayek, Friedrich A. (1944) *The Road to Serfdom*. Chicago: University of Chicago Press.

Hayek, Friedrich A. (1945) "The use of knowledge in society", *American Economic Review*, **35**, September, pp. 519–30.

Leoni, Bruno (1971) *Freedom and the Law*. Los Angeles: Nash.

Rae, Douglas, W. (1967) *The Political Consequences of Electoral Laws*. New Haven: Yale University Press.

Riker, William H. (1982) "Two-party systems and Duverger's Law: an essay in the history of political science". *American Political Science Review*, **76**, December, pp. 753–66.

Sunstein, Cass R. (1984) "Naked preferences and the constitution", *Columbia Law Review*, **94**, November, pp. 1689–732.

The Calculus of Consent:
Notes in Retrospection
WILLIAM C. MITCHELL

7.1 Introduction

Although the early 1960s was an exciting era for political scientists, it was an inauspicious time to publish *The Calculus of Consent* (1962). A theory based on methodological individualism or rational utility maximization flew in the face of the high-flying behavioralism then the rage among young, aspiring political analysts. Behavioralism's commitments stood and remain in stark contrast to those of *The Calculus*. It was Social Psychology versus one brand of Economics. And the latter lost; in fact, it was no contest.

To be sure, political scientists were not unfamiliar with economic reasoning about politics for many had read and even accepted various elements of *An Economic Theory of Democracy* (Downs 1957). The major generalizations of the book were but logically connected restatements of much that was conventional learning (especially in the interest-group approach) about American and British politics. All this could be readily accepted because Downs not only eschewed mathematical exposition, but he was never combative about his economic and methodological commitments. Accordingly, his theories of spatial competition and median voters, rational ignorance, and the role of ideology were readily acknowledged even when the overall framework of analysis was suspect. (However, see Stokes, 1963, for an early critique of the spatial model).

This mostly favorable reception of Downs was not, however, to be accorded by political science to *The Calculus of Consent* (Buchanan and Tullock 1969) or to Arrow (1951) or to Olson (1965). For quite some time I harbored the belief that perhaps Downs deserved his more ready acceptance not only because his book had a superior organization, but also because of its simple and highly lucid prose which deflected if not subverted potential critics. Today, I attribute both the greater indifference and hostility (on the latter, see, Brian Barry, 1965) toward Buchanan and Tullock to three factors: 1 the fact that *The Calculus* deals with a much more abstract and unfamiliar subject matter, namely, individual rational choice of constitutional rules; 2 the more strident positivist methodological stance of its authors; and 3 the apparent normative thrust of the text. In short, much of the book was so at odds with the common perceptions and professional commitments of ordinary political scientists that they soon dropped it either out of indifference or petulant exasperation and anger. Traditional political scientists placed little trust in abstract theory-building, whilst the behavioralists saw the world through the lens of social psychology which left little room for pure theory – especially rational theory about the importance of institutions in individual and collective choice. And, perhaps, worse, Buchanan and Tullock appeared in an age of "liberalism" at least within the academy to be outright "conservatives". They explicitly and repeatedly endorsed the rational pursuit of self-interest and a public interest based on the former.

7.2 The Messages of the Calculus

The fundamental concepts, propositions, and normative implications of *The Calculus* directly and unmistakably challenged core assumptions and ideals of "liberal" political theorists. Led primarily by Brian Barry, a small but talented group of liberal critics including Michael Taylor (1976), Robert Goodin (1976), Russell Hardin (1982), Howard Margolis (1982), Michael Laver (1981, 1983), Steven Rhoads (1985) and Elaine Spitz (1984) have all seen fit to respectfully, criticize, reject, modify, and occasionally ridicule, in part or whole, basic notions set forth or associated with *The Calculus of Consent*. This counterattack on the "economics of politics" continues to this day. Other political theorists, notably, J. Roland Pennock (1979), recognized the importance of but rejected significant elements of the argument. Marxist analysts, including C. B. MacPherson (1973, 1977) and their socialist offspring asserted either contrary views or, as has more often been the case, simply ignored the book. In fact, it is quite probable that many young graduate students at our best universities have little or no knowledge of the work and the body of thought it generated.

Space limitations prohibit a detailed summary let alone commentary on prevalent objections, but it remains quite clear that the philosophical critics are more or less united in their rejection of the basic framework, that is, the rational choices of utility-maximizing individuals constrained in their decisions by uncertainty rules of the game, their limited assets, and the structure of incentives and costs. Such critics variously stress non-rational components, altruistic motivations, and integrative rather than competitive elements in political life. To such theorists the utilitarian, contractarian (Wicksellian) foundations of Buchanan and Tullock's approach seem far-fetched – the work of "madmen". One is left with the impression that these analysts prefer a non-deductive analysis founded upon non-rationality, certainty, altruism, and unlimited resources.

If the reception accorded *The Calculus* by liberal political philosophers has been highly critical, its reception among positivist political theorists has been much more favorable perhaps because the positivists have been more concerned with the technical or "scientific" rather than the ideological imputations. In any case, Buchanan and Tullock are accorded major status in basic texts written by Riker and Ordeshook (1973) and Abrams (1980). And the pages of the major political science journals publishing public choice articles contain frequent references to *The Calculus*. Still, it must be said that political scientists working on public choice problems clearly rely more upon their positivist brethren than upon the Virginia School. Journal articles deal mostly with elections, voting, bargaining, party competition, coalition formation, strategies, etc., and do so employing formal tools and substantive theory emanating from game and social choice theory. Rarely does one find work based on constitutional problems, rent-seeking, demand-revelation, the Coase theorem, fiscal activities of the state, welfare states, and policy issues and outcomes. A "division of labor" clearly exists between political scientists and Virginia economists interested in public choice. Indeed, the latter economists speak of "public choice" while the political scientists label their work as "positive theory", or "formal social choice".

Although leading political philosophers and positivist political scientists pay considerable attention to *The Calculus*, ordinary, "run-of-the-mill" political scientists who teach American Government have hardly noticed the book. Unlike the elementary texts in economics, public finance, and price theory, conventional American Government textbooks contain no references to the Buchanan and Tullock classic or, indeed, any of their work. The famous cost curves of collective action found in *The Calculus* are now obligatory in political economy texts, but unheard of in political science textbooks. The only exception is Peter Aranson's *American Government* (1981), itself, in my view, one of the most remarkable texts in the history of contemporary political science. Although Aranson might best be viewed as a positivist he has shown an unusual proclivity for work in the Virginia mode. Still, most of the text is written from a positivist stance and is strongest on elections, party strategies, and voting. The book is rather weak on policy outcomes, although it does deal with constitutional reform from a basically Virginia perspective.

With a display of considerable courage the authors of *The Calculus* introduced an extraordinary array of profound ideas – ideas that after 25 years are still at the forefront of public choice: the notion of politics as exchange; the ideal of unanimity found in Pareto and Wicksell; minimizing the cost of collective action; asymmetric, uninternalized distributions of costs and benefits; and the efficiency of log-rolling. These revolutionary ideas are of uncommon worth. They serve at once to correct and deepen our understandings of seemingly apparent and attractive but flabby political ideas and ideals masking as eternal truths. Our ideas and ideals of democracy can never again be quite the same for Buchanan and Tullock have corrupted liberal academic innocence.

I should like now to consider, however, briefly, some of the above noted contributions. Their generalized economic (contractarian) theory of constitutions was primarily based on demand considerations, that is, public goods and externality arguments. However, they were far more explicit than political science in their discussions of the alternative courses of action available for dealing with the problems raised by the presence of externalities. Voluntary cooperation can sometimes if not often effectively offset the adverse affects of externalities. Since government intervention can itself impose costs and externalities, in deciding on appropriate policies, Buchanan and Tullock took into explicit account the costs and advantages of three alternatives: (1) purely individualistic decision-making; (2) voluntary organization; and (3) collective control. They then developed an elaborate, but highly useful, classification scheme as a first attempt to treat such a comparison systematically.

Two critical problems arise whenever one employs the contractarian paradigm to explain collective action: the lesser in importance is the anthropologist's and historian's familiar lament that few if any governments ever arose as depicted in contract theories, while the more important criticism rests on the observation that one cannot readily account for the capacity of governments to grow and become more powerful than would seem possible in any reasonable constitutional contract among utility-maximizers. The state becomes the more powerful and indeed the most powerful institution in society. How can this come about? Unaccountably, the authors of *The Calculus* did not anticipate such dire analytical possibilities. Subsequent work by Buchanan and Tullock strongly suggests that both became acutely aware of this critical lacuna in their original efforts. Most of their work since the early 1970s has in fact been devoted to clarifying how states become powerful far beyond the confines of original contracts, and in Buchanan's own work the concern has become one of rewriting the contract.

In this connection it should also be noted that *The Calculus*, although providing analytical possibilities for the state to grow, expenditures to multiple, and taxation to increase, did so largely within the familiar restrictive Downsian demand-based model. Demand forces led to log-rolling under simple majority rules and increases, indeed, inefficient increases in public expenditures. The authors of *The Calculus* not only saw log-rolling and simple majority rule as villains but differed with Downs on a fundamental empirical issue, namely, citizen perceptions of taxation and public benefits. Downs argued that voters were likely to be more conscious of taxes than public goods benefits, while Buchanan and Tullock saw it the other way around.

Although Buchanan and Tullock set forth a demand theory of governmental growth, their implicit estimates of growth rates appear to have been underestimated. Apparently fiscal growth would proceed in essentially incremental ways and amounts. While present in the analysis, redistribution and rent-seeking – now recognized as the chief sources of expansion – were still not major forces affecting the design of constitutions nor explanation of the growth of government.

7.3   Some Comments on the Calculus

Buchanan and Tullock investigated in detail some alternative voting rules, and raised serious questions about the special status which had been accorded to the majority voting principle. To them that principle was purely an arbitrary convention with many unattractive features, and they took the position that only the rule of unanimity has any real welfare significance. They argued that collective decision-making is always likely to incur external costs if decision-making is not unanimous, because then the controlling group is apt to approve legislation whose deleterious effects on others exceed the advantages to themselves. Only a rule which requires unanimous consent for any government action can lead to optimal results. Though this argument is relevant and illuminating, I – like many political scientists – remain somewhat and perhaps inconsistently ambivalent towards it. The obverse of a unanimity rule is the veto power which it gives to any one person if an arrangement is not initially optimal. It offers special advantages to anyone who can continue an arrangement whereby he profits at the expense of the rest of the community. A unanimity rule is, paradoxically, the ideal instrument for the preservation of existing externalities and inequities.

More generally, every voting rule not only specifies those whose approval will suffice to institute change, but it also designates residually what groups can prevent change. Moreover, in the set of all possible legislative decisions any given legislative proposal has what may be called its negative equivalent. In a society in which there are no trade restrictions it takes an affirmative vote to introduce them, but in one where such restrictions already exist it takes a negative vote to prevent their abolition. Thus a two-thirds voting rule, while it means that 67 percent of the voting members must approve a tariff, also empowers 34 percent of the legislature to prevent the elimination of a duty. Considering the range of possibilities between majority vote and the rule of unanimity, we can say that the more closely the arrangements approximate the latter, the smaller the group which we empower to perpetuate the inefficiencies and inequities of previous actions or failures to act. Majority rule, therefore, is certainly not entirely arbitrary, for as many theorists have noted it is the rule which may be said to minimize the tyranny of a conservative minority, while not at the same time offering any minority the unilateral power to institute change. Accordingly, there is very little distinction between imposing costs on others and preventing costs on others from being removed. Power resides both in the group which can impose and the one which can prevent. Majority rule is the one arrangement which makes the smaller of these groups as large as possible.

For similar reasons I cannot always follow the Buchanan-Tullock allegation that simple majority voting tends to produce over-investment by the public sector. They point out that any project whose costs and benefits are not uniformly distributed is likely to be approved by a majority vote, provided that it does not adversely affect more than 49 percent of the voters. But, as has been suggested by others (see Ferejohn, 1974), this argument works both ways. Suppose that a proposed public project offers small net costs to a majority of voters and very substantial net benefits to a significant minority. In that case, the project may on the same grounds be voted down despite the fact that on balance it may yield a net gain to the community.

Buchanan and Tullock provided an original and fundamental contribution in their analysis of log-rolling and its welfare effects. They argued convincingly that log-rolling is an essentially beneficial feature of the voting process. Log-rolling may be described as the free exchange of votes by legislators. And, as in the elementary theory of trade, generally such an exchange will only be made if it is beneficial to both parties. It constitutes another example of the substantial gains from trade. Economists can conclude that the prevention of log-rolling, like the prevention of the exchange of ration coupons can sometimes if not always be disadvantageous to society.

Some gains from log-rolling can be spelled out in somewhat greater detail. It is a device whereby a minority group can obtain the interest and support of the majority for issues which would otherwise have been ignored. Log-rolling is, as recognized by the authors, an important means for the protection of minority groups. Moreover, log-rolling transforms voting from a procedure which takes into account only ordinal preferences into one which can reflect intensities of feeling, that is, cardinal benefits. If I favor an item, I can only vote for it once, no matter whether my feelings about it are very strong or only moderate. But the number of votes on other issues which I am willing to trade in return for support of the bill which I advocate will vary with the degree of urgency with which I regard the measure. It follows from all this that log-rolling can permit the passage of legislation which increases the overall welfare and which would otherwise be lost. This device therefore emerges from the analysis as an integral part of the democratic machinery. Political scientists have long had an intuitive grasp of this critical institution, but until Buchanan and Tullock's exposition its detailed workings were never set forth. We now possess a much better understanding of those necessary conditions under which efficiency is promoted, as well as those in which it is not. And the keys (villains?) are the asymmetrical distributions of costs and benefits and majority rule.

7.4 Conclusions

In retrospect it now appears that *The Calculus* may have overemphasized its themes of politics as exchange and the state as a provider of public goods and overseer of externalities. Ironically, subsequent work by both Buchanan and Tullock has aided in undermining their brilliant classic. Political exchange is not a strict analogue of market exchange. And the state never came into existence to supply public goods nor has it often provided efficient solutions to externalities. The state is, itself, a monopoly driven by its own political objectives but *The Calculus* never really dealt with the state or government. One wonders how the book might now be rewritten.

Readers who expected an analysis of a on-going polity *à la* Downs must have been disappointed. The book did not treat ordinary voting choices, political party competition, bureaucracy, nor interest groups. Instead it raised the ultimate question of the rational basis of constitutional government. Most importantly, it did so in a quite remarkable way.

References

Aranson, Peter (1981) *American Government*. Cambridge: Winthrop Publishers.
Arrow, Kenneth J. (1951) *Social Choice and Individual Values*. New York: Wiley.
Barry, Brian (1965) *Political Argument*. London: Routledge & Kegan Paul.
Ferejohn, John A. (1974) *Pork Barrel Politics*. Stanford: Stanford University Press.
Goodin, Robert E. (1976) *The Politics of Rational Man*. New York: Wiley.
Hardin, Russell (1982) *Collective Action*. Baltimore: Johns Hopkins.
Laver, Michael (1981) *The Politics of Private Desires*. New York: Penguin.
Laver, Michael (1981) *Invitation to Politics*. Oxford: Martin Robertson.
MacPherson, C. B. (1973) *Democratic Theory*. Oxford: Clarendon Press.
MacPherson, C. B. (1977) *The Life and Times of Liberal Democracy*. Oxford: Oxford University Press.
Margolis, Howard (1982) *Selfishness, Altruism & Rationality*, Cambridge: Cambridge University Press.

Olson, Mancur (1965) *The Logic of Collective Action*. Cambridge, Mass.: Harvard University Press.

Pennock, J. Roland (1979) *Democratic Political Theory*. Princeton NJ: Princeton University Press.

Rhoads, Steven E. (1985) *The Economist's View of the World*. Cambridge: Cambridge University Press.

Spitz, Elaine (1984) *Majority Rule*. Chatham: Chatham House Publishers.

Stokes, Donald (1963) "Spatial models of party competition", *American Political Science Review*, **57** Spring, pp. 368–77.

III

The Vote Motive

8

Voting Paradox

DENNIS C. MUELLER

8.1 Introduction

One of the more important intellectual developments in the social sciences since the Second World War has been the metamorphosis of political man into economic man. The assumption that politicians and bureaucrats pursue the public interest has increasingly given way to assumptions of self-interested motivation on the part of these key actors in the political drama. Models built on the self-interest motive behind political behavior have produced a rich harvest of hypotheses that seem more in tune with political realities.

There is one area of positive political science, however, where the economic-man assumption has not produced hypotheses that fit the data well. I refer, of course, to the theory of the individual voter. The most important theorem about the individual voter to emerge from the public choice literature is the prediction that a rational, egoistic voter will not vote. This prediction is blatantly and routinely rejected by the data. Moreover, the most frequently given reason for why individual citizens vote is out of "a sense of civic duty" (see, for example, Ashenfelter and Kelley, Jr., 1975). But this explanation is tantamount to saying that individual voters participate in the political process to advance the public interest. Having tossed out advancing the public interest as a motivation for those at the top of the political system, one is forced to reintroduce this motivation to explain the behavior of those at the bottom of the system, or so it would seem. This paper explores the theory and evidence behind this paradox.

8.2 The Rational-Voter Hypothesis

(a) Expected Utility Maximization

The rational-voter hypothesis was first developed by Anthony Downs (1957, chapters 11–14) and later was elaborated upon by Gordon Tullock (1967, pp. 110–14), and William Riker and Peter Ordeshook (1968, 1973). In deciding between two parties or candidates the voter envisages the different "streams of utility" to be derived from the policies promised by each candidate. The voter calculates the expected utility from each candidate's victory, and rationally votes for the candidate whose policies promise the highest utility. Thus, voting is a purely instrumental act in the theory of rational voting. One votes to bring about the victory of one's preferred candidate. The benefit from voting is the difference in expected utilities from the policies of the two candidates. Call this difference B.

Of course, it is unlikely that one's vote decides the outcome of the election. One's vote has an impact on the outcome only when (1) the votes of all other voters are evenly split between the two candidate, or (2) one's preferred candidate would lose by one vote if one did not vote. Call the probabilities of these two events occurring $P1$ and $P2$, respectively. If one's preferred candidate has a 50/50 chance of eventually winning should the first election end in a draw, then the probability that a single individual's vote is instrumental in bringing about the victory of the voter's preferred candidate is $P = P1 + 1/2\ P2$. The expected benefits from voting are PB.

P is a subjective probability and depends on how close the voter expects the election to be. Let P be the voter's expectation of the percent of the vote his/her preferred candidate will get, that is, the probability that any one voter votes for the candidate. Then

$$P = \frac{3e^{-2(N-1)(p-1/2)^2}}{2\sqrt{[2\pi(N-1)]}}$$

P declines as N increases, and as P diverts from $1/2$.[1] Even when $p = 1/2$, however, the probability that a single vote decides the election is but 0.00006, when there are 100,000,000 voters. If there were some cost, C, to voting, then the expected benefits from one's preferred candidate's victory would have to be large indeed to make the voter's calculus produce an expected utility gain from voting $(PB - C > 0)$.

Several people have noted that the probability of being run over by a car

---

[1] Owen and Grofman (1984) derive the following formula for the probability that a voter's vote breaks a tie when N is odd

$$POG = \frac{2e^{-2(N-1)(p-1/2)^2}}{2\sqrt{[2\pi(N-1)]}}$$

Now P_1 is simply the probability that N is odd (0.5) times P_{OG}, and P_2 is the same. Thus, $P = 1/2\ P_{OG} + 1/4\ P_{OG}$, which is the formula in the text. See also Beck (1975), Margolis (1977), Mayer and Good (1975).

going to or returning from the poles is similar to the probability of casting the decisive vote.[2] If being run over is worse than having one's preferred candidate lose, then this potential cost of voting alone would exceed the potential gain, and no rational self-interested individual would ever vote. But millions do, and thus the paradox.

If voting cannot be explained as a rational, self-interested act, then it must either be irrational or non-self-interested. We shall argue below that it is the former, but first we examine two attempts to reconcile it with the rationality postulate, and the arguments that voting is an ethical, altruistic, selfless act.

(b) A Taste for Voting

One way to reconcile voter-rationality with the act of voting is to posit the existence of benefits stemming from the act itself, but not dependent on the consequence of the act, that is, not depending on whether the vote is decisive. Individuals may have a patriotic or civic itch, and voting helps scratch that itch, yielding benefits (utility) D.[3] Thus, a person votes if $PB + D - C > 0$. With PB tiny, the act of voting is explained by the private gains (psychic income) from the act of voting itself, D, exceeding the personal costs of going to the polls, C. Voting is not undertaken as an instrumental act to determine the winning candidate, but as a private, or symbolic act from which satisfaction is derived independent of the outcome of the election.

This modification of the rational-voter hypothesis does reconcile the act of voting with individual rationality, but does so by robbing the rational, self-interest hypothesis of all of its predictive power. Any hypothesis can be reconciled with any conflicting piece of evidence with the addition of the appropriate auxiliary hypothesis. If I find that the quantity of Mercedes autos demanded increases following an increase in their price, I need not reject the law of demand, I need only set it aside in this case by presuming a taste for "snob appeal". But in so doing I weaken the law of demand, as a hypothesis let alone as a law, unless I have a tight logical argument for predicting this taste for snob appeal.

So it is with rescuing the rational, self-interested voter hypothesis by assuming a taste for civic duty. If this taste explains the act of voting, what else might it explain? If the voter is carried to the poles by a sense of civic duty, what motivation guides his actions once there? Does he vote for the candidate whose policies advance the voter's narrow interests, or does his sense of civic duty lead him to vote for the candidate whose victory is most

---

[2] B.F. Skinner (1948, p. 265), appears to be the first to have used the probability of an auto accident as a foil to destroy the rational-voter hypothesis, writing some nine years before Downs and cited in Goodin and Roberts (1975). Meehl (1977) also uses it.

[3] See Riker and Ordeshook (1968). Tullock (1967, p. 110) described these personal, psychic gains from voting as a negative cost, C.

beneficial to the general, public interest? If voters can be moved by civic duty, why not politicians and bureaucrats? Without a theory explaining the origin, strength, and extent of an individual's sense of civic duty, merely postulating a sense of civic duty "saves" rational egoism by robbing it of its predictive power.

(c)   The Rational Voter as Minimax-Regret Strategist

In a much discussed article, John Ferejohn and Morris Fiorina set out to show one means of rescuing rational choice theorists from this embarrassing predicament of the voting paradox (1974, p. 525). They recognize that the Achilles heel of rationality is the tiny, but positive probability that a vote changes the outcome of an election. They then posit that voters may be using a decision strategy that does not weigh each possible event by its probability, but rather gives all events equal weight, like the minimax-regret strategy. Under this decision rule one calculates not the actual pay-off for each strategy choice-state of the world combination, but the regret, that is, the loss one would experience in choosing the given strategy should this state of the world occur, as opposed to the best alternative strategy under this state of the world. One then chooses the action which minimizes the regret. Voting for one's second choice is not surprisingly a dominated strategy. So the decision reduces to whether to vote for one's first choice, or abstain. There are essentially two relevant states of the world to consider: *SI* the outcome of the election is independent of whether one votes, *SD* by voting the individual produces the victory of his/her preferred candidate by either breaking a tie or forcing a run-off, which the candidate wins. If one votes and the outcome is independent of one's vote, one regrets voting because one has incurred C to no avail (see table 8.1, cell a). If the outcome is independent of one's vote and one abstains, one has no regrets (b), likewise if one votes and casts the decisive vote (c). If the net gains from having one's candidate's victory (B) exceed the costs of voting (c), then one's maximum regret occurs when one abstains, when one's vote would have been decisive (d). The minimax-regret strategy is to vote.

Table 1   Minimax-regret options

		States	
		S_I	S_D
	Vote	(a) C	(c) O
Strategies			
	Abstain	(b) O	(d) B–C

The minimax-regret strategy is extremely conservative, and leads to rather bizarre behavior when applied to other decisions or even when extended within the voting context, as several critics have stressed.[4] Suppose, for example, a voter is indifferent to the Republican and Democratic candidates. His/her minimax-regret strategy is then to abstain. Suppose now the Nazi party enters a candidate. Now the minimax-regret criterion forces the voter to the polls to avoid the possible although highly unlikely event that the Nazi candidate wins, *and does so by a single vote.*

Few situations in everyday life in which individuals routinely employ minimax-regret strategies come to mind. Indeed, it is easier to think of examples where people exhibit the reverse tendency. Losing one's home and possessions must be a disaster at least comparable to having one's second choice for president win, and probably occurs with no less probability than that one's vote decides an election. Yet most people do not protect themselves against losses from floods even when insurance is sold at rates below acturial value (Kunreuther et al., 1978). Is it reasonable to assume that the same person is a risk taker with respect to home and personal possessions, but becomes a minimax-regret conservative when deciding whether or not to vote?

Ferejohn and Fiorina seem to think so. They cite Levine and Plott (1977) in support of the "possibility that individuals act as if they vary their decision rules in response to the decision context" (1975, p. 921). People also vote. The issue is not whether these things happen, but whether they can be explained and predicted using the rational egoism postulate. If individuals commonly switch from extremely risk-averse strategies to risk-taking strategies, how are we to predict their behavior? What theory tells us which situations elicit which strategy? Merely to be able to rationalize a given action *ex post* as possibly consistent with the use of a given decision strategy in this situation does not suffice to justify the rational egoism postulate as the foundation of a *general* behavior theory.

(d) The Rational-Voter Hypothesis: the Evidence

Ferejohn and Fiorina's major defense of their thesis rests upon empirical evidence they present in support of their hypothesis. The key determinant of voter turnout under the minimax-regret hypothesis is $B\text{-}C$. The costs of voting are difficult to define and measure, but data on the perceived differential between candidates are gathered in surveys like those conducted by the University of Michigan Survey Research Center. These may be used as a measure of B. B also figures prominently in the Downsian expected-utility model, as does P. Ferejohn and Fiorina's test of the minimax-regret

---

[4] Beck (1975), Goodin and Roberts (1975), Mayer and Good (1975) and Meehl (1977).

hypothesis is to see whether differences in B and P are significantly related to voter abstentions. Under minimax-regret only B should be related to voter turnout, the probability of the voter being decisive does not matter. Under Downsian expected-utility maximization both B and P should be related. The choice between the hypotheses rests on whether P, the probability that a voter's vote is decisive, is systematically related to abstentions.

Examining pre-and post-election survey results for 1952, 1956, 1960 and 1964 they find the minimax-regret hypothesis supported five times, the Downsian hypothesis only once (1975). In their sample about 90 percent of the respondents claimed to have voted. This is a much higher percentage than is typical of the USA and suggests a non-random sample or mis-representation of voter behavior. More importantly the variation in abstention rates is likely to be too small to allow one to run tests against other variables. A look at some additional evidence is warranted.

One of the first papers to present empirical evidence in support of the full rational-voter hypothesis is by Riker and Ordeshook (1968), from which we have taken the $R = PB + D - C$ formulation of this hypothesis. Riker and Ordeshook examine 4,294 responses to the 1952, 1956 and 1960 pre-presidential SRC questionnaires. They cross-tabulate responses to see whether P, B and D have a significant impact on the probability of an individual's voting. They find that when one holds the levels of the other two variables fixed, P, B and D all tend to have a significant impact on the probability of voting in the way the rational-voter hypothesis predicts. Thus, the Riker-Ordeshook results support both the instrumental-vote portion of the rational-voter hypothesis (PB matters), as well as the tastes (D) matter portion.

Although P, B and D all seem related to voter behavior in the manner the rational-voter hypothesis predicts, the quantitative importance of D in the Riker-Ordeshook data set is much greater than that of either P or B. The difference in probability of voting between those with high P (that is, those who thought the election would be close), and those with low P, ignoring both B and D, is 78 percent versus 72 percent. Eighty-two percent of those with high values for B voted, as opposed to 66 percent of those with low Bs. However, 87 percent of those with high Ds voted, against only 51 percent of those with low Ds. D was operationalized by Riker and Ordeshook through the questions related to citizen duty. Thus, a high sense of citizen duty has a quantitatively much larger impact on voter turnout, over a low sense of citizen duty, than do high values of either P or B over low values of these variables. Both parts of the rational-voter hypothesis are supported in the Riker-Ordeshook study, but the tastes component has the greater quantitative impact.

Among the most ambitious tests of the rational-voter hypothesis in terms both of sample size and number of variables included is that of Orley Ashenfelter and Stanley Kelley, Jr (1975). They examine the responses of 1,893 individuals surveyed by the SRC in connection with the 1960 and

1972 presidential elections. They relate individual answers to the question "Did you vote?" to a large set of variables grouped under the headings:

1 Personal characteristics
2 Cost variables
3 Strategic value of voting
4 Interest in campaign
5 Obligation toward voting

These variables can be related to the rational-voter hypothesis

$$R = PB + D - C \qquad\qquad 8.2$$

with C obviously related to group 2 variables; P and B both related to 3; B and possibly D related to 4; and D and 5 related. The personal characteristics of each individual (education, income, age, etc.) could be related to any one of the components of R, and do not clearly discriminate among the hypotheses.

Ashenfelter and Kelley's results give mixed support for the rational-voter hypothesis. Several measures of the cost of voting are statistically significant and of the right sign. Most important among these were the existence of a poll tax and literacy tests, legal in 1960 but abolished by 1972. A six-dollar poll tax in 1960 reduced the probability of an individual voting by 42 percent (p. 708). This result gives one a rough idea of what the distribution of $PB + D$ is for a large fraction of voters. Several of the other variables introduced to proxy the costs of voting do not perform well, although multicollinearity among the cost variables is a problem.

Turning to proxies for P and B, Ashenfelter and Kelley did not find that a voter's perception of whether the race is close or not had a statistically significant relationship to the probability of voting (p. 717). On the other hand, this proxy for P was of the correct sign (t value of 1.4 in the pooled regression), and the difference in the percentage of voters who thought the 1972 Nixon landslide would be close and the percentage that thought the Nixon-Kennedy 1960 election would be close was so great (10 percent versus 60 percent), that the difference in the levels for this variable between 1960 and 1972 is enough to explain 40 percent of the change in turnout between 1960 and 1972 (pp. 7201). Both of these findings are of considerable importance in explaining an otherwise perplexing inconsistency in the literature on voter participation, and we shall return to them.

Of the variables that might measure an individual's perception of the differences between the candidates (B), the answer to the question "How do you think you will vote?" proved to have the most explanatory power. If, at the time of the survey, an individual was undecided as to how he/she would vote, there was a 40 percent lower probability that this individual would vote at all (p. 717). If an individual's indecision arises because of a small perceived difference between the two candidates, a small B, then this result offers considerable support for the rational-voter hypothesis. But if indecision concerning how one will vote stems from indecision over whether one will vote, that is, one is not interested in the election, then the impact of the finding is less clear. Some people may simply prefer to remain aloof from the political process.

Individuals who felt a "strong obligation" to vote did so with a 30 percent higher probability; those with a "very strong obligation" voted 38 percent more often (pp. 719–20). These variables, measuring a sense of obligation to vote, had substantial explanatory power. Their impressive performance underlines the importance of the D term in the rational voter's calculus.

Ashenfelter and Kelley conclude that the theory of voting that is best supported by the evidence is that which posits a sense of duty or obligation as the primary motivation for voting. The variables with the greatest quantitative impact on voting are education, indecision, the dummy variables representing the sense of an obligation to vote, and certain cost variables (p. 724). This study offers rather strong support for the Tullock-Riker-Ordeshook interpretation of rational voting, which sees the D and C terms in the $BP + D - C$ equation as dominating the voting decision. As noted above, indecision might arise from a small B term, but indecision might also detract from the D term, if the sense of obligation to vote is weakened by not knowing for whom one should vote. Education should *ceteris paribus* reduce the importance of the BP term, since higher education levels should make one less susceptible to the misconception that one's vote makes a difference (that P is large). Education's positive impact on voting must then come through the D and C terms.

A very similar pattern of results appears in Morris Silver's (1973) analysis of 959 SRC questionnaires from the 1960 election survey. Several cost variables are significant, as are interest in the campaign, sense of citizen duty, and education. Whether the individual thinks the election will be close or not did not have a significant impact on the probability of voting. Thus, the only support for the BP portion of the rational-voter hypothesis in Silver's results comes through the "interest in the campaign" responses, if one assumes that these measure B, although Silver regards them as an index of D.

The same general picture of the voter's decision reappears in the analysis of survey results for some 2,500 voters in the 1968 presidential election using Opinion Research Corporation and SRC data by Brody and Page (1973). They focus upon the importance of indifference, the perceived difference between candidates, and alienation – the difference between a voter's position and his/her preferred candidate's position, in explaining abstentions. Abstentions increase with both indifference and alienation, but not by enought to confirm a purely instrumentalist interpretation of the act of voting. Forty-three percent of the 201 individuals who saw no difference between the candidates ($B = O$) voted nonetheless. Forty-four percent of the 174 who were both alienated and indifferent chose to vote (p. 6). For these voters and probably for many of the others, the D and C terms of R must explain the decision to vote.

A fifth test of the rational-voter hypothesis using SRC data, although explicitly built on Downs's formulation, is more difficult to interpret. Frohlich, Oppenheimer, Smith, and Young (1978, hereafter FOSY) cons-truct proxies for B, P and d from the SRC questions by combining various questions using different weights. They then make various assumptions about the distribution of the unknown C variable, and use combined B, P, D and C[5] to predict both turnout and choice of candidate for the 1964 presidential election. The assumption that C is lognormally distributed works best, and with this assumption they can predict turnout with an R^2 of 0.847.[6] But FOSY do not report their results in such a way as to allow one to gauge the relative importance of BP, D and C in explaining turnout, although the assumption concerning the distribution of C is important. However, the individual's opinion as to the efficacy of his/her vote (the proxy for P) does appear important, suggesting that P plays a bigger role in explaining turnout in the FOSY study than it did in those of Ferejohn and Fiorina, and Ashenfelter and Kelley.

The five preceding studies relate the characteristics and opinions of an individual voter to that person's decision to vote. A second set of studies tests the rational-voter hypothesis by relating aggregate figures on voter turnout, at say the state level, to characteristics of the population of voters in that state. These studies have basically tested to see whether P, the probability that a voter's vote changes the outcome, has a significant impact on voter turnouts. They have done so by regressing turnout figures on p, the expected vote of the leading candidate, and N, the size of the jurisdiction. Reference to the formula for P

$$P = \frac{3e^{-2(N-1)(p-1/2)^2}}{2\sqrt{[2\pi(N-1)]}} \qquad 8.3$$

indicates that both p and N are inversely related P in a non-linear way. Table 8.2 summarizes the results of eight studies, abstracting from the functional

[5] They formulate the $R + BP + D - C$ equation slightly differently, but their formulation and the one used here are equivalent.

[6] As with the Ferejohn and Fiorina SRC sample, a whopping 90.9 percent of the subjects reported having voted, raising issues of representativeness or misrepresentation.

The Vote Motive

Table 8.2 Impact of the probability of a vote's being decisive on voter turnouts

Study	Sample (Time period)	p^a	n^b
Barzel and Silberberg (1973)	122 gubernatorial elections 1962, 1964, 1966, 1968	− (0.01)	− INS
Silberman and Durden (1975)	400 congressional districts 1962	− (0.01)	− (0.01)
Tollison, Crain and Paulter (1975)	29 gubernatorial elections 1970	+ (0.10)	− INS
Kau and Rubin (1976)	50 states 1972 presidential	+ INS	− (0.01)
Settle and Abrams (1976)	26 national presidential elections, 1868–1972 omitting 1944	− (0.01)	
Crain and Deaton (1976)	50 states 1972 presidential	− (0.01)	− INS
Cabula and Murphy (1980)	35 states 1976 presidential	− (0.01)^a	
Foster (1984) Barzel-Silberberg	50 states 1968 presidential 1972 presidential 1976 presidential 1980 presidential	+ (0.05) − (0.01) − INS + INS	+ INS − INS − INS − INS
Foster (1984) Kau–Rubin	50 states 1968 presidential 1972 presidential 1976 presidential 1980 presidential	+ (0.05) − (0.01) + INS − INS	− INS − INS + INS − INS
Foster (1984) Silberman–Durden	200 states pooled 1968, 1972, 1976, 1980 presidential	− INS	− (0.10)
Foster (1984) Crain–Deaton	200 states pooled 1968, 1972, 1976, 1980 presidential	− INS	− (0.01)
Foster (1984) Wolfgram–Foster	200 states pooled 1968, 1972, 1976, 1980 presidential	− (0.10)	− INS

[a] p expected (actual) per cent of vote for leading candidate.
[b] *N* size of jurisdiction.

[c] Proxy for *ex ante* measure of closeness used, proportion of Democrats in the lower house for all states with more than 50 per cent Democratic representation.

form used to introduce p and N. Each study differs from the others with respect to choice of functional form, and choice of other variables included. But we focus here on just p and N. A negative coefficient for each variable is interpreted as consistent with what the rational-voter hypothesis predicts. Only signs and significance levels are given in the table. Cebula and Murphy (1980) attempt an *ex ante* measure of p by limiting their sample to states with a Democratic majority in the lower house, and estimating p as the fraction of the house which is Democratic. Foster's (1984) last set of results employs a similar *ex ante* measure of p but for both Republican and Democratic majorities. All other studies assume rational expectations on the part of voters, and measure p by the actual split in the vote between the candidates on election day.

Considering first the studies in the upper half of table 8.2, we observe that both p and N generally are of the correct sign and more often than not have statistically significant coefficients. From these studies one is inclined to conclude that voter turnouts are positively related to the probability of a single vote's being decisive.

The bottom half of table 8.2 summarizes the results of Carroll Foster's (1984) re-estimation of the models from four studies as well as the estimates for his own model using data for the 1968, 1972, 1976 and 1980 presidential elections. Instability in the coefficient estimates across cross-sections precluded pooling the data to re-estimate the Barzel-Silberberg and Kau-Rubin models, so the results for the individual cross-sections are presented. In general, voter turnouts are not related to p or N in Foster's retesting of the rational-voter hypothesis. Outside of the Nixon landslide in 1972, p does quite badly. N performs only moderately more consistently.

Foster concludes 'that the perceived probability of a tied election at the state level is not a powerful or reliable factor in explaining across-state variation in voter participation rates in presidential elections' (p. 688). This conclusion seems justified. But p and N have the predicted sign more often than not, and when their coefficients are significant they are with but one exception of the correct sign. Here the Ashenfelter-Kelley results with regard to voter perceptions of the closeness of an election should be recalled. They found that there was a statistically weak and quantitatively small positive effect on the chances of an individual voting if the individual thought that the election was close. Changes in voter perception of the closeness of an election should vary considerably from one election to another. A pre-election Gallup poll projection of a candidate's getting 60 percent of the vote makes the candidate's victory a virtual certainty. Few would bet against a candidate with pre-election poll percentages in the 54–6 range. The difference in prior probabilities between an election that is 'too close to call', like the 1960 Kennedy-Nixon contest and the 1972 Nixon landslide over McGovern, is the difference between a coin flip and a sure bet. With these shifts in odds, even if only some voters are weakly influenced by changes in their perception of the closeness of the contest, large changes in turnout may ensue. This consideration may explain why the closeness of the race in each state seems to have had a significant impact on voter turnouts in Nixon's 1972 landslide win (Crain and Deaton, 1977; Foster-Barzel-Silberberg and Foster-Kau-Rubin, 1984), and why efficacy affected voter turnouts in Johnson's 1964 landslide (FOSY, 1978).

In some ways the weak performance of differences in P in explaining voter turnouts supports the overall view of the voter as a rational egoist more than it contradicts this image. Even when the probability of each voter's voting for one of the candidates is 0.5, the probability of a single vote being decisive in a polity of 100,000,000 is only 0.00006. As Riker and Ordeshook (1968) note regarding their finding that voter turnout is responsive to changes in P, this finding implies an unusually elastic response by voters to changes in probabilities. If drivers responded to changes in the probability of accidents to the same degree, heavy rain would find the roads abandoned. Riker and Ordeshook (1968) suggest that the highly elastic response of voters to changes in P may be due to the persuasive impact of television and radio announcements claiming that "your vote counts" (1968, pp. 38–9). Consistent with this explanation for the importance of *perceived* closeness of the election are the results of Tollison, et al. (1975). They found an enhanced impact for the closeness variable in states with relatively large newspaper circulation. 'Information concerning the expected outcome [tends] to make more people vote in close races' (p. 45). But if voters are so easily misled concerning the importance of their vote, one's confidence in the intelligence of the rational voter is weakened. While *naïveté* and rationality are not strictly opposites, the existence of the former does undermine the importance of the rationality assumption somewhat.

The results reviewed here suggest that changes in P and voter abstentions are weaker than Riker and Ordeshook assume. If so, then voters are less naive about their ability to change the outcome of the election, and thus behave in what seems like a more sophisticatedly rational way. But in so doing they confirm the more cynical interpretation of voter rationality, that is, the non-instrumentalist view that voting is determined solely by its entertainment-psychic income value (D), and private costs (C). This interpretation raises the issue, in deriving a theory of voting, of the determinants of D and C. From whence springs a sense of civic duty, and how does one predict its variability across individuals and over time?

8.3 The Ethical-Voter Hypothesis

Unless one escapes the voting paradox in the tautological way of postulating a taste for (psychic income from) voting (the D term), one must either reject the postulate that voters are rational or that they act in their (narrowly defined) self-interest. One group of scholars has chosen the second alternative.[7] They view the voter as having two sets of preferences, an ethical set and a selfish set. The latter includes only one's own utility, the former includes the utilities of others, or one's perception thereof. In some situations, for example the consumer in the market place, one uses one's selfish preference to decide, one maximizes one's utility as conventionally defined. In others, one employs one's ethical preferences. Voting is assumed to be one of those situations in which one's ethical preferences govern. Voting is presumed to improve the welfare of others by, say, improving the quality of the outcomes of the political process (better outcomes arise when all vote), or by helping to maintain democratic institutions. The D term in $R = PB + D - C$ is essentially the effect of one's vote on the welfare of all others.[8]

This Jekyll and Hyde view of man's nature has a long and distinguished ancestry. Indeed, its ancestry is so long and distinguished that one cowers from contradicting it. I have no substantive objections to this conceptualization of the voter's decision, as a way to rationalize the consistency of the rationality assumption and the act of voting. The importance of 'a sense of civic duty' in explaining voting resonates with this 'ethical-voter' hypothesis. But the ethical-voter hypothesis suffers from the same deficiency as the 'taste for participation' explanation for voting. Instead of providing us with a hypothesis with which we can develop a theory of voting and perhaps of other cooperative-social behavior, it provides an *ex post* rationalization for the act. It provides the end for a story about voting, not the beginning for a behavioral theory of voting.

Elsewhere (1986), I have suggested that the kind of ethical-selfish dichotomy presumed in the ethical theory of voting might be operationalized as a predictive theory by assuming that each individual i maximizes an objective function of the following form:

$$O_i = U_i + \Theta\Sigma U_j \qquad\qquad 8.4$$
$$i \neq j$$

A purely selfish voter would set $\theta = 0$, a fully altruistic voter would set $\theta = 1$, as in Harsanyi (1955). In either case the individual is behaving rationally in the sense of maximizing an objective function. In either case the analyst benefits from the most important advantage of the rationality assumption, clear predictions about human behavior, in this case in the form of first order

[7] See Goodin and Roberts (1975), Margolis (1982) and Etzioni (1986). Harsanyi's (1955) approach is the same, although he does not discuss the act of voting. See also Arrow's (1963, pp. 81–91) discussion.
[8] This is the way FOSY describe the term in their Downsian test, also.

conditions to the maximization of 8.4 with θ equal to either zero or one. But the first order conditions for (2) differ, in general, if one sets $\theta = 0$, or $\theta = 1$. How does one know which assumption to make? From the SRC surveys it would appear that some individuals think of voting as a selfish act ($\theta = 0$), others as an ethical one ($\theta = 1$). How does one differentiate between selfish and ethical voters? Moreover, in situations where the ethical decision variable is continuous for example, how much to contribute voluntarily to the provision of a public good), rather than 0, 1 as with voting, it appears that some θ less than one but greater than zero is required to make an individual's observed behavior consistent with the maximization of (2). How can one predict when an individual will behave selfishly and when ethically or the degree to which one's ethical preferences govern one's actions, when ethical behavior is not a simple either/or decision. To make these predictions one needs to do more than merely posit the existence of ethical preferences, one needs a theory of how ethical preferences are formed, what determines their strength, what triggers their use. One needs a theory of learning, which probably must be found in the area of psychology or sociology.

8.4 Ethical Preferences as Selfish Behavior

Behaviorist psychology seems to offer the best description of the learning process.[9] Actions followed by rewards increase in frequency. actions followed by punishment decline in frequency. Man learns to avoid doing that which brings about pain, and to do that which produces pleasure. When one observes how man learns, it is difficult to reject the postulate that man is innately a selfish animal. The same principles appear to describe the learning processes of all animals. Man differs from other animals not in how he learns but in what he learns. Man is capable of learning far more complex behavioral patterns than are other creatures.

Ethical behavior is learned. Much of this learning takes place when we are children. When we commit acts that harm others we are punished by our parents, teachers and other adult supervisors. Actions that benefit others are rewarded. Ethical behavior patterns learned as children can be maintained at high frequency levels through adulthood by only occasional positive and negative reinforcement.[10] what we normally describe as ethical behavior is inherently no more or less selfish than what we call selfish behavior. It is a conditioned response to certain stimuli governed by past reinforcement experience.

There are several advantages to using behaviorist psychology to explain

[9] For reviews of the basic principles of behavioral psychology, see Notterman (1970) and Schwartz and Lacey (1982), chapter 1–6.
[10] Ibid.

ethical behavior. First, it allows us to work with a single conceptualization of man, a conceptualization consistent with the selfish egoism postulate underlying both economics and public choice. Second, it allows us to develop a purely positive theory of behavior, free from the normative prescripts that often accompany the Jekyll-and-Hyde view of man. Third, it gives us some insight as to what variables might explain when individuals behave in what is commonly described as an ethical manner, and when they do not. Home environment during childhood, education experience, religion, community stability and any other factors which might affect an individual's ethical learning experience, become possible candidates as explanatory variables in a positive theory of ethical behavior.

Thus, to explain ethical behavior like voting I propose retaining the self-interest assumption of public choice, and dropping or at least relaxing the rationality assumption. I propose dropping the fiction, which is the heart of our operationalization of the rationality assumption that individuals conciously maximize the objective function in (8.4) with $\theta = 0$. Individuals do not consciously maximize anything, as the many critics of the rationality-maximization assumption have pointed out down through the years. Moreover, in situations involving ethical choices, the usual defense of the rationality-maximization assumption, that the implications fit the data well, typically does not stand up. For example, the predictive power of the selfish-utility maximization assumption collapses in prisoners' dilemma situations.

The same empirical objection can be raised against assuming that in a prisoners' dilemma an individual pulls out his/her ethical preferences and rationally maximizes (8.4) setting $\Theta = 1$. This assumption fails by predicting far more ethical behavior than we observe.

Equation (8.4) can be useful in describing behavior in situations involving ethical choices, however, if we assume that individuals act *as if* they were maximizing (8.4), with some θ not necessarily equal to zero or one. The argument is similar to Alchian's (1950) argument that competition eliminates less profitable firms, leaving only the most profitable, whose actions resemble those they would have chosen had they consciously been maximizing profit even when they were not. It is in society's collective interest in certain contexts, which we might characterize as prisoner's dilemma situations,[11] to establish institutions that condition people to behave

---

[11] Voting, as an instrumental act, is not well characterized as a prisoners' dilemma. For most prisoners' dilemmas, for example stealing and not stealing, collective welfare increases as the fraction of players choosing the cooperative strategy increases. But the outcome when 80 percent of the population vote may be identical to that when 40 percent vote, and even when different may not be better.

If individuals vote not to secure the victory of a given candidate, but as an act of civic duty motivated by the belief that democratic institutions are strengthened by citizen participation, then the prisoners' dilemma analogy holds.

as if they were maximizing (8.4) with $\theta = 1$. While this degree of cooperative behavior is seldom achieved, the conditioning process is usually successful in eliciting some degree of cooperation. Observed behavior thus resembles that which one would expect if individuals consciously maximized (8.4) with some $\theta > 0$, even though (because) individual behavior is governed by social conditioning.[12] Under this interpretation θ is a behavior parameter to be explained by the individual's or group's conditioning history, not a choice variable set equal to zero or one depending on whether the individual has chosen today to be Hyde or Jekyll.

8.5　The Selfish Voter

Normally, when we model individual behavior, an individual's past history plays no part in the analysis. Sunk costs are sunk, bygones are bygones, and all that matter are the future consequences of an individual's actions. With respect to voting, this conceptualization of the voting act boils the number of relevant variables down to three: the benefits from the preferred candidate's victory, B, the probability of one's vote bringing about this victory, P, and the costs of getting to the polls, C.

Modelling individual behavior as conditioned by past learning shifts attention from the future payoffs from different actions to the past history of the individual. The list of potential explanatory variables is expanded considerably.

We have already made the point that years of education might, if voters were purely rational and egoistic, be expected to be negatively related to the probability of voting. The uneducated might be duped by television advertisements to believe their vote would count, but the more educated should remain rationally cynical regarding the efficacy of their vote.

One learns more than probability theory in school, however. One learns also to cooperate. Number of years of successfully completed schooling measures the amount and strength of conditioning in the numerous cooperative games played in a school environment. By the time one graduates one has been rewarded again and again for going by the rules, and doing what is expected, and one has usually been punished on those occasions when one has broken the rules. One expects those with more education to behave more cooperatively, to break fewer rules be they driving laws or social mores, and to do more of what is expected of them as a citizen.

---

[12] Darwinian selection will play a role in determining which social institutions survive or even which social groups. If the collective gains from cooperation are large, those groups which are more successful at eliciting cooperative behavior (including individuals to behave as if $\theta = 1$) will have higher survival chances. Evolutionary forces may also select gene structures more conducive to the teaching and learning of cooperative behavior, when cooperation raises individual survival chances.

Years of education have proven to be positively and significantly related to voter turnout in virtually every study (Campbell, Converse, Miller and Stokes, 1964, pp. 251–4; Milbrath, 1965; Kelley, Jr, Ayres and Bowen, 1967; Verba and Nie, 1972, pp. 95–101; Silver, 1973; Brody and Page, 1973; Ashenfelter and Kelley, Jr, 1975).

Income is another variable, which invariably picks up the wrong sign in explaining voter turnout from what a straightforward application of the rational egoism postulate would imply. The higher one's income, the higher the opportunity cost of time, and *ceteris paribus* the lower the probability that one goes to the polls.[13] yet income is consistently, strongly positive correlated with the probability of voting (Dahl, 1961 and Lane, 1966 as cited by Frey, 1971; Milbrath, 1965; Kelley, Jr, Ayres and Bowen, 1967; Dennis, 1970; Verba and Nie, 1972, pp. 95–101; Silver, 1973; Silberman and durden, 1975; Ashenfelter and Kelley, Jr, 1975; Crain and Deaton, 1977; Foster, 1984).

Income, like a graduation certificate, is a mark of success at playing by certain rules of the societal game. (Of course, some individuals accumulate income by successfully breaking the rules, but I doubt that many of these persons are part of the SRC survey panels.) Individuals with high income are more likely to go by the rules and to live within the social mores. Moreover, their high incomes are evidence that they have been rewarded for doing so, since money is society's chief token reinforcer. High-income individuals like the highly educated can be expected to break fewer rules, and to behave in other socially cooperative ways, like voting.

There are other explanations for why income and education might be positively related to political participation, of course, and some of these are more compatible with the rational egoism postulate.[14] Without denying the possible relevance of these explanations, I nevertheless favor starting from a behavioralist view toward voting and other forms of cooperative behavior, both because this approach offers a more natural explanation for why these and other background characteristics of the voter matter, and because this approach offers greater potential for developing additional hypotheses about individual behavior in prisoners' dilemma-type situations like voting.[15]

[13] See discussion of Russell (1972), Fraser (1972) and Tollinson and Willett (1973).

[14] See in particular Frey (1971), and ensuing discussion by Russell (1972), Fraser (1972), Frey (1972) and Tollinson and Willett (1973).

[15] Much has been made in recent years of the decline in voter turnouts in presidential elections since 1960. In any presidential election, over half of the voters are rewarded for going to the polls in that this action is followed by their preferred candidate's victory. In this way, majority rule tends to sustain political participation. Since 1960, however, three presidents have been elected whose performance in office must have been a great disappointment to their supporters: Johnson because of Vietnam, Nixon because of Watergate, Carter because of Carter. Thus, voting for the winning candidate was punished, and this punishment may explain the drop in the frequency with which individuals go to the polls. Barring a Vietnam or Watergate between now and 1988, Reagan's obvious good performance in the eyes of his supporters should increase voter turnouts, if this line of reasoning is correct.

8.6 Normative Implications

All of the public choice literature as it pertains to the outcomes of committee voting, or elections assumes that voters vote, whether sincerely or strategically, to attain that outcome promising them the highest benefits. All of public choise is based on the assumption that it is the attainment of B, in the equation $R = PB + D - C$, which determines the way in which an individual votes.

The logical foundation for this assumption is significantly undermined in elections or committees in which the number of voters is large. P is then infinitesimal, the PB term vanishes and considerations other than the instrumental value of the vote determine whether or not an individual votes, or at least they ought to if the individual is both rational and sufficiently intelligent to make a reasonable guess as to the magnitude of P.

The empirical literature reviewed here is reassuring with respect to both the intelligence and rationality of voters in that it indicates that P has a rather weak (statistically) and inconsistent relationship to the decision to vote. The primary explanation for why individuals vote comes from the D and C terms in R as Downs (1957) and Tullock (1967) first asserted. What then are the implications of this conclusion for the rest of the public choice literature that assumes voters are voting to maximize B? If PB does not explain why individuals vote, can B explain how they vote? If it does not, what does?

Brennan and Buchanan (1983) have posed these questions. They emphasize that the knowledge that one's vote has a negligible effect on the outcome of the election frees one to vote in ways inconsistent with one's own interest. One can vote in a totally whimsical fashion secure in the knowledge that the satisfaction of this whim through voting will not affect one's welfare in any other way.

Given the apparent importance of the D term in explaining why individuals vote, we need to draw out the implications of this "taste" variable for the question of how they vote. Do individuals who are motivated to vote because of D nevertheless vote to bring about some purely selfishly-determined B once they get to the polls, or do they perhaps give some weight to the impact of the outcomes on the welfare of others?

A few studies exist which examine the rationality of an individual's vote in improving the voter's narrowly defined self-interest. One of the easiest of these to interpret is Jeffrey W. Smith's (1975) analysis of voting in Oregon Intermediate Election Districts. Voting takes place on whether the tax burdens of the districts should be equalized or not, with equalization raising the tax rates of some districts and lowering those of others. A simple application of the self-interest hypothesis implies a vote for equalization if it lowers one's taxes, against it if it raises them. The percentage favoring equalization was positively related to whether one gained from equalization, and was larger for large gains (Smith, 1975, p. 64).

Percentage favoring equalization of large gainers   60.7[16]
Percentage favoring equalization of small gainers   52.9
Percentage favoring equalization of small losers   46.1
Percentage favoring equalization of large losers   32.7

Bloom's (1979) analysis of voting on tax classification in Massachusetts provides similar support for a private-interest explanation for voting. Caution should be exercised in generalizing from these results, however. In each case the voter is essentially confronted with the question of whether he/she prefers a higher or lower tax rate *ceteris paribus*. Such issues must raise the importance of private interest to its highest level. Yet in Smith's study over 40 percent of the population voted to raise their tax rates. Some factors beyond private interest must have influenced the voting of this substantial fraction of citizens.

A tougher test of the private-interest explanation for voting comes on issues where the "public interest", that is, the welfare of others, is clearly affected by an issue as well as one's own welfare. Transfer payments present a good example. The narrow private-interest assumption is that all recipients of transfers vote for them, all payees against them. This assumption underlies Meltzer and Richard's (1981) model of the growth of government using the median voter theorem, and Peltzman's (1980) explanation based on candidate competition. Gramlich and Rubinfeld (1982) found from an examination of the responses of 2,001 households in Michigan to a telephone survey that transfer recipients (the aged, unemployed and those on welfare) had only a moderately higher tendency to vote against a tax limitation proposal than non-recipients. A more significant difference occurred for public employees, yet even here, 42 percent of those voting voted to *restrict* expenditures.

Sears, Law, Tyler and Allen, Jr (1980) examined Center for Political Studies survey data for the 1976 presidential election. Their concern was "to assess the relative roles of self-interest and symbolic attitudes in producing policy attitudes and issue voting on four controversial policy areas" (unemployment, national health insurance, busing of school children for racial integration, and crime). They concluded that "in general, symbolic attitudes (liberalism-conservatism, party identification, and racial prejudice[17]) had

---

[16] Large gainers (losers) had their tax rates lowered (raised) by equalization by more than $1 per $1,000 of assessed value.

[17] The importance of racial prejudice as a determinant of voter behavior reinforces the case for using behavioral psychology to explain individual actions in social interaction situations, like prisoners' dilemmas, as opposed to a pure, rational-egoist-game-theoretic explanation, or a dual preference explanation.

The typical rational-egoist explanation for cooperative behavior in a prisoners' dilemma is to posit an indefinite sequence prisoners' dilemma supergame with each player playing the tit-for-tat strategy (Taylor, 1976; Axelrod, 1984). Such an explanation is consistent with

strong effects, while self-interest had almost none" (p. 679). They also reviewed several studies reaching similar conclusions with respect to the relative importance of self-interest. While survey results are susceptible to different interpretations, this literature strongly suggests that considerations beyond one's narrowly defined self-interest influence a citizen's vote, once he/she is at the polling booth.

If the act of voting is explained as a cooperative response to a perceived prisoners' dilemma by individuals who have been conditioned to behave in prisoners' dilemma situations as if they were maximizing equation (2) with $\theta > 0$, then it is tempting to assume that they behave analogously once inside the voting booth. Furthermore, it is tempting to characterize the objective

$$O_i = U_i + \theta \sum_{j \neq i} U_j$$

function as i's (implicit) conceptualization of the public interest. That is, it is tempting to interpret the literature reviewed above as suggesting that voters, who vote because of a sense of civic duty, vote according to a (conditioned) conceptualization of the public interest. If this interpretation were to be sustained, it would leave us with the following paradox. Suppose we take as given the assumption that candidates act as if maximizing their self-interest and not the public interest when campaigning and in office and do so by choosing policies to maximize their expected votes. If, however, voters vote for that candidate who comes closest to their conception of the public interest, then candidates will adopt policies consistent with a particular conception of the public interest, albeit not necessarily their own, personal conception. The public-interest conception of politics is pulled from the ashes by the selfish, but ethically-conditioned, voter's behavior[18]

It is fitting for this volume in honor of Tullock, himself a problem-poser, that we close this essay as we began with a paradox.

$O_i = U_i + \theta \sum_{j \approx i} U_j$ over the supergame with $\theta = 1$.

Racial prejudice can be characterized as *as-if* maximization of O_i with $\theta < O$ for some racial group. That racial prejudice is a conditioned behavioral response to certain stimuli is an easily defended proposition. But what kind of supergame and supergame strategies lead one to behave as if one maximizes (2) with negative θ?

I suppose those who favor explaining cooperative behavior as the maximization of a second, ethical set of preferences, would explain racial prejudice by assuming yet a third set of preferences. Now we have Mr Hyde, Dr Jekyll and Simon Legree. To explain sexism we assume a fourth set of preferences, and so on. However useful this approach is to characterizing different behavior in different situations, it does not take one anywhere in developing a theory to explain and predict behavior.

[18] Gordon Tullock (1984) argues similarly.

References

Alchian, Armen A. (1950) 'Uncertainty, evolution and economic theory', *Journal of Political Economy*, **58**, June, pp. 211–21.

Arrow, Kenneth J. (1963) *Social Choice and Individual Values*. New York: Wiley.

Ashenfelter, Orley and Kelley, Stanley, Jr. (1975) 'Determinants of participation in presidential elections', *Journal of Law and Economics*, **18**, December, pp. 695–733.

Axelrod, Robert (1984) *The Evolution of Cooperation*. New York: Basic Books.

Barzel, Yoram and Silberberg, Eugene (1973) 'Is the act of voting rational?', *Public Choice*, **16**, Fall, pp. 51–8.

Beck, Nathaniel (1975) 'The paradox of minimax regret', *American Political Science Review*, **69**, September, p. 918.

Bloom, Howard S (1979) 'Public choice and private interest: explaining the vote for property tax classification in Massachusetts', *National Tax Journal*, **32**, December, pp. 527–34.

Brennan, Geoffrey and Buchanan, James (1983) 'Voter choice and the evaluation of political alternatives', mimeo, George Mason University.

Brody, Richard A. and Page, Benjamin I. (1973) 'Indifference, alienation and rational decisions', *Public Choice*, **15**, Summer, pp. 1–17.

Campbell, Angus (1964) Converse, Philip E., Miller, Warren E. and Stokes, Donald E. *The American voter*. New York: Wiley.

Cebula, Richard J. and Murphy, Dennis R. (1980) 'The electoral college and voter participation rates: an exploratory note', *Public Choice*, **35**, pp. 185–90.

Crain, W. Mark and Deaton, Thomas H. (1977) 'A note on political participation as consumption behavior', *Public Choice*, **32**, Winter, pp. 131–5.

Dahl, Robert A (1961) *Who Governs? Democracy and Power in an American City*. New Haven: Yale University Press.

Dennis, Jack (1970) 'Support for the institution of elections by the mass public', *American Political Science Review*, **64**, September, pp. 269–80.

Downs, Anthony (1957) *An Economic Theory of Democracy*. New York: Harper and Row.

Etzioni, Amitai (1986) 'The case for a multiple utility conception', mimeo, George Washington University.

Ferejohn, John A. and Fiorina, Morris P. (1974) 'The paradox of not voting: a decision theoretic analysis', *American Political Science Review*, **68**, June, pp. 525–36.

Ferejohn, John A. and Fiorina, Morris P. (1975) 'Closeness counts only in horseshoes and dancing', *American Political Science Review*, **69**, September, pp. 920–5.

Foster, Carroll B. (1984) "The performance of rational voter models in recent presidential elections", *American Political Science Review*, **78**, September, pp. 678–90.

Fraser, John (1972) 'Political participation and income level: an exchange', *Public Choice*, **13**, Fall, pp. 115–18.

Frey, Bruno S. (1971) 'Why do high income people participate more in politics?' *Public Choice*, **11**, Fall, pp. 101–5.

Frey, Bruno S. (1972) 'Political participation and income level: an exchange, reply', *Public Choice*, **13**, Fall, pp. 119–22.

Frohlich, Norman, Oppenheimer, Joe A., Smith, Jeffrey and Young, Oran R. (1978) 'A test of Downsian voter rationality: 1964 presidential voting', *American Political Science Review*, **72**, March, pp. 178–97.

Goodin, R.E. and Roberts, K.W.S. (1975) 'The ethical voter', *American Political Science Review*, **69**, September, pp. 926–8.

Gramlich, Edward M. and Rubinfeld, Daniel L. (1982) 'Voting on spending', *Journal of Policy Analysis and Management*, **1**, Summer, pp. 516-33.

Harsanyi, John C. (1955) 'Cardinal welfare, individualistic ethics, and interpersonal comparisons of utility', *Journal of Political Economy*, **63**, August, pp. 309–21.

Kau, James B. and Rubin, Paul H. (1976) 'The electoral college and the rational vote', *Public Choice*, **27**, Fall, pp. 101–7.

Kelley, Stanley, Jr, Ayres, Richard E. and Bowen, William G. (1967) 'Registration and voting: putting first things first', *American Political Science Review*, **61**, June, pp. 359–79.

Kunreuther, Howard et al. (1978) *Disaster Insurance Protection*. New York: Wiley.

Lane, Robert E. (1966) 'Political involvement through voting', in Seasholes, B. (ed.) *Voting, Interest Groups, and Parties*, Glenview, Ill. Levine, Michael E. and Plott, Charles R. (1977) 'Agenda influence, and its implications', *Virginia Law Review*, **63**, May, pp. 561–604.

Margolis, Howard (1977) 'Probability of a tied election', *Public Choice*, **31**, Fall, pp. 135–8.

Margolis, Howard (1982) *Selfishness, Altruism, and Rationality*. Cambridge: Cambridge Unversity Press.

Mayer, Lawrence S. and Good, I.J. (1975) 'Is minimax regret applicable to voting decisions?' *American Political Science Review*, **69**, September, pp. 916–17.

Meehl, Paul E. (1977) 'The selfish citizen paradox and the throw away vote argument', *American Political Science Review*, **71**, March, pp. 11–30.

Meltzer, Alan H. and Richard Scott F. (1981) 'A rational theory of the size of government', *Journal of Political Economy*, **89**, October, pp. 914–27.

Milbrath, Lester W. (1965) *Political Participation*. Chicago: Rand McNally.

Mueller, Dennis C. (1986) 'Toward a more general theory of egoistic behavior', Presidential Address, Public Choice Society, Baltimore, March.

Notterman, Joseph M. (1970) *Behavior: A Systematic Approach*. New York: Random House.

Owen, Guillermo and Grofman, Bernard (1984) 'To vote or not to vote: the paradox of nonvoting', *Public Choice*, **42**, pp. 311–25.

Peltzman, Sam (1980) 'The growth of government', *Journal of Law and Economics*, **23**, October, pp. 209–88.

Riker, William H. and Ordeshook, Peter C. 'A theory of the calculus of voting', *American Political Science Review*, **62**, March, pp. 25-42.

Riker, William H. and Ordeshook, Peter C. *Introduction to Positive Political Theory*. Englewood Cliffs: Prentice Hall, 1973.

Russell, Keith P. 'Political participation and income level: an exchange', *Public Choice*, **13**, Fall, pp. 115–18.

Schwartz, Barry and Lacey, Hugh *Behaviorism, Science, and Human Nature*. New York: Norton.

Sears, David O., Law, Richard R., Tyler, Tom R. and Allen, Harris M., Jr. 1980
'Self-interest vs. symbolic politics in policy attitudes and presidential voting'.
American Political Science Review. 74, September, pp. 670–84.

Settle, Russell F. and Abrams, Burton A. 'The determinants of voter participation: a
more general model', *Public Choice*, 27, Fall, pp. 81–9.

Silberman, Jonathan I. and Durden, Gary C. 'The rational behavior theory of voter
participation: the evidence from congressional election', *Public Choice*, 23, Fall, pp.
101–8.

Silver, Morris 'A demand analysis of voting costs and voting participation', *Social
Science Research*, 2, August, pp. 111–24.

Skinner, B.F. (1948) *Walden II*. New York: Macmillan 1948.

Smith, Jeffrey W. 'A clear test of rational voting', *Public Choice*, 23, Fall, pp. 55–67. 1975

Taylor, Michael J. (1976) *Anarchy and Cooperation*. New York: Wiley.

Tollinson, Robert, Crain, Mark and Paulter, Paul (1975) 'Information and voting: an
empirical note', *Public Choice*, 24, Winter, pp. 43–9.

Tollinson, Robert D. and Willett, Thomas D. (1973) 'Some simple economics of
voting and not voting', *Public Choice*, 16, Fall, pp. 59–71.

Tullock, Gordon (1967) *Toward a Mathematics of Politics*. Ann Arbor: University of
Michigan Press.

Tullock, Gordon (1984) 'A (partial) rehabilitation of the public interest theory',
Public Choice, 42(1), pp. 89–99.

Verba, Sidney and Nie, Norman H. *Participation in America*. New York: Harper and
Row, 1972.

9

The Robustness of the Voting Paradox
CHARLES R. PLOTT

9.1 Introduction

Dennis Mueller has provided us with an excellent review of data that bears on the question of why people vote. He has attempted to provide a coherent theory of a very complex pattern of behavior and he has presented us with paradoxes and challenges in a well-written and well-documented paper.

The data are fascinating, but the theory he weaves to explain it is less so. My reservations begin with the formulation of the problem, but my major reservation rests on the primary structure of Mueller's theory.

The opening remarks of the paper claim 'The most important theorem about the individual voter to emerge from the public choice literature is the prediction that a rational egoistic voter will not vote'. Notwithstanding the fact that Tullock's writing can be referenced as a source of this "theorem" the statement is not true. The solution of the voter game involves mixed strategies (Palfrey and Rosenthal, 1983; 1985). All voters always not voting would be just as irrational as all voters always voting. Exactly what behavior is "rational" might be very context related depending upon the preference of the electorate and the positions of the candidate.

The relationship of the mixed strategy equilibrium to Mueller's equation (1) is not clear at all. The comparative statics of the Nash equilibrium can be complicated and perhaps perverse. Consequently, the relevance of the specifications in table 8.1 remains to be established. In other words, the comparative static properties of equilibrim behavior are unknown so the implications of the tests are unclear. We do not know how equilibrium turnout should vary with the parameters Mueller lists.

9.2 The Essence of the Voting Paradox

Let me now turn to the structure of the theory. The essence of the model is a Bergson-Samuelson social welfare function with an index that identifies the person to whom it belongs. In order to see this, let x denote the social state and note Mueller's additive function:

$$O_i = U_i (x) + \sum_{j=i} U_j (x). \qquad 9.1$$

Now notice that this functional relationship is simply a special case (additive) of the general welfare function:

$$O_i = W^i(U_i(x), \ldots, U_n(x)). \qquad 9.2$$

Presumably, Oi is the objective function that guides i's choices over social states in light of his own feelings about the well-being of himself and others. This is the classical Bergson-Samuelson welfare idea applied to voting. I have argued elsewhere that such theories of personal ethics do not escape the Arrow-type impossibility problems and that alternative theories exist that have a degree of plausibility (Plott, 1972; 1976). It follows that I am unconvinced by the internal consistency of models such as Mueller's. I am also skeptical about tests of such theories as is alluded to in Mueller's section on the prisoner's dilemma. Tests are very difficult because in prisoner's dilemma experiments the repeated-games nature of contests serves to add competing hypothesis which are consistent with the data. There is no need to pursue this discussion here and I add it only because Mueller appears to have overlooked this difficulty with tests of the theory.

The real difficulty with Mueller's theory appears when the theory is applied to the voting problem. Mueller does not indicate explicitly how the theory is to be applied but the following seems to be a straightforward extension of the analysis. Let the position x_1 and x_2 of the candidates be evaluated through the objective function $O_i(x)$. The subjective value difference in positions is of course $B = O_i(x_i) - O_i(x_2)$. The measure is in the ethical units of of course. Using this benefit measure, the expected value of the individual vote is PB where P is the probability that the vote is decisive. But Mueller argues that P is so small as to make this quantity zero. Thus in the Mueller theory, there is no incentive to vote. The theory seems to suffer from exactly the same problems as those Mueller criticizes.

References

Palfrey, Thomas R. and Rosenthal, Howard (1983) 'A strategic calculus of voting', *Public Choice*, 41, pp. 7–53.

Palfrey, Thomas R. and Rosenthal, Howard (1985) 'Voter participation and strategic uncertainty', *American Political Science Review*, 79, March, pp. 62–78.

Plott, Charles R. (1976) 'Axiomatic social choice theory: an overview and interpretation', *American Journal of Political Science*, 20, August, pp. 511–96.

Plott, Charles R. (1972) 'Ethics, social choice and the theory of economic policy', *Journal of Mathematical Sociology*, 2, February, pp. 181–208.

IV

Interest Groups

10

Parchment, Guns, and the Maintenance of Constitutional Contract

RICHARD E. WAGNER

10.1 Introduction

James Buchanan and Gordon Tullock's *Calculus of Consent*, with its apt subtitle *Logical Foundations of Constitutional Democracy*, is the *locus classicus* for the contemporary interest in constitutional political economy.[1] This work introduced the conceptual distinction between constitutional and post-constitutional levels of collective choice. Particular post-constitutional choices were seen as depending upon the nature of constitutional constraints. Consequently, particular policy outcomes are more or less a 'natural' product of people pursuing their interests through political processes, as this pursuit is shaped and constrained by constitutional rules. Undesirable or inefficient outcomes, then, call for, and require, constitutional, as contrasted with legislative, remedy.

There is a close analogy between statistical decision theory and constitutional political economy. Suppose a bottling machine fills quart bottles to between 31.9 and 32.1 ounces, 99 per cent of the time when running properly. Just because one bottle the bottler inspects has 32.2 or 31.8 ounces does not mean that the machine is malfunctioning and production should be halted for repairs. A 'bad' or 'inefficient' outcome, an under or overfilled bottle in this case, is consistent with an efficiently working machine. Moreover, the range of outcomes that come off the assembly line is a "natural" consequence of the 'constraints' under which the bottling machine works. And if it is decided that too many bottles are being overfilled or underfilled, the remedy does not call for legislative tinkering through readjusting the levels in the individual bottles, but rather calls for some maintenance or retooling of the bottling machine, that is, 'constitution' reformation.

---

[1] For a collection of recent essays on constitutional political economy, see Richard McKenzie (ed.), (1984).

Within political processes, particular policy outcomes are like the individual bottles coming off the assembly line. A bottle that is underfilled does not imply that there is something wrong and improvable in the process that produced that underfilled bottle. And if a judgment is reached that too many of the policy equivalents of the underfilled bottles are being enacted, remedy must focus on correcting the constitutional-institutional process that produce those policy outcomes.

A constitutional contract is viewed, metaphorically, as offering an escape from the prisoners' dilemma that the members of society would otherwise be caught in, (Buchanan (1975; 1977). A constitution is a form of treaty among what otherwise would be warring factions, and it provides a framework for the conduct of government. However, that treaty is not self-maintaining, so the constitutional contract may be subject to erosion. The formation of constitutional contract has received considerable attention in the literature on constitutional political economy; the maintenance of constitutional contract has received much less attention.[2] Yet the models of constitutional political economy carry implications about incentive-compatible processes of constitutional interpretation, enforcement, and maintenance, implications that diverge significantly from prevailing processes of constitutional interpretation and enforcement. After examining this divergence, I shall consider some principles of constitutional construction and maintenance that emerge from the preceding consideration of constitutional erosion.

10.2 Constitutional Contract as Escape from Anarchy

The prisoners' dilemma is the central model of constitutional political economy, for it is commonly used to illustrate the gains from trade that can be captured by making the leap from anarchy. This theme is developed in several of the essays in Tullock (1972). A common representation of that model is illustrated by figure 10.1. There it is assumed that each person faces a choice between two strategies for economic conduct: 'exchange' and 'predation'. Exchange involves a limitation on the types of economic activity that people pursue, in that the only way people may relate to each other economically is through mutual agreement. Someone who wants to manufacture shirts must get the agreement of others to supply him with labor, materials, and other imputs, and to sell the shirts he must get the agreement of consumers to buy them. By contrast, predation involves no such limitation on economic activities. Someone who wants to manufacture and sell shirts can engage in exchange, but is not limited to exchange. He may, for instance,

---

[2] Some pertinent issues concerning constitutional maintenance are raised in Juergen Backhaus (1978) and Randall Holcombe (1980).

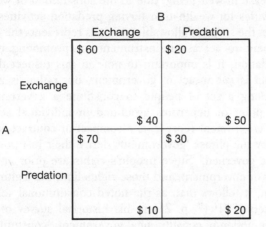

Figure 10.1   The prisoners' dilemma

try to take shirts from someone else, he may try to force people to work for him, he may try to prevent people from competing with him through working at home, and he may try to prevent people from buying imported shirts.

In such a world of 'anything goes' in which predation is an admissible economic strategy, people will, of course, invest less in exchange and more in predation. This investment in predation will in turn include offensive investment in predatory activities, as well as defensive investment against being victimized by the predatory activities of others. Figure 10.1 illustrates the social consequences of these alternative sets of rules governing economic relationships. If both parties adhere to the rules of exchange, the incomes of A and B will be $60 and $40 respectively. But if both engage in predation, those incomes will be only $30 and $20 respectively. These lower incomes reflect both the offensive and the defensive costs of predation.

The case for constitutional contract rests on a recognition that there are situations, as illustrated by figure 10.1 and the prisoners'-dilemma model generally, in which even though the outcome of people pursuing their own interests will be generally undesirable, people individually will have little incentive to act differently, because to do so would leave them even worse off. With respect to Figure 10.1, if B follows a strategy of exchange while A engages in predation, A's income will rise from $60 to $70, but B's income will fall from $40 to $10; but if B should also resort to predation, his income would rise to $20, which is less than what it would have been had both parties refrained from predation, but more than it would have been had B alone refrained from predation.

A constitutional contract represents conceptually an agreement to abide by the rules of exchange and to refrain from predation, the result of which is a general increase in well-being, due to the substitution of wealth-creating exchange activities for wealth-transferring predation activities. The agreement to restrict the scope of allowable activities represents the establishment of a government to act as an instrument for promoting exchange and deterring predation. It is important to note in this respect that a constitutional contract is *not* an act of government, but rather is an antecedent agreement among a set of people to constitute a government. From a Lockean-like point of departure grounded in individual self-ownership, constitutional government represents a compact or contract among people, as expressed by the phrase 'governments derive their just powers from the consent of the governed.' Since people's rights are prior and superior to particular acts of government, and those rights limit the legitimate activities of government, it follows that, as the noted constitutional scholar Charles McIlwain observed (1947, p. 21) in his historical survey of thought and practice on the notion of constitutional government: 'constitutional government is by definition limited government'. The very *raison d'être* of constitutional government is that the Government is subject to limits that reside in people's prior rights of person and property, and most clearly is not itself the arbiter of those limits.

But 'government' is an abstract noun, and there is no inherent reason for real governments to act in the manner envisioned by the models of constitutional contract. Government may, for instance, become an instrument of predation, with those who gain control of government authority using that authority to prey upon others. If the possession of government authority were permanent, as in authoritarian regimes, save for revolutions and coups, the outcome would be servitude or slavery. This outcome would be represented by a movement toward the southwestern or northeastern cells of figure 10.1, depending upon whether *A* or *B* gained control of governmental authority. By contrast, if the possession of governmental authority were temporary and revolving, as characterizes democratic regimes, the outcome would be a movement toward the jointly predatory outcome illustrated by the southeastern cell of figure 10.1. While these two cases involve differing distributional consequences, they both also involve an erosion of the aggregate gain that escape from the prisoners' dilemma through constitutional contract promised.

Constitutional contract, then, must also involve appropriate controls upon the enforcing agent, government, to maintain the joint gains that constitutional contract promises. There are, of course, numerous instances of government acting as an agent of predation. Indeed, the theory of rent-seeking, initiated by Gordon Tullock (1967) and surveyed and summarized by Robert Tollinson (1982), is nothing but an examination of government as an instrument of predation. As noted above, restrictions on the ability of people to manufacture clothing in their homes is predation, for it represents an effort by some people to restrict the exchange activities of others, and is just as much predation as would be an outright raid to plunder the output of people who work at home. Similarly, prohibitions on the ability of people to install lawn-sprinklers without a license constitutes predation, for effort is deflected from exchange into the prevention of exchanges that would otherwise take place. The list of predatory activities is long and growing, as the rapidly expanding literature on rent-seeking shows, and in all cases those activities involve both a transfer of wealth to the predator and a diminution in the aggregate level of wealth.

Ordinary legislative processes will not 'naturally' prevent government from becoming an instrument of predation. Indeed, the prisoners' dilemma model in conjunction with the theory of rent-seeking explains that the 'natural' or unconstrained outcome is the substitution of predation for exchange within legislative processes, unless constitutional constraints manage successfully to restrain the use of predation. Without such constraints, ordinary legislation will promote some substitution of predation for exchange, as a byproduct of the efforts of people, legislators and citizens alike, to exploit the profit opportunities they face, as these are shaped by the existing constitutional rules. Better outcomes, those that encourage exchange and discourage predation, require alternative constitutional rules that reduce the political profitability of legislation that represents predation relative to that which represents exchange.

10.3 Legislation, Adjudication, and Constitutional Erosion

It is a commonplace assertion that the constitution is what the Supreme Court says it is. As a positive statement about prevailing constitutional interpretation, this statement is hard to dispute these days, even though this may not have been so in the days of Andrew Jackson and the *Cherokee Indian Cases*, in which President Jackson is reported to have said: "John Marshall has made his decision, now let him enforce it.'[3] These days, the degree to which constitutional contract is maintained or erodes would seem to depend ultimately upon the rulings the Supreme Court makes. Such a perspective upon the Court leads naturally, of course, to a focus on the principles that the Court follows in declaring what is constitutional and what is not.

There are obvious disparities between what the constitution plainly says as judged by anyone who can read, and what the constitution is viewed as

---

[3] For a discussion of the *Cherokee Indian Cases*, see Charles Warren (1922, vol. I, pp. 729–79). The quotation, along with a discussion of some questions regarding whether Jackson actually made the remark, as against simply sharing the sentiment the remark expresses, appears on p. 759.

saying as reflected in Supreme Court decisions. The positive or empirical description of constitutional provisions that emerges from reading Supreme Court decisions and constitutional law books bears, in many instances, faint resemblance to the constitution as written and amended. Such scholars as Richard Epstein (1985), Peter Aranson (1985), Bernard Siegan (1980), and Terry Anderson and Peter Hill (1980), among others, have documented the large and expanding gap between what the terms of the constitutional contract plainly state and what the actual terms are as these are interpreted through Supreme Court decisions.

While it is clear that a massive degree of anti-constitutional amendment has been accomplished through 'interpretation', there is, to be sure, some inherent degree of ambiguity as to what constitutes interpretation as against amendment. The Fourth Amendment strictures about 'unreasonable searches and seizures' is surely one example where there is inherently considerable ambiguity about what constitutes 'unreasonableness'. Rummaging through a trash can without a search warrant may be viewed as unreasonable by some and reasonable by others, and a ruling either way seems unlikely to be part of a systematic process of substituting predation for exchange. By contrast, it is clear that between the Ninth and the Tenth Amendments, which in turn limit the Federal Government to its delegated powers and reserve all other powers to the states or to individuals, the Federal Government has no constitutional authority to establish a nationwide speed limit, let alone to engage in the various transfer programs that constitute the welfare state. At the same time, Court rulings that have effectively repealed those amendments are understandable as part of a process of substituting predation for exchange.

As Epstein (1985) explains, a vast array of legislation of the past half-century violates the Fifth Amendment's strictures that seek to prevent government from taking private property, unless it *justly* compensates the owner and unless the property is to be put to a *legitimate public use*. For example, there is no way that the court's unanimous decision in *Hawaii Housing Authority* v. *Midkiff*, 467 US 229, supporting the state of Hawaii's scheme for land redistribution, can be squared with the plain language of the Fifth Amendment that requires any taking of property not only to be compensated, but also to be for 'public use'. There is clearly some interpretative differences among referees about when a receiver is judged to have fumbled and when the pass was judged to be incomplete, but the disparity between what the constitution plainly says and what the Supreme Court interprets it to say, goes far beyond differences of interpretation and involves changes in the rules of the game.

In Epstein's view the Supreme Court is the guardian of the constitution. He accepts the prisoners'-dilemma formulation of the social gains offered by constitutional contract, and views the Supreme Court as the agent that makes it possible to avoid the Hobbesian dilemma of the enforcing agent, the state, becoming an instrument of predation. In particular, in Epstein's view, the Fifth Amendment's strictures against the taking of private property for public use without just compensation bear an important part of the burden of preventing the interests represented by legisaltive majorities from using the state as an instrument of predation. For this to happen, however, requires the Supreme Court to enforce the Fifth Amendment by making sure that both just compensation is paid and that the taking is for public use. Epstein considers most legislation of the past half-century unconstitutional, based on a comparison of the legislation in question with what the constitution plainly says.

The principle that 'the king can do no wrong' has no place in the American constitutional order by virtue of our not being a monarchy, but the principle that 'the legislature can do no wrong' has no place in that order either, despite our having a republican form of government. The very idea of constitutional government is that the authority of government is limited, out of recognition that, in the absence of such limits, the Hobbesian dilemma will assert itself and the state will be used as an instrument of predation by winning factions.

It is certainly convenient to view the Supreme Court as the guardian of the constitutional contract, by its declaring when it is that the legislature does do wrong. Yet there has been a growing body of court opinon to the effect that the legislature can indeed do no wrong, at least with respect to a substantial portion of human activity. *Lochner* v. *New York*, 198 US 45 (1905), in which the court held invalid legislation by the state of New York that prevented people from agreeing to work in a bakery for more than 10 hours a day or 60 hours per week, is a ruling that supported exchange over predation. Yet this was a five-to-four decision, with the dissenting opinion written by Justice Harlan asserting the principle that the legislature can do no wrong: "[Whether] or not this be wise legislation is not the province of the court to inquire. Under our systems of government the courts are not concerned with the wisdom or policy of legislation."   Within a generation of *Lochner*, the principle that the legislature can do no wrong had become firmly ensconced in the declarations of the Supreme Court. For instance, in *Nebbia* v. *New York*, 291 US 502 (1934), the court upheld a regulation by the state of New York that established minimum prices for the sale of milk. The Court sided with the New York legislature in its substitution of predation for exchange, and said so by declaring that 'a state is free to adopt whatever economic policy may reasonably be deemed to promote public welfare, and to enforce that policy by legisaltion adapted to its purpose. The courts are without authority... to override [such a policy].' And in *Ferguson* v. *Skrups*, 372 US 726 (1963), the Court unanimously upheld a state law restricting the debt-adjusting business to lawyers, declaring that 'it is up to the legislatures, not the courts, to decide on the wisdom and utility of legislation.' One of the more pithy statements of the principle that the legislature can do no wrong is expressed in the unanimous opinion in *Berman* v. *Parker*, 348 US 26 (1954), when Justice Douglas wrote: '...when the legislature has spoken, the public interest has been declared in terms well-nigh conclusive. In such cases the legislature, not the judiciary is the main guardian of the public needs to be served by social legislation.' Those who look to the Supreme Court to prevent legislatively-sponsored predation certainly cannot draw much solace or grounds for optimism from the strong tendency of the court to adopt the position that the legislature can do no wrong. If the Supreme Court is regarded as the guardian of the constitution, there has clearly been a massive failure by the guardian. The Court accepts the legislature as sovereign, and rules accordingly. It is always possible to exhort the Court to rule differently. This is, for instance, Epstein's proposed remedy, as well as those who propose to appoint different justices. However, to exhort the justices to change their calls raises the question of why the justices should make such changes, and why they should now be amenable to exhortation. But before addressing the failures of existing processes of constitutional maintenance, it would seem useful to consider the nature of those processes that would be compatible with the conceptual framework of constitutional political economy.

10.4 Consentaneous Principles of Constitutional Enforcement

The idea of constitutional or limited government raises the age-old question of how government's adherence to the constitutional contract can be maintained, once it is recognized that government acts both as a participant in the division of labor in society and as a referee as to the propriety of the actions of the various participants. When government possesses this dual capacity, there is always a question of whether the refereeing will be impartial or discriminatory, which in turn is the age-old question of whether the sphere of *gubernaculum* (government) can be kept subservient to the sphere of *jurisdictio* (law).

The mere signing of a treaty or ratification of a constitutional contract does not eliminate the prisoners' dilemma in which the participants are caught. That dilemma is inherent in social life, it cannot be vanquished, but at best held in check, (Tullock 1974). The prisoners' dilemma model also describes the incentive to engage in post-contractual opportunism. Whether such opportunism will be exploited depends upon the profit opportunities that people think such exploitation offers. A constitutional contract may be looked upon as a mutual agreement to limit predation, but constitutional parchment itself cannot limit predation. The only thing that can limit predation is its unprofitability, and any such unprofitability surely requires more than a parchment barrier to predation.

The social dilemma of there being both joint gains from all participants agreeing to follow a set of rules that constrains personal conduct and potential personal gains from violating those rules also pervades the playing of ordinary games. The players in a basketball game may agree to rules that enjoin them from grabbing the jersey of other players. Yet there will be many cases where a player can gain an advantage by doing just this. But without some process for proper rule-enforcement, the game will become less productive to the participants as the equivalent of predation displaces the equivalent of exchange.

It is not surprising that constitutional political economy has developed the analogous distinction between choosing the rules of a game and selecting strategies for playing the game. The choice of rules in this case represents the choice of constitutional constraints upon the subsequent playing of the game. This conceptual distinction between constitutional and post-constitutional choice conforms closely to real-world processes of rule-formation and game-playing, which do follow the two-stage decision process envisioned by constitutional political economy. The rules of the game are agreed to in advance of play, as are the referees. Referees are selected *consentaneously* by the participants to enforce the rules those participants have agreed to play by. The referees are *not* makers or amenders of rules. This is not to deny that they will have to make judgment calls about which people might disagree. What one referee calls an incomplete pass might be called a fumble by another. What one referee calls goal-tending might be judged a blocked shot by another.

Despite what would seem to be an inherent degree of ambiguity between rulings that merely interpret the rules and rulings that amend the rules, there is really little ambiguity with respect to the actual conduct of games. What maintains the distinction between interpretation of the rules and amendment of the rules is the *process* by which referees are selected and maintain their position. Not only are they chosen by the agreement of all participants, but also they are subject to continual and consentaneous reaffirmation by the participants. It is the presence of a consentaneous test involving a process of periodic reaffirmation of referees that makes it possible to determine whether amendment has replaced interpretation. If judges are reaffirmed consentaneously, it is reasonable to infer that rules are being interpreted but not amended. But the absence of consensus would mean that the rules are being amended and property rights redefined for the benefit of some of the participants at the expense of others.

The process of interpretation and enforcement envisioned within the framework of constitutional political economy is, following the analogy with rules of the game, a consentaneous one in which the participants agree to the choice of referees, who are the interpreting and enforcing agents. It is critical to note in this conceptualization that the enforcing agent, normally the Government, does not make the rules and is not involved in the definition and assignment of property rights. Rather those rights are prior to government, and as a reflection of the use of those rights an enforcing agent is selected out of recognition of the gains that can be secured by restricting the scope for predation. Moreover, the operation of the enforcing agent is monitored by the participants, and the enforcing agent can continue in office only through maintaining the consent of the participants.

10.5   Actual Processes of Constitutional Interpretation

The actual process of constitutional interpretation and enforcement differs substantially from the type of process that is consistent with the maintenance of constitutional contract within the models of constitutional political economy: models which distinguish between the players choosing the rules of the game on the one hand and agreeing to abide by those rules during subsequent play on the other hand. Within the spirit of constitutional political economy, the referee or the state does not make or amend the rules, but only enforces them. The players themselves, and they alone, can make or amend the rules.

But is the Supreme Court analogous to the officials of a game? If the members of the Court were selected consentaneously by the participants and subject to periodic reaffirmation by the same consentaneous process, the Court would indeed possess an analogous position. But the Court is not subject to periodic reaffirmation. And it is certainly not subject to any consentaneous affirmation by the participants who are asked to abide by its decisions. Indeed, the massive controversy that often greets Court appointments, along with the growing interest-group campaigning that has entered into lobbying over appointments to the Supreme Court, argues strongly that the Court is not part of a consentaneous process of rules interpretation, but rather is engaged in an anti-constitutional process of rule amendment via "interpretation". Consequently, government is not a *follower* of rules, as is envisioned by the models of constitutional political economy, and indeed, by the very idea of constitutional government, but rather is a *maker* of rules, as expressed by the statement that the legislature can do no wrong (because it is the source of rights).

While a great deal of normative discourse speaks of the Supreme Court as being the guardian of the constitution and of maintaining the constitutional contract, there is no positive model that explains how the Court would have either the interest or the ability to do so. James Madison was correct in asserting in *Federalist* (No. 51): "In republican government, the legislative authority necessarily predominates." Within the central features of American republicanism, the legislature controls both the jurisdiction and the budget of the Supreme Court, and has the ability to eliminate all courts inferior to the Supreme Court. While the president does have the ability to nominate members to the Supreme Court, they must be confirmed by the Senate. More than this, the president, and the executive branch generally, cannot act without appropriations from the legislature. Moreover, the legislature can impeach the president, while at most the president can force the legislature to operate with a two-thirds majority through the veto power.

The suzerainty of the legislature seems clear. Without the enforcing agent, the Court, having an independent source of revenue, and one that varies inversely with the amount of predation countenanced, along with the ability to maintain that independence, it is hard to see how it could be otherwise. If this suzerainty was in doubt before, it was surely affirmed by the legislative response to the Supreme Court's ruling in *Chisholm* v. *Georgia*, 2 Dallas 419 (1793), where the Court had held that a citizen of one state could sue another state in federal court. The Eleventh Amendment to prohibit this was ratified within five years. In this case the legislature responded through constitutional amendment, as it has done a few times since, but in many cases it has resorted simply to legislative enactment. For instance, in *Leisy* v. *Hardin*, 135 US 100 (1890), the Court held invalid an Iowa statute prohibiting the sale of alcoholic beverages. That same year, Congress passed the Wilson Act, which gave states the right to regulate the sale of alcoholic beverages. When the Court ruled in 1944 that insurance was interstate commerce, Congress enacted legislation giving states control over the regulation of insurance. And when it ruled in 1953 that the Federal Government had dominion over tidelands, Congress enacted legislation giving control to the states.

Landes and Posner (1975) model the independent judiciary as an agent of the legislature, not of the present legislature, but of some weighted average of legislatures past. By contrast, if judicial appointments were subject to periodic renewal, the judiciary would be an agent of the present legislature. In either case, a model of the judiciary as an agent of the legislature falls fully withing the framework of American republicanism. If the Supreme Court is an agent of the legislature, even if some weighted average of past legislatures rather than simply the present legislature, the legislature becomes the principal interpreter of the constitution, with the Supreme Court serving as the legislature's agent in the process of interpretation. This is not to say that the agency relationship works perfectly, but only that the Court is not independent of the interests of the legislature, but rather is largely reflective of those interests.

The position of the judiciary as an agent of the legislature says nothing, by itself, about whether the judiciary will support or oppose legislation that substitutes predation for exchange. It says only that the judiciary will tend to support the interests of some weighted average of past legislatures. It is the same with the ordinary game situations envisioned by constitutional political economy: the referees of a game are agents of the players. The difference between the existing process of rules interpretation and enforcement and that envisioned by constitutional political economy is due principally to the consentaneous nature of the process under constitutional political economy, as against its majoritarian nature under present institutions. The agency relationship is real with respect to games, but only formal with respect to constitutional contract. As envisioned within constitutional political economy, the referees are continually subject to reaffirmation through agreement among the players, making the officials real agents of the players. But with respect to the interpretation and enforcement of constitutional contract, a Court that is the agent of the legislature, whether the present one or some weighted average of past legislatures, is not thereby an agent of all the players, but only of a subset – even if a continually revolving subset.

Whether the judiciary will support the substitution of predation for exchange through legislation will depend, in light of this agency relationship, upon the character of incentives within the legislature. A legislature will encourage predation over exchange if there are profits from doing so. A legislature that is consistent with the models of constitutional political economy would be consentaneous in nature, such as is illustrated by Knut Wicksell's (1896) proposal for legislative organization. Such a legislature would not be a source of property rights, but rather would be reflective of people's uses of those rights. But should government become a maker of rules for others, rather than being an adherent to the same rules as others, a "market" will naturally arise to secure favorable rules and favorable interpretations of those rules. Under institutions that allow for non-consentaneous governance, there will be profits to be made through governmental encouragement of rent-seeking predation. Accordingly, the constitution would not serve to limit government, but rather would be something that is created by government via a process of constitutional interpretation. The Court would be a participant in processes of rent-seeking legislation through increasing the durability and value of such legislation.[4]

So long as government is organized according to majoritarian principles, its participation in economic life will contain a significant predatory component, because there are profits to be acquired from the supply of such rent-seeking legislation. It is, of course, possible for accidental forces to

---

[4] For empirical support of this thesis of constitutional litigation as establishing, within the Landes-Posner framework, more highly valued statutes than ordinary legislation, see Mark Crain and Robert Tollinson (1979).

generate conditions under which predation will give way to exchange, even when political institutions reward rent-seeking. This is illustrated by certain cases of deregulation, as with airlines, for instance. But it is inconsistent to invoke rent-seeking to explain the development of public regulation, and then to look upon deregulation as the sudden disappearance of rent-seeking. Deregulation would seem better represented as a temporary confluence of different rent-seeking interests negating each other. For instance, and as just one illustration among many, if the firms in an industry want regulations that raise price while the consumers want regulations that lower it, and if the value of this regulation is independent of the value of other pieces of legislation, the resulting outcome will depend on the relative valuations to the contending factions. If those valuations are equal, which admittedly is an assumption that clashes with the general presumption that concentration defeats diffusion, it is possible for the zero regulation, competitive output to result.

However, such an outcome would not be described as representing the transformation of a rent-seeking political process into some aggregate wealth-maximizing process; the same rent-seeking process remains in place, only in this one particular legislative market, the value-maximizing outcome is, for now, zero legislation. However, this condition is fragile, for there is no reason to expect the roughly equal valuations to persist. For example, instead of producers being opposed by a unified group of consumers, there may be opportunities for transfers among consumers, as through cross-subsidization, in which the cartel gain is shared between producers and a subset of consumers, as well as by the politicians who establish and maintain the cartel. The substainability of deregulation would seem to depend on underlying political reform that diminishes the ability of legislatures to interfere with property rights and that requires them to operate consistently within the framework of such rights.

10.6 Maintaining Constitutional Contract

The number of particular formats through which a program of constitutional maintenance might be implemented is limited only by the analyst's imagination. To recite a variety of such possibilities would be well beyond the scope of this chapter, which is more concerned with some general principles of constitutional construction that are pertinent to the maintenance of constitutional contracts. Within a republican system of government, however, the legislature is supreme, and the constitution will, by and large, be what the legislature wants it to be. The model of Landes and Posner about the independent judiciary is but a reflection of the essential nature of republican government. This was well recognized by James Madison, as well as by the anti-federalists, all of whom recognized that constitutional control was not so much a matter of dividing governmental authority between legislative, executive, and judicial branches, as it was a matter of arranging legislative authority in some polycentric manner as that described by the idea of concurrent majorities – (Ostrom, 1971).

With the legislature being predominant in republican polities, the basis of legislative organization becomes central to any consideration of constitutional maintenance. Exchange will dominate predation in constitutional interpretation and enforcement so long as such interpretation yields higher returns to the members of the legislature. Such an approach to constitutional reform as that advanced by Hayek (1979) perhaps illustrates one possibility of such a division of legislative interests. Hayek proposed that there be two distinct legislative bodies: (1) a Legislative Assembly; and (2) a Governmental Assembly. The Legislative Assembly, which would be essentially a revision of the British House of Lords, would be selected from among people forty-five years of age or above who would serve for 15 years, and this assembly would have the function of enacting general law that would remain in force for a long period of time. These laws would include those relating to the distribution of tax burdens among people, but would not deal with the actual amount of taxation. The Governmental Assembly would be constituted in the same way as the British Parliament, with the intention being that its particular choices about such governmental matters as budgets would be made in conformity with the general rules chosen by the Legislative Assembly.

The extent to which such an approach might work would depend on the powers each assembly possessed, as well as the degree of similarity or diversity between their interests. There is no strong reason to believe that the interests of the Legislative Assembly would be markedly more favorable to exchange and hostile to predation than those of the Governmental Assembly. Random selection of members would surely work more strongly in this direction than would ordinary electoral processes. Yet these people would be serving largely as a matter of honor and would be engaged in the provision of public goods, for which they would face weak incentives.

An alternative approach in this same vein might involve a change in the method of paying legislators. Predation-enhancing legislation is enacted despite its diminution of aggregate wealth because the concentrated gains it offers to supporters dominates the diffused losses elsewhere. To the extent government undertakes those protective and productive activities that promote the common welfare, while refraining from undertaking those activities that retard it, the total wealth of the society increases. But under the prevailing institutional arrangements, legislators can gain by supporting programs that transfer wealth to particular interests, even though aggregate wealth is diminished in the process.

This negative outcome is facilitated because legislators have a direct stake not in the common or aggregate wealth of the members of the nation, but only in the particular wealth positions of the members of the various warring factions that compete for rents. Madison thought that concurrent majorities among bodies with differing interests would produce a resultant outcome that promoted the general welfare. In a somewhat different application of the same principle that Madison sought to implement, legislators could perhaps be compensated through a balanced portfolio of stocks, bonds, and other assets, which might be constructed to operate similarly to stock options and related incentive plans in corporations. To the extent this could be done, the incentive for each legislator to promote the general welfare might be strengthened.

A legislator who had a significant number of unemployed youths in his district, and who might support some job-creation program despite its demonstrated ineffectiveness, because most of the cost would be placed elsewhere, and who recognized that a reformation of minimum wage and child labor legislation would actually be more effective overall, would be more inclined to support such legislation. The reason is that the legislator would share in all the gains *and* losses of legislation. To the extent such a balanced portfolio could be put into effect, legislators would tend to be rewarded in direct proportion to the general increase in national wealth, rather than in proportion to the particular favors conferred upon the beneficiaries of particular legislation.[5]

10.7 Concluding Remarks

While the prisoners'-dilemma model illustrates nicely the potential gains that constitutional contract offers, the parchment that constitutional contract represents does not in itself assure the maintenance of that constitutional contract. Constitutional parchment does not eliminate the potential gains to individual acts of predation or rent-seeking. The elimination of those gains, and with it the maintenance of the constitutional contract, requires the elimination of the profitability of predation and rent-seeking. So long as the political system is one in which government is a maker of rules for others, rather than being an adherent to the same rules as others, a "market" will naturally arise to secure favorable rules and favorable interpretations of those rules. The problem of controlling legislators so that their personal interest corresponds to the promotion of the common interest does not

---

[5] In a quite different context, W.H. Hutt (1982) has proposed a system of *shared entrepreneurship* between workers and owners as a way of overcoming the faction that often characterizes present labor-management relations.

resolve itself naturally, but can be resolved only through appropriately constructed institutional constraints.

Within the framework of American republicanism, the Supreme Court has no enduring ability to maintain the constitutional contract, even if its members should wish to take on that assignment, unless the legislature itself is constituted so that the interests of its members are more fully advanced by promoting the substitution of exchange for predation than by selling predatory legislation to rent-seekers. Constitutional maintenance requires a preponderance of legislative interests on the side of exchange rather than predation. Parchment itself cannot stop guns, and it is guns, metaphorically speaking, when arrayed predominantly against the use of government as an instrument of predation, that provides for constitutional maintenance. Relatedly, Paul Rubin's (1977) model of common law efficiency depends on both parties having an equal interest in the establishment of a precedent. If this equality of interest is not present, the presumption of common-law efficiency vanishes. In assessing both the efficiency of common law and the maintenance of constitutional contract, what matters is the strength of interests – guns – and not some abstract principle – parchment *per se*.

References

Anderson, Terry L., and Hill, Peter J. (1980) *The Birth of a Transfer Society*. Stanford, CA: Hoover Institution Press.

Aranson, Peter H. (1985) "Judicial control of the political branches: public purpose and public law", *Cato Journal*, 4 Winter, pp. 719–82.

Backhaus, Juergen (1978) "Constitutional guarantees and the distribution of power and wealth", *Public Choice*, **33**, no. 3, pp. 45–63.

Buchanan, James M. (1975) *The Limits of Liberty: Between Anarchy and Leviathan*. Chicago: University of Chicago Press,

Buchanan, James M. (1977) *Freedom in Constitutional Contract*. College Station: Texas A & M University Press.

Buchanan, James M. and Tullock, Gordon (1962) *The Calculus of Consent*. Ann Arbor: University of Michigan Press.

Crain, W. Mark and Tollinson, Robert D. "Constitutional change in an interest-group perspective", *Journal of Legal Studies*, **8**, January, pp. 165–75.

Epstein, Richard A. (1985) *Takings: Private Property and the Power of Eminent Domain*. Cambridge, Mass.: Harvard University Press.

Hayek, F.A. (1979) *The Political Order of a Free People*. Vol. III of "Law, Legislation, and Liberty", Chicago: University of Chicago Press.

Holcombe, Randall G.(1980) "Contractarian model of the decline in classical liberalism", *Public Choice*, **35**, 3, pp. 277–86.

Hutt, W.H. "Every man a capitalist", *Policy Review*, **22**, Fall, pp. 141–53.

Landes, William M. and Posner, Richard A. (1975) "The independent judiciary in an interest-group perspective", *Journal of Law and Economics*, **18**, December, pp. 875–901.

McIlwain, Charles H. (1947) *Constitutionalism: Ancient and Modern* (revised ed). Ithaca, NY: Cornell University Press.

McKenzie, Richard B. (1984) (ed.) *Constitutional Economics*. Lexington, Mass.: D.C. Heath.

Ostrom, Vincent (1971) *The Political Theory of a Compound Republic*. Blacksburg, VA: Center for Study of Public Choice.

Rubin, Paul H. (1977) "Why is the common law efficient?" *Journal of Legal Studies*, 6, January, pp. 51–63.

Siegan, Bernard H. (1980) *Economic Liberties and the Constitution*. Chicago: University of Chicago Press.

Tollison, Robert D. (1982) "Rent-seeking: a survey", *Kyklos*, 35, 4, pp. 575–602.

Tullock, Gordon (1967) "The welfare costs of tariffs, monopolies, and theft", *Western Economic Journal*, 5, June, pp. 224–32.

Tullock, Gordon (ed.) *Explorations in the Theory of Anarchy*. Blacksburg, VA: Center for Study of Public Choice.

Tullock, Gordon (1974) *The Social Dilemma*. Blacksburg, VA: Center for Study of Public Choice.

Warren, Charles (1922) *The Supreme Court in United States History*, 2 vols. Boston: Little, Brown.

Wicksell, Knut (1958) "A New Principle of Just Taxation", Richard A. Musgrave and Alan T. Peacock (eds). *Classics in the Theory of Public Finance*, London: Macmillan, pp. 72–118.

11

Public Choice and the Choices of the Public

ARTHUR SELDON

11.1 The Denial of Public Choice

Public choice is the latest fruitful development in economic analysis. Yet, if the term is interpreted incautiously, it could be a misnomer. It is the correct label for the processes by which the people indicate preferences and make decisions collectively by mechanisms ranging from committees of half a dozen round a table in a small room speaking for 50 citizens, to vast chambers housing 500 elected to represent perhaps 200 million. The representatives decide "in public", in the presence of others, rather than individually, "in private", without consulting or debating with others. "Public choice" is the analysis of group or collective decision-making by debate and voting, in contrast to "private choice" by individual decision-making, by offering money in markets.

Yet in the short 30 years since the 1950s, when the protagonists of public choice rediscovered and built on the insights of three Frenchmen (de Borda, Laplace and Condorcet) who wrote in the late eighteenth century, "public choice" has revealed that collective decision-making by representatives usually or often misinterprets or thwarts the choices that the public would wish to make as individuals. For much of the burgeoning literature of public choice analyses the defects in the mechanisms by which collective decision-making is designed to reflect the choices of individuals and the remedies required by reforming the rules and procedures in the mechanisms and by other measures.

Why has the machinery failed – at least so far? Somehow it has been difficult to devise voting systems which accurately reflect individual preferences. Somehow the voters' intentions are blurred by the time their representatives come to put them into effect. Representatives do not always represent faithfully, not because they do not wish to do so, but because they do not know what those represented want. The representatives may also find it advantageous to make "deals" with other representatives to support one another's chosen measures, which they may not favor. The measures may be designed to favor organized pressure groups at the expense of the generality of citizen-voters as a whole. The politicians voted into office and political power are not always able to induce their officials to execute their intentions. And there are other obstacles that come between individual voters and their representatives in the US Congress, the British Parliament, the French National Assembly, the German Bundestag, the Italian Chamber of Deputies, the Swedish Riksdag, the Spanish Cortes, the Israeli Knesset, and so on.[1]

These are the political defects that public choice examines to discover why the American dream of representative institutions, shared by other democracies in the industrial West – government of the people, by the people, for the people, seems to have perished from the earth.[2] That is the austerely analytical side of the coin of public choice. The other side is the search for reforms that could make the dream come true after all. So public choice examines methods of enabling or inducing voters to reveal their real preferences, or to indicate their choices more directly than in a roundabout way through representatives, methods of limiting government to the functions it cannot avoid so that the scope for misinterpreting voter preference is minimized, of reducing the power of organized groups to importune political representatives, of reforming the overriding constitution to restrain the power of a transient majority, and so on. Public choice faces reality, but offers hope.

Gordon Tullock has contributed original ideas to many aspects of public choice. Other essays in this book by specialists in different disciplines discuss them in some detail. My observations reflect on encounters with Tullock over 16 years to spur (or provoke) him to explain, amplify and refine his thinking in my personal quest to discover why representative government fails to serve the governed and how it might yet succeed.

11.2 Another Scot to the Rescue of the English

In view of my "special relationship" with Tullock as a presenter in Britain of

---

[1] Public choice analysis is ubiquitous. The parochial assertion by a senior Cambridge (England) economist, R. C. O. Matthews, that "much of it is inapplicable without considerable modification to countries other than the United States" is hardly supported by Peter Bernholz's public choice approach to international relations. Matthews, Master of Clare College, Cambridge, Introduction to *Economy and Democracy*, Macmillan, London, 1985. Bernholz, University of Basel, *The International Game of Power*, Mouton Berlin, New York, Amsterdam, 1985.

[2] For a British citizen it was an inspiring experience to stand near the spot where Abraham Lincoln used these evocative words in 1863, four months after the Battle of Gettysberg, where Tullock, Charles Rowley and I had repaired as an act of spiritual renewal on 3 August 1986. Lincoln's short, simple description of democracy has lived longer than the two-hour address of the orator Edward Everett that preceded it.

his stream (or torrent) of public choice, my account of his influence will –
firstly – necessarily be an individual one.

In 1976, (by coincidence, 200 years after the publication of Adam Smith's
Wealth of Nations) I asked Tullock, also of Scottish ancestry, to expound the
elements of public choice for the then largely uninstructed British (although
another Scot, Alan Peacock, had, with others, laboured in the vineyard). In a
short time he wrote *The Vote Motive*.[3] In 1970, at my prompting, he had
written *Private Wants, Public Means*,[4] in which he portrayed government as a
device for dealing with externalities and as the source of injury to the
community. In 1979, I inadvertently led Tullock into a brisk encounter with
Lionel Robbins at a seminar in Britain on the role of the British bureaucracy,[5] when Robbins found Tullock's strictures too strong meat (see below). In
1986, I embroiled Tullock even further in contemporary British public
policy by asking him to offer a public choice diagnosis of the combative
exchange between Department of Education bureaucrats and university
academics on the possibility of making schools competitive (see below).

Is a decade a long time in economics?[6] How do the propositions of public
choice explain recent developments in representative government?

11.3 Median Voters and Conviction Politicians

In 1976 Tullock suggested that a central proposition of public choice: the
theory that the preferences of the median voter tended to dominate political
markets under a range of not implausible assumptions, helped to explain why
politicians who followed the vote motive (he instanced Johnson, Wilson,
Nixon, Heath) were more likely to be elected than those who sought to
maximize the "public interest" (Goldwater, Powell, McGovern).

Recent developments in Britain (and elsewhere) permit tentative testing. I
hasten to add that if the "facts" do not fit Tullockian thinking they do not
necessarily unseat the hypothesis in the absence of a better hypothesis. Yet
ten years later in 1987 I wonder how he would incorporate into median voter
theorizing the emergence of a fourth political party and its alliance with an

[3] Institute of Economic Affairs, 1976 (James Buchanan had reservations about the IEA's
choice of title).
[4] This title was suggested by Charles Goetz.
[5] The proceedings were published in *The Taming of Government*, Institute of Economic
Affairs, London, 1979.
[6] The former prime minister, Harold Wilson, once justified a change in policy by what is
frequently interpreted as a cynical excuse – "A week is a long time in politics" – which
suggests the intriguing reflection in the economics of politics that no politician can be
condemned for disclaiming his bond, political party manifestoes are designed to have little
informative value as a guide to the voter of politicians' intentions and are less useful than a
business prospectus, and the scope for political promises to disguise intentions and mislead
voters undermines the rationality of voting.

existing party to form a third political force. In 1965 Anthony Downs had written[7] "New parties arise when either (a) a change in suffrage laws sharply alters the distribution of citizens along the political scale, (b) there is a sudden change in the electorate's social outlook because of some upheaval such as war, revolution, inflation or depression." The third force in British politics did not arise from "sudden change". It reflects the long-term secular change in the socio-economic conditions of supply and demand. "Consensus politicians" presumably reflect the median-voter theorem. President Ford in 1975 said: "We are going to stay in the middle", though Carter in 1976 seems to have edged even closer to the median. But "conviction politicians" must believe they can shift the distribution of voter preferences in their favor. Prime Minister Margaret Thatcher said in March 1986: "If we heed the grumblers, we would be bending and turning with every twist in the opinion polls. . . our style is to decide what is right, not temporarily convenient."; "Applause dies with the day. Belief lives on;. . . We are more than a one-generation society." These are remarkably "disinterested" declarations to come from a politician. Conviction politicians take the median preference not as the last word on policy formation but as a datum to be reshaped. The median preference may still minimize voter disappointment and communal dissatisfaction, but in a few years it has in Britain been shifted to the market-oriented libertarian Right (or "New Right" as it is called by the Left). The British experience is echoed in the USA most clearly, but also in France, Italy, Spain, and New Zealand.

11.4 The Frustration of the General Will by Group Interest

The role and power of group interests also requires refinement in public choice theory. As the bible says: "The poor always ye have with you" (St John, xii, 8). Group interests have also been with us always. Two British parliamentarians separated in time by $1\frac{1}{2}$ centuries lamented the power of such interests to suborn democratic institutions. In May 1822 a Member of Parliament, well-known for his economic writings, David Ricardo, complained that the House of Commons had been "tormented. . . with constant solicitations to sacrifice the public good to particular interests". In September 1986, 164 years later, a British Minister, the Home Secretary, Douglas Hurd, warned his colleagues in Parliament: "Members of Parliament and Ministers both need to shake themselves free to some extent from the embrace of pressure and interest groups [which] interpose themselves between the executive and Parliament." He went on to condemn "the deference with which politicians regard [these]. . . serpents constantly

---

[7] *The Economic Theory of Democracy*, Harper and Row, New York, 1965.

emerging from the sea to strangle Laocoon and his sons in their coils". [Laocoon – the priest in Greek legend who warned the Trojans against the wooden horse.] (*The Times*, 20 September 1986).

In 1965, Mancur Olson[8] argued that the (political) public goods conferred on their members made group interests difficult to organize except (as with government) by coercion. Since coercion is easier the better group interests are organized, the economy and the polity is distorted in favor of the more organized against the less organized. The rent-seeking interests have appeared among workers and employers.

In Britain the trade unions' power to organize was strengthened during the period 1974–9 by a government that increased their legal privileges – giving them a wide range of means of coercion, from closed shops to secondary strikes and general immunity from rules applicable to corporate bodies – which enabled them to threaten general industrial dislocation. In 1977 Charles Rowley[9] thought that only "a brave (foolhardy?)" government would withdraw these legal privileges. It was then difficult to foresee the early emergence of a radical government under Conservative leadership. But Rowley seems to have anticipated how it would emerge: "a majority of the population would welcome the transition if the costs were not likely to be imposed on them." He contemplated two constitutional essentials: proportional representation (PR) and separation of powers in a written constitution. The first is now much more possible than at any time in British history. The new Social Democrat/Liberal Alliance has said it would demand PR for its collaboration in a "hung" Parliament, which some political observers think likely. And the French adoption of PR could, ironically, strengthen support for PR from the Conservatives (to forestall a Labour Government), although the Prime Minister is opposed to it. A written constitution is still a distant prospect, but Rowley's example of an outsider who captured the popular vote (Carter), although difficult, could be emulated by the Social Democrat leader, Owen, in 1992. Yet the power of the damaging trade union interest was evidently broken, *without* constitutional reform,[10] in 1979 by a persuasive appeal over its head to the neglected long-term (and long-suffering) interest of the voter from new "leadership in tune with the majority of the electorate"[11] under the inspiration of an elemental idea. Observers, sympathetic and hostile, are united in calling the new idea "market forces", even if they are divided in applauding its (political) preacher as a brave Boadicea or damning her as a wicked witch. The British worm turned; and it is

[8] *The Logic of Collective Action*, Harvard University Press, Boston, 1965.

[9] *Trade Unions: Public Goods or Public "Bads"?*, IEA, London, 1978.

[10] The British constitution is unwritten (although there are written constitutional "conventions").

[11] Rowley, C. K. (1984) "The Political Economy of British labour laws", *University of Chicago Law Review*, **51**, 4, Fall, pp. 1135–60.

unlikely to return to its subservience whichever party controls government in the 1990s. The power of vested interests to "torment" the legislature seems to have been weakened (below).

Mrs. Thatcher is now held to have done what Goldwater, Powell and McGovern failed to do. In 1979 the then (Labour) Government was almost the instrument of the trade unions that are now seemingly powerless to resist de-socialization on a scale that would have been thought "politically impossible" as recently as 1979. Resistance has in the 1980s erupted into violence (mining, local government, printing), but has not prevailed. In the mid-1970s economic liberalization, epitomized by the reversal of post-war socialization into "privatization", seemed a Utopian dream. Now almost everything seems possible – even education vouchers. And no party in political power is likely to restore the unions to their pre-1979 dominance. If a decade is a long time in politics, is it a long time in the economics of politics? Does public choice analysis comfortably accommodate recent developments?

So much for rent-seeking by the workers – or rather their representatives organized as trade unions. An American rent-seeking interest from industrial management presented public choice analysis with a conundrum. Chrysler was evidently "saved" by an act of sophisticated rent-seeking by the President, Lee Iacocca.[12]

"As early as the summer of 1979, it was clear that only drastic measures could save the Chrysler Corporation;" . . . If we were going to survive, we needed help. . . .

Ideologically, I've always been a free-enterpriser, a believer in survival of the fittest. When I was President of Ford, I spent almost as much time in Washington as in Dearborn. Then I went to the capital . . . to get the government off our backs. When I was back in Washington as Chairman of Chrysler to make the call for government help, everybody said: "How dare you?" I answered "It's the only game in town."

The Chrysler episode of successful lobbying for a government guarantee for a loan, which included "talking" to the Italian caucus, comprising Republicans and Democrats, seems a clear specimen of rent-seeking. But Iacocca mixed transparent special pleading with the persistent claim that Chrysler's difficulties were due ultimately to government over-regulation. "I had a week of hell in Congress trying to explain that. They say "'It was stupid management.'" I told them "'It's 50 percent our fault, 50 percent your fault.'" What if most Western economies, and their industrial enterprises, have costs raised by over-regulation – of prices, wages, safety standards,

[12] The encounters with Congressmen (and women) in Washington are recounted in graphic detail by Lee Iacocca and William Novak, *Iacocca – An Autobiography*, Sidgwick and Jackson, London, 1984; Bantam Books, New York, 1986.

taxes, so that firms organize themselves as rent-seekers to offset the over-regulation? Is rent-seeking that is designed to neutralize "direct political allocation" a "bad" or a "good" thing?[13]

11.5 Convergence with Three Parties?

In 1976 Tullock baldly presented the political response to voter power: ". . . if there are only two parties, we will find [the politicians] selecting positions [policies] very close together; if more than two, the parties will be further apart".

Until 1979 two major parties alternated in British government; the Liberal third was insignificant: it was last in sole office in 1915. Convergence of policy duly crystallized in the 35-year post-war consensus from 1945 to 1979 on Fabian public ownership for efficiency in industry, the Beveridge welfare state and the Keynesian cure for unemployment and inflation. Socialism reigned, despite alternating Labour and Conservative governments, for almost as long as the Whig dynasty in the early eighteenth century. The Conservative objection to government control of the economy, or socialism, was that it was undesirable unless it was conducted by Conservatives.

Since the 1983 General Election three parties (or rather coalitions) with comparable opinion poll support have alternated as the voters' (median?) preference. Labour and the Conservatives have been joined in the political market by the unwelcome Alliance of the historic Liberals and the fledgling Social Democrats. The expected divergence in policies has been (in effect, whatever the distinctive battle-cries to create political product differentiation) increasingly replaced by three-party convergence on market-oriented policies. The Conservatives were the first in 1975, although their Tory paternalists are resisting the capture of the Party by the Whiggish libertarians. The unexpected development was a declaration by the Social Democrat leader in 1983 in the market-oriented journal *Economic Affairs* that echoed the German social market economy.[14] And now in 1986 Labour has recently emerged with a disavowal of systematic re-socialization if re-elected and a tentative approach to markets in economic policy.[15] Perhaps Anthony Downs would now list, as the source of new political parties and the influence on them of median preferences, gradual change in "social outlook"

[13] J. M. Buchanan, "Rent Seeking and Profit Seeking", in *Towards a Theory of the Rent-Seeking Society*, Texas A & M University Press, 1980.

[14] David Owen, "Agenda for competitiveness with compassion", *Economic Affairs*, October 1983.

[15] The Deputy Leader recently entitled a Fabian Lecture *Socialism and Markets*: he inveighed against markets urged by the "New Liberals" (Hayek, Friedman, Powell, Owen) but reprimanded socialists for failing to see the case for markets on the grounds of freedom and efficiency.

from the market forces of *embourgeoisement* and technological advance as well as the sudden change from upheavals of war and revolution.

The median-voter theorem could still be vindicated if the internal party coalitions rearranged themselves into two new separate coalitions, one based on the Thatcher liberal Conservatives, the other on the Alliance led by the Owen Social Democrats, each offering a discrete conception of the content and timing of a market-oriented policy. The remaining paternalists and étatists could then form insignificant rumps with lingering representation in Parliament but little political significance. The tendency to convergence would be stronger than in West Germany in the 1960s because *embourgeoisement* and technology have advanced rapidly in the last 20 years. But the German experience is instructive, though Tullock was skeptical at the 1984 Meeting of the Mont Pelerin Society in Cambridge, at which I failed to arouse interest in the possibility of political convergence in Britain.

11.6 Democracy, Vested Interests and the Underground Market

Tullock stated in 1976 that "a new discovery in the economics of politics [might] invalidate not only [public choice analysis of voting as a means of collective control of government] but also the whole idea of democratic government!" But in the last ten years the public experience of representative institutions, in Britain and probably elsewhere, reinforced by the unprecedented critique by *politicians* of the political process,[16] has visibly weakened respect for democratic politics. There is an increasing public sense in Britain (and elsewhere) that representative government is unrepresentative of the sovereign people because it yields to organized producer interests (the "rent-seekers"). In the last ten years democratic government almost everywhere has been influenced more by "demos" (street demonstrations) than by *demos*. To gain a hearing individuals have to form groups with slogans and take to the streets with banners to compete with the organized teachers, miners, nurses, railwaymen and others. This is the price-effect of vested interests politics: if you yield to them, they multiply. In this milieu, where infrequent election votes count less than well-timed electronically-amplified "voice" between elections, every man has to become a politician and engage in the political life. If he does not, and most cannot, his protest lies in tax rejection of the legitimacy of the political system.

---

[16] A sophisticated example is the critique of British government by David Howell, a Minister in the 1970–4 Government under Edward Heath and a Cabinet Minister in Mrs Thatcher's Government of 1979–83. Despite the handicap of learning economics from the Keynesians at Cambridge, he argues that democratic politics has failed to keep pace with rapidly changing technology and the decentralized institutions it makes possible and, in time, will enforce. *Blind Victory*, Hamish Hamilton, London, 1986. Democracy, it seems, lags behind market forces.

Tullock could be right to shock American and British citizens into the realization that "the whole idea of democratic government" could be "invalidated" by refinements in public choice analysis, but it could, even before that, be discredited by revealing the imperfections in the political process that prevent it from executing the public will. Men are not more venal in politics than in business or academia, but they are exposed to inducements that make them appear to be.

If representatives are prevented by defective electoral machinery, from reflecting the preferences of the represented, the reason must be in part the very nature of representative government. Some evidence that indirect representation is less accurate than direct voting is provided by the results of referenda in Switzerland. The defects of the welfare state are less evident in Switzerland than in other Western countries because their citizens' preferences are less liable to be misinterpreted, obscured or distorted as much as they can be in nominal democracies: "Federalism and direct participation of the citizens in local, regional and, to a certain extent, also in federal votes about welfare issues slowed down the emergence of the welfare state."[17] This conclusion is reached by Walter Rüegg, Professor of Sociology at the University of Berné. ". . . the thought of a welfare state is politically dead in Switzerland." Again, indirect voting through representatives in a legislature seems to be the main source of the misrepresentation of the citizen. And the remedy seems to be to devise techniques for reducing the chain of "commands" between citizens and legislators.

Until the faith of voters in the political process is restored, the rejection of unrepresentative government which frustrates the choices of the public may be expected to take the form of evasion of the legislation produced by imperfect democracy. Classical liberals, who uphold the rule of law, find it dangerous to give any countenance to such forms of escape from unrepresentative government. But if there is no other escape, and voting offers no instrument of control over flawed representatives, it is not surprising if evasion of the law spreads in Western democracies.

Yet there is hope. If the representative role of democratic government is distorted by the pressure of rent-seekers, it may be that the citizen is learning from experience to fight shy of politicians who seek power by pre-election commitments to strident vested interests. The failure of former Vice-President Walter Mondale in the 1984 Presidential Election was seen by some in Britain as a political climateric, in which special interests succumbed to the more general will.

In Britain, also, a political party, Labour, financed by a powerful, although shrinking, interest has lost two General Elections to a party that made a

[17] "Social Rights or Social Responsibilities? The Case of Switzerland", in S. N. Eisenstadt and Ora Ahimeir, (1985) *The Welfare State and its Aftermath*, Croom Helm, London and Sydney, in association with the Jerusalem Institute for Israel Studies, Jerusalem.

general, moralistic appeal over its head, and could lose a third in 1987. R. W. Johnson, in an assessment of party prospects, writes: "this ... "'federation of the fragments' was the strategy adopted in 1983, when Labour's Manifesto was cobbled together by every possible sort of radical pressure group. . ."; "It was a disaster. The electorate was sick of parties in hock to pressure groups of any kind". (*The Times*, 29 September 1983) Here again, the analysis of rent-seeking may require refinement in the light of recent developments. Moral appeal in politics may be more rewarding than material interest.

So far, at least in the more stable democracies, the rejection of government takes the main form of tax evasion in the underground economy, which should indeed raise a silent cheer from classical liberals, since it is in principle as much resistance to unacceptable political coercion as the French Resistance was to the Nazi occupation. If rent-seeking, another Tullock "invention" (or, rather, discovery, since it was in existence), takes the form, *inter alia*, of extracting "unearned" income in the political process to supplement income earned in the market, the underground is not only the haven of tax rejectors. It is even more fundamentally a return to the free market of individuals with commercial talents who have to compensate for the lack of political skills required to extract favour from government. Those who cannot "join" government by "voice" are "beating" it by "exit". To over-simplify: the politically adroit seek, though they may dissipate, rents by importuning the state with the interest group activities analyzed in public choice theory; the politically maladroit, who are also probably the culturally less well-endowed, return to commerical skills in the "anarchical" underground which has no government to dispense favours to politically active rent-seekers. The growing underground, now perhaps a fifth or a quarter of some Western economies,[18] is still largely under-studied by economists. (Does it reduce inequality in incomes? Can it ever be insignificant in any interventionist economy? Is the cost, in lost production, of suppression larger than the gain in tax revenue? Is there a case for amnesty?)

11.7 Bureaucracy Challenged

In a British seminar in 1979,[19] a month before the British General Election, Tullock portrayed bureaucracy as a major cause of as well as a product of big government: they inflated each other inter-actively. Many in Britain are still

---

[18] Friedrich Schneider, "The shadow economy in Europe and America", *Economic Affairs*, early 1987.
[19] The papers were reproduced in *The Taming of Government*, IEA, London, 1979.

attached to the notion of "civil servants" as sea-green incorruptibles who interpret "ministers" holy grail of the public interest. The notion that to make a man a public official is to make him a public benefactor is a long time dying.

Tullock had more "shocks" in store for the British: promote competition within bureaucracies, he urged; contract out functions to the market; reduce salaries until voluntary resignations reach the desired reduction in numbers; most shocking of all, withdraw the vote from bureaucrats and their families. Despite some exceptions (notably Rowley and Peacock)[20] British economists had tended not to examine closely the bureaucracy and government. But Mrs. Thatcher's Government is the first significantly to confront the bureaucracy during the post-Second World War period. Contracting out of government services that are not public goods is proceeding; competition between bureaus has been increased by creating a Manpower Services Commission to train children from the age of fourteen for industry in competition with the Department of Education. But salaries have yet to be reduced. And the bureaucrats' vote remains. The British bureaucracy remains, pained and puzzled, but unbloody and unbowed.

An IEA Paper on education,[21] which drew on the Tullock interpretation of the British education bureaucracy, and quoted his dismissive conclusion, "The only real mystery is why anybody pays any attention to them", fuelled the new British debate that started in 1979 on the power of the bureaucracy to obstruct reform by reducing taxes and generally "rolling back" the state. The relationship of master and servant has been replaced by open warfare. The air is now full of government thinking on measures to discipline the bureaucrats; and in education *The Times* and other commentators have discussed government intentions to replace the culturally-conservative Department of Education by a new industry-oriented Department of Education and Training to emphasize the preparation of young people for a life of work. The Government, it seems, has refused to "join" the bureaucratic system and has thought of "beating" it by replacement, evasive action, and benign neglect. The British are absorbing Tullock and Niskanen (and others) on the economics of bureaucracy.

11.8   Optimum Government, Vanishing Public Goods and Constitutional Reform

Whatever the constitutional reforms designed to restrain government, the task is easier the smaller the province of public goods. In an early work on

---

[20] *Welfare Economics: A Liberal Restatement*, Martin Robertson, London, 1975.
[21] A. Seldon, *The Riddle of the Voucher*, IEA, London, 1986.

the limits of government,[22] Tullock reviewed the scope of public goods defining it rather more widely than he might now. Rapid technical change in the last 15 years is enabling the market to supply activities – civil security, pollution avoidance, urban planning (by special function streets) and others – whose non-excludability of free riders and/or non-rivalry have been thought to make them unavoidably the function of government.[23] In general, at least in Britain, where a referendum or constitutional reform to discipline the government pork-barrel would be massively resisted by recipient producer interests – from landowners, miners, railwaymen, and motor car manufacturers to prima donnas, pop-stars and assorted culture cranks – we may have to rely rather on emergent market alternatives that dispense with monopoly supply by government.[24] Constitutional reform has to confront the obstruction of the political process and its vested interests; market forces can find ways round or through them, not least because markets are no respecters of politics.

11.9 Tullock the Positivist

Before economics was almost drowned in a sea of spurious statistics,[25] Robbins used to speak of the economist's gift of introspection, and Arnold Plant praised concise elucidation of a proposition, as in Machlup's "drei Minuten Wirtschaftslehre". Another distinguished Austrian has said that the revival of microeconomics was essential for the future of liberalism. For the time-cost it has incurred and the harm that it has done, macroeconomics has proved to be a wasteful diversion that has distracted economists from refining micro-theory. Whether by instinct or by analysis Tullock has, by his austere positive microeconomics, helped to rescue economics from the dominance of macro-thinking.

His general avoidance of normative exposition was stated explicitly in a criticism of Amartya Sen in a recent book.[26] Sen had argued that famines

[22] *Private Wants, Public Means*, Basic Books, New York and London, 1970.

[23] The Belgian lawyer, Dr Frank van Dun, argues the case in "Public goods from the market", *Economic Affairs*, IEA, London, 1984, and the Belgian economist, Professor Boudewijn Bouchaert, in "Public goods and the limits of liberty", *Economist Affairs*, London, 1986/7.

[24] I suggest a crude empirical short-cut to the identification of public goods: if you can price it, it is *not* a public good. "Charge where you can, tax where you must" could be a workable rule-of-thumb for a liberal society.

[25] A noted econometrician, the British economist Sir Alan Walters, who was driven by tax rapacity to the USA, has graphically epitomized the excesses of mathematics in economics by his recollection that for a time not long ago mathematically-minded economists "regressed virtually everything on everything else". "The Rise and Fall of Econometrics", *The Unfinished Agenda*, IEA, London, 1986. The question remains: would they have done so if their income had come not from government hopefully fertilizing externalities, but from students paying fees strictly by results in obtaining degrees to earn a living?

[26] *Poverty and Famines*, Oxford University Press, New York, 1981.

were a reflection of shortage not of food but of purchasing power. The poor should therefore be supplied with purchasing power. Tullock objected that this was delivering "a moral lecture" and engaging in "political activity" which he found "extremely distasteful".[27] "I try to avoid imposing my own values on the reader." I find Tullock unnecessarily austere. Economists do not have to be philosophic eunuchs to win respect for their intellectual work. People who work in the social sciences understandably develop values, and it is better to declare them so that the reader or audience can allow for them.

11.10　Conclusions

A conclusion I draw from the literature of public choice, and from much of Tullock's work, is that government has a propensity to expand rather than contract. The direct benefits to politicians and bureaucracies of big government are self-evident. A telling example is anti-trust law. Even classical liberal economists were for decades generally in favour of trust-busting. Some have changed their minds.[28] But the politicians and the officials (of course) continue to advocate it strongly. An inescapable inference, it seems to me, is that democratic, representative government will tend to be too big rather than too small with intervention excesses slow to be revised. In short, the reality of democratic politics establishes a public choice predilection in favour of too little rather than too much government.

And that is a proposition in positive public choice that Tullock certainly would accept.

---

[27] *The Economics of Wealth and Poverty*, Wheatsheaf Books, Brighton, England, 1986.
[28] The conversion is explained in Basil Yamey, "The New Anti-Trust Economics", *The Unfinished Agenda*. op. cit.

12

Bureaucracy
WILLIAM A. NISKANEN

12.1 In the Beginning

Gordon Tullock uses economics the way a bright child uses a new hammer, alternately building something and smashing something. That is part of his charm. Few of us who have been exposed to Tullock's hammer will ever be quite the same.

But that is the mature Tullock. His first book and major contribution to the theory of bureaucracy developed from a quite different process. After training as a lawyer and experience in the foreign service, Tullock "discovered" economics as a way to make sense of his own experience. The first contribution to an economic theory of bureaucracy was the result of that discovery process.

One cannot imagine such a contribution arising from the academy. At that time, most of the scholarly literature on bureaucracy was a normative mishmash of Max Weber's sociology and Woodrow Wilson's vision of public administration. There was little relevant literature in economics. Few economists had addressed the behavior of people *within* firms or bureaus. The one prior book on bureaucracy by an economist, Ludwig von Mises (1945), had little analytic content. Fortunately, as far as I can discern, Tullock had read none of this literature. His own contribution reflected a fine mind, a broad reading of history, an independence of established scholarly traditions, and the central insight, but not the techniques, of an economist.

12.2 The Politics of Bureaucracy

The book published as *The Politics of Bureaucracy* in 1965 was based on a more lengthy manuscript completed in 1957, prior to Tullock's first academic appointment or more than casual exposure to economics. In *Chapter 2*, James Buchanan describes how he transformed the 1957 manuscript into the final book (1986), primarily by excising most of Tullock's personal narrative. The result was a summary of Tullock's perceptions about bureaucracy, but one which lacked an explanation of how he came to these perceptions. ,

The focus of this book is on the relations of people *within* organizations, where the costs of withdrawing from these relations are high to both parties. In this sense, there is some political element in most market relations, to the extent that the cost of withdrawing from these relations is not zero. Similarly, there is some economic element in most relations within organizations, to the extent that the cost of withdrawing from these relations is not infinite. Tullock focuses on the political end of this spectrum. Although these relations are analyzed elsewhere as bilateral monopolies, Tullock does not use either this term or the formal analysis of this type of relation. For someone who has never married, however, Tullock has a very subtle understanding of bilateral monopolies.

In fact, there is little "economics" in this book, except that Tullock's use of the central motivational assumption of economics produces some important insights about bureaucratic behavior. These insights, however, derive less from economic theory than from Tullock's fertile mind. There is no use of marginal analysis, a limitation that gets Tullock into some trouble. For example, Tullock (1965, p. 69) concludes that a subordinate will only support those policies that are consistent with the current information of his superior; this conclusion is clearly wrong if the incremental benefits (to the superior) of an alternative policy are higher than the incremental costs (again, to the superior) of assimilating the additional information. Machiavelli makes a similar mistake in advising a prince ". . . to discourage absolutely attempts to advise him unless he asks it" (1952, p. 117). Most of us can identify some organizational mistakes that are due to advice that was not offered or to questions that were not asked, but few general problems of organizations are due to an insufficient supply of information. The method of argument is also quite different from most of economics. There is no formal model or any use of algebra. Most of the references are to obscure historical treatises or to contemporary novels. There is no formal empirical analysis. The several graphs look most like television station test patterns and convey about as much information. At that time, Tullock's economics was more a mindset than a technique.

Machiavelli's *The Prince* (1952) was the closest model to Tullock's book on bureaucracy. Machiavelli focuses primarily on the behavior of the sovereign and his immediate subordinates. Tullock focuses primarily on the behavior of middle-level bureaucrats and their immediate superiors. Both assume that people will pursue their own interests and not the interests of others or the moral standards of the community. Both use a mix of historical and contemporary examples, plus an appeal to the understanding of the reader to make their point. Both recognize that their analyses will shock some readers – Machiavelli with apparent indifference, Tullock with apparent delight.

The primary contribution of Tullock's book was a set of "mental experiments" addressed to the relation of organizational structure and performance. In a pyramidal structure, Tullock concludes, output will increase at a slower rate than input as a function of the number of layers of supervision. This decline in efficiency is a consequence of the progressive loss of control from the top down and the progressive loss of information from the bottom up. He then addresses the effects of a large number of techniques to limit these losses – the executive officer, a staff system, random inspections, cost accounting, etc. One gains a better understanding of why some large organizations are as bad as they are. The book, however, lacks any sense of why some other large organizations are as good as they are. In the absence of any economies of scale or scope, there is no reason for either firms or bureaus. Only a balancing of the marginal gains and losses of scale and scope can provide a basis for an optimal sizing rule. Tullock concludes that "Most modern governmental hierarchies are much beyond their efficient organizational limits", a conclusion with which I agree, but one which is not self-evident from the Tullock experiments (1965, p. 177).

One of my favorite sections of the book is his description of the promotion process in a bureaucracy, by analogy to a gaseous diffusion plant (several other characteristics of a bureaucracy could also be described by this term). This approach leads to some interesting insights about the relations between efficiency and morality. The promotion process in any organization will select against moral behavior (in the sense of serving the interests of the whole organization), unless the incentive system is such that self-serving behavior and moral behavior are the same. In this sense, bureaucratic behavior is likely to be moral only when the organization is efficient – the reverse of the conventional perspective that moral behavior is a necessary condition for efficiency. This contrast in perspectives deserves re-emphasis. An economist's prescription is to design the organization (and its relations to other organizations) to be efficient, and moral behavior will follow. The gurus of public administration from Confucius to Wilson, in contrast, have long promoted training in moral behavior, with the wistful hope that efficiency will follow.

The relation between efficiency and freedom is more complex. An inefficient bureaucracy provides substantial freedom for what Tullock calls "bureaucratic free enterprise". An increase in efficiency necessarily reduces this dimension of discretion. An efficient organization may permit substantial discretion in the choice of means to serve the objectives of the organization, except where some coordination of the means is valuable, but cannot permit the freedom of actions that do not serve the organization. On the job, a government employee probably has more freedom than a private employee. A richer concept of freedom, however, would focus on the freedom to make alternative contract relations, rather than the freedom within a contract of one's choice. Among societies, there is ample evidence that efficiency requires such freedom of contract.

Tullock finally concludes that the problems of bureaucracy cannot be solved, at least within the Government. He may be right, but his analysis and evidence are not sufficient. Many large private organizations, operating in a competitive market, are quite efficient, adaptive, and creative. So the efficiency problems that he attributes to government organizations are probably due more to their external relations than to their internal structure. His skepticism about solving the problems of bureaucracy leads him to recommend more reliance on local governments and a reduction in the scope of governmental activities – prescriptions that are probably correct in any case.

He proved to be a poor prophet, however, by concluding in 1965 (p. 224) "that the 'ideological climate' [for these ideas] is more favorable than it has been in many years." Such naive optimism has sustained many of us through a continued expansion in the roles and relative spending by government under administrations of both parties. As of 1986, the "ideological climate" may be even more favorable, but increasingly irrelevant. I wonder how much longer such optimism can be sustained. Maybe I am just tired. On the other hand, the narrow bureaucracy problem may be declining. The continued growth of government programs, spendings, taxes, and regulation since 1965 has not involved *any* increase in total federal employment. The efficiency of the bureaucracy is still not impressive but may not be the important thing.

12.3   The "Dynamic Hypothesis"

Tullock made one other published contribution to the theory of bureaucracy. In a book review (1972), he made a few brief favorable comments about my book and then proceeded to sketch his own theory of the growth of the bureaucracy. This theory was only slightly expanded in a 1974 article: "dynamic hypothesis on bureaucracy". The two elements of this hypothesis were that (1) the demand for the services of a bureau is the sum of the private demand and the demand by bureaucrats: and (2) the bureaucrats face a choice of responding to an increase in demand by increasing the numbers or the wages of bureaucrats. The unsurprising conclusion is that an increase in demand would probably lead to an increase in both the numbers and wages of bureaucrats. A part of the problem of this paper is that it did not reflect institutional reality. The wage scales are not set by each bureau but on a government-wide basis. For each individual, the only action that can increase his wage is a promotion. For each bureau, the only action that can increase average wages is an increase in average employment grades. A general wage increase is dependent on an increase in the total demand for government employees, a condition that is not much affected by the actions of each bureau. For the most part, the Government wage scale is probably best considered exogenous to the behavior of an individual bureau. There remains the intriguing question why total federal employment has not changed much in 20 years, but this hypothesis provides no insight about this issue. This little contribution is best described as an experimental test vehicle that did not get off the ground.

12.4 Odds and Ends

In the summer of 1966, Tullock made two other contributions to understanding bureaucracy, only one of which has been acknowledged. At that time he was a visiting senior staff member at the Institute for Defense Analyses (IDA), where I was his division director.

Motivated by our joint interest in the process of promotion in a bureaucracy, Tullock designed an ingenious test. Examining the records of the graduates of West Point during the late 1930s who had achieved the rank of colonel or higher, Tullock looked for the distinguishing characteristics of those who were promoted to the rank of brigadier-general. (At that time, only about 10 per cent of colonels were promoted.) The results were disturbingly consistent with Tullock's suspicions. This critical promotion was closely associated with cadet rank at West Point but was independent of academic rank. The characteristic of their later record that was most closely associated with this critical promotion was distinguished performance in staff work. Some combat experience increased the probability of promotion but distinguished performance in combat did not. For a young man entering West Point, the optimal career path to become a brigadier-general, thus, appeared to be popularity among your classmates, an early superficial wound, and a subsequent career as a "horseholder" for senior officers. The army, apparently, selects its generals on the basis of their peacetime skills. These results were too sensitive for a defense research firm to publish early in the Vietnam war. More studies of the type pioneered by Tullock would contribute to a better understanding of our major public and private bureaucracies.

In his forward to *The Politics of Bureaucracy*, James Buchanan writes:

Once this basic theory of the behavior of the individual unit is constructed, it becomes possible to begin the construction of a theory of the inclusive system, which is composed of a pattern of interactions among the individual units. By the nature of the systems with which he works, administrative hierarchies, Tullock's "theory of organization" here is less fully developed tha[n] is the analogous "theory of markets". A more sophisticated theory may be possible here, and, if so, Tullock's analysis can be an important helpmate to whoever chooses to elaborate it. (1965, p. 3)

Shortly after this book was published, Tullock had the direct opportunity to be this important helpmate, during his brief period at IDA, by prodding me to develop my inchoate views on the relation between a bureau and its "sponsor", the critical element of a theory of the market for the services of bureaus. By separate paths, we had both come to believe that bureaus act as if they are maximizing their budgets (an hypothesis, by the way, that I now believe is inferior to an hypothesis that bureaucrats act to maximize their "discretionary" budget, the difference between the actual budget and that necessary to supply the output expected by the sponsor). In a role that Buchanan had served for him, Tullock encouraged me to believe that I had something important to say, if I could abstract from my own experience as a defense analyst. My own book on *Bureaucracy and Representative Government* (1971) grew out of that brief productive interaction. That may not be Tullock's major contribution to an economic theory of bureaucracy, but it is the one for which I was, and am, most grateful.

References

Buchanan, James (1986) 'The qualities of a natural economist' chapter 2 of this book.

Machiavelli, Niccolo (1952) *The Prince*. New York: New American Library.

Mises, Ludwig von (1944) *Bureaucracy*. New Haven: Yale University Press.

Niskanen, William A. (1971) *Bureaucracy and Representative Government*. Chicago: Aldine-Atherton.

Tullock, Gordon (1965) *The Politics of Bureaucracy*. Washington: The Public Affairs Press.

Tullock, Gordon (1972) 'Review of bureaucracy and representative government', *Public Choice*, **12**, Spring.

Tullock, Gordon (1974) "Dynamic hypothesis of bureaucracy", *Public Choice*, **19**, Fall.

V

Rent-Seeking

13

Is The Theory of Rent-Seeking Here to Stay?

ROBERT D. TOLLISON

13.1 Introduction

Government, as all students of public choice know, is not free. Yet until very recently the cost of government intervention in the economy has been under-estimated. The reason for this is that the economic theory underlying such measurements was incomplete. In 1967, Gordon Tullock offered a picture of what a complete economic theory of the cost of government looks like when he invented what has come to be called the theory of rent-seeking.[1] The purpose of this chapter is to assess the evolution of Tullock's idea in the literature, with special attention given to the problems and conundrums that presently dog rent-seeking theory.

There is, moreover, some market evidence that Tullock's concept of rent-seeking should be taken seriously. Using 1984 citation data, Tullock's 1967 paper, "The Welfare Costs of Tariffs, Monopolies and Theft", ties for second among his most cited works, and is the only article-length publication in his top five list (see table 13.1). I have not checked, but I would also guess that citations of this paper have greatly increased over the past several years. I am, therefore, not dealing with a backwater of Tullock's work, but rather a peak, and a growing peak at that.

---

[1] There is a debate about what to call the behavior described by rent-seeking. The name is from Krueger's 1973 paper by the title, "The Political Economy of the Rent-Seeking Society". Bhagwati objects to the rent-seeking terminology, preferring instead the appellation, Directly Unproductive Activities (DUP) (see, for example, Bhagwati, Brecker, and Srinivasan, 1984). His interest in the relationship between the theory of second-best and rent-seeking is apparent in his preferred terminology. Others, such as North (1984), simply want to identify rent-seeking as economic behavior subject to constraints, that is, as an application of the maximizing paradigm of economic theory. I have no strong feelings about what we call the behavior at issue here, though "rent-seeking" does just fine so long as the analysis is spelled out and carried through properly.

Table 13.1   Gordon Tullock's five most cited works – 1984

Book or article	Number of 1984 citations[9]
The Calculus of Consent	49
The Politics of Bureaucracy	17
'The welfare costs of tariffs, monopolies, and theft'	17
Towards a Mathematics of Politics	10
Economics of Income Redistribution	7

[9] Citations to *The Calculus of Consent* are found under James M. Buchanan and are counted as 1.

Source: Social Science Citation Index, 1984.

The chapter proceeds as follows. Section 13.2 is definitional: in the simplest terms, what does rent-seeking mean? Section 13.3 further develops the theory of rent-seeking in the context of a government-created monopoly right. Section 13.4 examines the concept of equilibrium in rent-seeking contests. Section 13.5 introduces the concept of rent-protection. Section 13.6 discusses durable and nondurable monopolies and their welfare implications. Section 13.7 considers the possible links between income distribution and rent-seeking activities. Section 13.8 considers the relationship between politcal order and rent-seeking. Section 13.9 briefly introduces the positive economic side of rent-seeking theory. Section 13.10 concludes the chapter.

13.2   Rent-Seeking Defined

Economic rent is a familiar concept to economists. Simply, it is a return to a resource owner in excess of the owner's opportunity cost. Economic analysis has identified various categories of such returns (not all distinct one from the other) – quasi-rents, monopoly rents, inframarginal rents, and so on. Rent-seeking in the sense of seeking quasi- or temporary rents is nothing more than the normal profit-seeking incentive that motivates economic behavior. Such behavior is healthy for an economy; it allocates resources to their most highly valued uses, creates new products and values, and so on (Buchanan, 1980b). This behavior is not what Tullock's concept of rent-seeking means. Positive or negative temporary rents compel entry or exit, and hence impact on economic output. The economy gets something in return for temporary rents (more or less product).

Rent-seeking arises where output is given and fixed, as in the case of monopoly rents. Output cannot be augmented by definition, so expenditure to capture monopoly or contrived rents do not yield any additional products for the economy. It was such expenditures that Tullock categorized as wasteful.

Perhaps the most useful way to think about rent-seeking is in terms of using real resources to capture a pure transfer. Since expenditures to take a dollar from A and give it to B produce nothing, they are wasted from the point of view of the economy at large; they are zero-sum at best and are probably negative-sum (Tullock, 1980b). A lawyer, for example, employed to transfer a dollar from A to B has an opportunity cost in terms of the lawyer output he or she could have produced alternatively. This opportunity cost is the social cost of rent-seeking.

Rent-seeking is perhaps most usefully illustrated in the context of government interference in the economy to promote monopoly and economic regulation. The most efficacious way to promote monopoly rents in an industry is to pass a law to restrict output and to license entry. As individuals and firms seek government's favor to operate in the industry, rent-seeking occurs because such competition cannot expand output in the industry, which is fixed by law. It is not necessary, however, to have government to have rent-seeking. Private collusion among firms to fix prices, for example, has all the attributes of a rent-seeking game. Likewise the Mafia, competitive advertising by oligopolists, and the competition among siblings for inheritances are other possible examples of rent-seeking in a private context.[2]

Another definitional point is useful. Once government has intervened in the economy to create rents, the implications of rent-seeking behavior are difficult to escape (Buchanan, 1980b). Transfers will beget rent-seeking competition to capture them on some margin. If rents are created in the civil service, queues and "extra" educational investments will arise to dissipate them. Proffered tax reductions will induce entry into tax-favored classes. The same holds on the expenditure side of the budget. Basically, rent-seeking is a cost of government activity in general.

Finally, the theory of rent-seeking has positive and normative elements. The latter, which will occupy the bulk of this chapter, consists of devising theories of how the social costs of rent-seeking can be measured. This is the welfare economics part of rent-seeking theory. The former involves using the struggle to capture or to protect rents to explain the behavior of interest groups, legislators, regulators, voters, and other relevant actors in the political economy.

---

[2] The latter example is a matter of some dispute in the literature; see Buchanan (1983); and Anderson and Brown (1985). Also, one could argue that each of these examples of rent-seeking in a private setting are somehow related to government in the limiting case. Competitive advertising by oligopolists, for example, takes place because agreements among firms on such matters are illegal under the anti-trust laws. See DiLorenzo (1984).

13.3   The Social Costs of Rent-Seeking

The purpose of this section is essentially to repeat the analysis of Section 13.2 in a slightly more complicated way. Hopefully, by the end of this discussion, we will be in a position to discuss the strengths and weaknesses of rent-seeking theory in more detail.

Following the above semantics, a useful way to analyze the social costs of rent-seeking is to consider the case where government promotes monopoly power in the private sector with a law or regulation (see figure 13.1.)

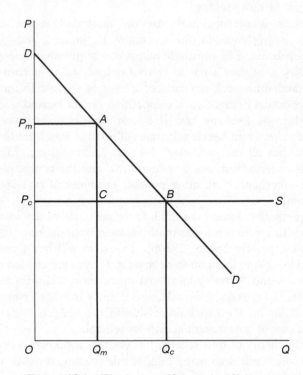

Figure 13.1   The basic welfare trade-off diagram

At the original competitive equilibrium, $P_c Q_c$, consumer surplus in this industry is DBP_c. However, no one guarantees that consumers will get this real income; it is essentially up for grabs in the economic system. This being the case, let us assume that producers seek to capture part of the surplus by obtaining economic regulation of their industry. Price rises to P_m, as the regulatory program restricts industry output to Q_m. The marginal revenue curve is omitted to avoid cluttering the diagram.

In the old theory of monopoly (Harberger, 1954), producers succeeded in capturing $P_m ACP_c$ as a *transfer* from consumers (those who continue to buy the product at P_m). Consumers were made poorer to the same extent that the monopolist was made richer. Interpersonal judgments aside, the economy was seen as unaltered by such transfers. ABC, however, vanished from the economy as a result of the monopoly, and this real income was captured by no-one. Hence, ABC was called the deadweight cost of monopoly or regulation. The fact that ABC was empirically small led to a complacency about monopoly and regulatory power in the economy, and to less interest among economists in the formal theory of monopoly (Mundell, 1962).

Tullock looked at this same type of analytical model, but posed the following question: what if $P_m ACP_c$ is not a simple transfer from consumers to producers? Suppose, instead, that those producers who aspire to be regulated have to spend real resources to capture the potential transfer of $P_m ACP_c$? By asking such questions, Tullock was led to discover the concept of rent-seeking.

Let us suppose a simple rent-seeking game. There is a fixed number of bidders for a government monopoly right, say 20. The monopoly right has a known and fixed value of $100,000. All bidders are risk neutral. Thus, each person bids $5,000 for a one-in-twenty chance of winning the $100,000 pool of rents; at a social level, $100,000 is spent to capture $100,000. In this case, $P_m ACP_c$ is exactly or perfectly dissipated, and the social costs of the monopoly is a trapezoid, $P_m ABP_c$, which consists of the Tullock or rent-seeking costs, $P_m ACP_c$, and the Harberger or deadweight cost of monopoly, ABC. Tullock's invention thus provided a framework for increasing the social costs of monopoly and regulation by a significant amount, in the limit, the value of the monopoly profits at stake, making the theory of monopoly and regulation more interesting and richer to study as a result (Kreuger, 1973; Posner, 1975).

Of course, the stylized example here over simplifies. For example, I did not say what happens to the payments made by the rent-seekers. They clearly flow to the public sector in some form. At an elementary level, each bidder may have spent $5,000 in taking regulatory officials out to dinner. Thus, the cost of rent-seeking in this case consists in the difference between the value of the in-kind transfer to the officials and its cash equivalent. In other words, not all of $P_m ACP_c$ is wasted; the officials place some value, though less than $100,000, on being taken out to dinner.

But this is a simple problem in rent-seeking theory. There are more interesting complexities that derive from this basic model, which I address in the sections that follow. Space does not allow a detailed elaboration of any of these issues. In each case, I endeavor to give the flavor of the problems at stake and to cite the relevent literature for those who would like to know more.

13.4   Equilibrium

The case where rents are exactly dissipated represents an example of competitive rent-seeking. With free entry and exit for bidders, the rent-seeking contest comes to reflect an equilibrium structure of bids and bidders. In the above example, rents are perfectly competed away with 20 bidders. Thus, even though the winner earns $95,000 on his or her bid, the game is presumably in equilibrium, and this prize is only a normal return investment in rent-seeking. If government, for example, were to seize the monopoly with no compensation, bidders would adjust their bids in the next round of rent-seeking.

Competitive rent-seeking is a popular equilibrium hypothesis in the literature (Posner, 1975). This is because it yields the exact dissipation result, which makes empirical work on the costs of rent-seeking easier. Rectangles and trapezoids are exact areas, which can be reasonably estimated. The exact dissipation model is thus like perfect competition; it is a useful, though not necessarily descriptive, analytical construct for increasing our understanding of how the world works.

This does not mean, however, that all rent-seeking contests are perfectly competitive in nature. Tullock (1980a) has offered classes of models where rent-seeking is imperfectly competitive in the sense that the competitive process for rents leads to over- or under dissipation of the available rents. These cases are interesting, and they are obviously generated by assumptions about limitations on the number of bidders, imperfect information, and so on. They are not very popular, however, because imperfect dissipation makes the problem of deriving reduced-form equations with which to estimate rent-seeking costs much more difficult and case-specific (Fisher, 1985). One can no longer simply estimate the area of a trapezoid; rather, the task is to estimate the area of something more or less than a trapezoid that is a function of behavior in the economy. This is clearly a harder modeling task.

As between Tullock's analysis of over- and under-dissipation possibilities, I do not find the over-dissipation possibility to be very plausible. In this case, rent seekers are somehow led to bid more than the value of the prize. While this is perhaps possible once, through the distortion of information to rent-seekers about their expected chances of winning, such behavior should not persist for long. The regulator/bureaucrat should only be able to lie once. In the next round of rent-seeking, bids will be adjusted to reflect "true" probabilities of winning; bureaucratic promises will be properly discounted.

Underbidding, where rent-seekers bid in the aggregate less than the value of the prize, is another matter. There are several plausible bases for underbidding equilibria, including risk aversion (Hillman and Katz, 1984), comparative advantage among monopolizing inputs (Rogerson, 1982), and game-theoretic considerations (Tullock, 1980a, 1985). As stressed above, such considerations make the problem of analyzing the costs of rent-seeking more difficult and case-specific.

The point is that the concept of equilibrium is important in rent-seeking theory because it informs us as to how costly such behavior is likely to be in the real economy. Under-dissipation means less waste of rents (though as we shall see later, perhaps more monopoly). Theory is in its infancy in this area. At present, the literature (Corcoran, 1984; Higgins, Shughart, and Tollison, 1985) suggests that exact dissipation best describes the long-run tendency in games where the prize is fixed and there is free entry and exit of bidders. Tullock (1985) is quite adept, however, at undermining such results, and as he puts it, returning us to the bog of under-dissipation.

All this is to say that exact dissipation appears to be a good general conjecture about equilibrium in rent-seeking contests, but that this theory must be adapted to the circumstances of any particular case of rent-seeking. Like the model of perfect competition, the model of exactly dissipated rents is simply a vehicle and starting point for helping us to understand the real world.

13.5   Rent Protection

Not only do individuals use real resources to seek transfers, but they also are sometimes required to use real resources to protect their rents from encroachment by rent-seekers. This behavior is called "rent avoidance" in the literature; I choose to call it "rent protection". The basis for such behavior is clear. Not all "suppliers" of wealth transfers find it economically rational to allow their wealth to be taken away (why spend a dollar to save a dime?). Some will find it cost-effective to fight back (spend a dollar to save two dollars).

Let us use the simple example of an excise tax on a competitive industry to illustrate the potential of rent protection thoery. Figure 13.2 illustrates. Here, as a result of an excise tax on the industry's product, industry supply shifts from S to S'. The traditional analysis of this case stresses three basic results: (1) ABC is the deadweight cost of the tax; (2) $EACF$ is the tax revenue that is transferred to government; and (3) the incidence of the tax is split between consumers (C) and producers (P) as a function of the elasticities of demand and supply.

Enter rent protection. Assume that consumers (C) are unorganized and have no rational incentives to organize to resist the loss of consumer surplus that the tax imposes on them. However, let producers be organized and prepared to lobby against the tax. In the case at hand, producers may

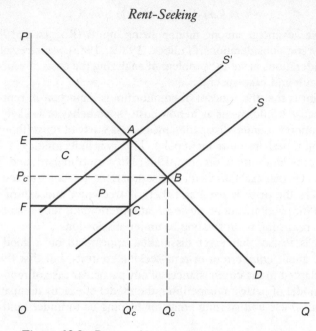

Figure 13.2   Rent-seeking in a heterogeneous market

rationally spend up to their loss of producer surplus, P_cBCF, to resist the tax or to keep it from being higher than it is. This is the amount of wealth that the tax takes away from the industry. These expenditures are a rent-seeking (rent-protecting) cost in Tullock's terms, and so must be added to the traditional cost of the excise tax, ABC, to obtain the total social cost of excise taxation in this case. The total cost of the excise tax thus equals P_cBCF plus ABC.

Now the traditional or optimal taxation analysis is in a little bit of trouble. It is a mainstay of optimal taxation theory that the excess burden imposed by selective excise taxation (ABC) is minimized, for a given amount of revenue raised, when such taxes are placed on commodities with relatively inelastic demand curves. Unfortunately, this optimal taxation rule cannot stand up to the above analysis. It is quite easy to show that when P_cBCF is counted as part of the cost of excise taxation, taxing an industry with a more elastic demand curve, but no organized, rent-protecting opposition to the tax, is socially preferable. Moreover, considerations of monopoly only strengthen the analysis.[3]

In sum, then, the concept of rent protection can be brought into conventional economic analysis, perhaps to yield new and interesting insights about the way the world works. For example, the idea that excise

[3] For the basic analysis, see Lee and Tollison (1985).

taxes in the face of organized industry opposition are not a good idea undercuts the tax program of most countries with respect to such commodities as beer and cigarettes. Moreover, virtually all welfare analyses of monopoly and regulation ignore rent-protection activities of organized opponents of such governmental programs. A more general welfare analytics will include traditional deadweight costs, rent-seeking costs, *and* rent-protecting costs.[4]

13.6 Durability

The durability of monopoly rights poses some interesting issues for the theory of rent seeking.[5] Consider the following limiting case. The monopoly right is granted forever, and all Tullock-type expenditures to capture the right are made *ex ante* by rent-seekers. In this situation, the Tullock costs are *sunk*. The economy is forever poorer by the amount of Tullock spending; abolishing the monopoly right cannot get the Tullock expenditures back.

Now consider the case where Tullock costs have not been completely capitalized. That is, the holder of the monopoly right must engage in some rent protection expenditures each period as there are threats to the political status of his or her monopoly. In this situation, *if*, for example, the monopoly is deregulated *permanently*, the ongoing Tullock expenditures can be returned to the economy.

The moral of this story about durability for anti-trust and regulatory reform efforts is clear. The gains from deregulation are greater where Tullock costs have not yet been capitalized. Others things being equal, the most cost-effective program of deregulation is to concentrate on industries that fight back, for here the social gains from deregulation are largest. There is less point in taking action with, say, old, quiet monopolies.

Mind you, this is a point about social gains. Consumers, on the whole could not, care less whether monopoly rents have been capitalized. But still the logic of the argument is to point out where it is in the political economy that the gains from deregulation are potentially the highest. This is paradoxically where deregulation is fought the hardest. Such are the implications of rent-seeking for anti-thrust and regulatory reform.

13.7 Rent-Seeking and The Distribution of Income

Pre-Tullock, the effect of monopoly on the distribution of income was clear:

[4] See Baysinger and Tollison (1980) for an effort along these lines.
[5] The following is adapted from McCormick, Shughart, and Tollison (1984). Also, see Landes and Posner (1975) for a positive theory of the durability of legislation.

the monopolist got richer and consumers got poorer (Comanor and Smiley, 1975). In the rent-seeking approach, the impact of monopoly on income distribution is a murkier issue. Of the original formulators of the theory, only Posner (1975) relates his analysis to the distribution of income. He states: "There is no reason to think that monopoly has a significant distributive effect. Consumers' wealth is not transferred to the shareholders of monopoly firms; it is dissipated in the purchase of inputs into the activity of becoming a monopolist" (1975, p. 821).

Posner's argument seems logical. Rent-seeking dissipates monopoly rents, translating potential transfers into social costs. The effect of monopoly on the distribution of income in the rent-seeking society would thus appear to be nil. Unfortunately, this argument does not stand up.

Rent-seeking has a pronounced impact on the distribution of income – the winner of the monopoly right becomes wealthier. Using the simple example employed by Posner, suppose that there are $1 million in rents to be captured and ten risk-neutral bidders for a monopoly right. The allocative effects in the problem are clear. Each bidder bids $100,000 for the franchise; $1 million is spent to capture $1 million; at a social level the monopoly rents are exactly wasted. But Posner is incorrect to imply that the example does not embody a distributional consequence. Clearly, one of the ten bidders wins the competition, and receives a net return on his efforts of $900,000. The resulting income distribution is different than that which prevailed before the monopoly right was created, in this example significantly different. Simply, nine people are $100,000 poorer, and one is $900,000 richer.

Without more information, one cannot say in this stylized example whether rent-seeking increases or decreases the degree of inequality in the distribution of income. The winner in this case could, for example, have been poor relative to the nine losers, and his victory would have leveled the income distribution to some extent. It seems a little far-fetched, however, to think that rent-seeking generally promotes any leveling in the income distribution of an economy. Set in a world of tradition, class, privilege, power, and differential organization costs, rent-seeking most likely promotes more inequality in the distribution of income.

Perhaps even more realistically, there will not be an equal distribution of rent-seeking ability in a society. Thus, the mechanism by which rents are assigned is likely to affect the distribution of wealth to the extent that Ricardian rents are earned in rent-seeking. Consider a regulatory hearing mechanism for assigning rents, and suppose that some lawyers or economists earn inframarginal rents in rent-seeking. On average, these individuals will be wealthier than their marginal competitors and wealthier than they would be without a rent-seeking mechanism of the particular type that rewards their skills. The choice of such a transfer mechanism increases the demand for lawyers (and possibly economists) above that which would hold with (say) an auction mechanism for assigning monopoly rents. So, first of all, the mechanism will alter the distribution of wealth by occupation. Moreover, if the requisite talents of the favored occupation cannot be reproduced at constant costs, the inequality of wealth in society may be further affected. For example, suppose the qualities of a good businessman/speculator are more fungible among the population than the qualities of a good lawyer. Then, inframarginal rents will accrue to the best of the legal profession in regulatory hearing cases, whereas with an auction no Ricardian rents would be earned. The distribution of wealth would differ between these two societies as a consequence.

The main point, then, is that rent-seeking will affect the distribution of income. This is not an empirical chapter. Estimating the actual impact of rent-seeking on income distribution has not been done and would be a formidable task. Perhaps Posner is right. If anyone looked, the actual impact of rent-seeking on income distribution would be trivial. This seems doubtful, however, given the rather large role that government has assumed in the economy and the degree to which government largesse figures prominently in the circular flow of income.[6]

13.8 Rent-Seeking and the Political Order

What is the relationship between the political order and the amount of rent-seeking that it begets? There are no easy answers here; in fact, to my mind, there are no answers at present. Let me explain.[7]

Rent-seeking can be seen as a two-stage game. First, there is competition to control the political apparatus that creates, enforces, and assigns rent flows. This is related to issues such as who controls the legislature, or how monarchs are selected. Second, there is the rent-seeking behavior that we have been discussing thus far in the chapter, namely, the competition to capture the rents that inhere in particular instances of monopoly and regulation. These two stages are linked in the discussion that follows, presenting a problem of some importance for rent-seeking theory.

The problem is easy to exposit. At base, in a world where Tullock waste is exact and complete, there is no marginal incentive to create monopolies. Investments in monopoly creation lead only to a normal rate of return. Political entrepreneurs will seek higher return margins of political investment. There thus exist incentives to convert Tullock waste into transfers,

---

[6] For more discussion along these lines, see Higgins and Tollison (1985).

[7] Again, see Higgins and Tollison (1985) for a more elaborate version of the argument in this section.

which make the creators of monopoly rents better off. Better to receive a transfer than to see transfers wasted.

In this context, consider two types of worlds. In one, Tullock waste is exact and complete. Here, the incentive to create monopoly will be low because there are no excess returns from doing so, but the social cost per instance of realized monopoly will be high. In the other world, politicians have succeeded in converting rent-seeking costs into transfers. There are thus significant excess returns to monopoly creation; hence, there will be more monopolies in such a society. Returns to politicians are only transfers and not waste in this society, but this society will have more monopolies and more Harberger losses than the first society.

The dilemma is now clear – which society will be wealthier? There does not appear to be an *a priori* way to say: one society has less monopoly and more waste per monopoly; the other has more monopoly and less waste per monopoly. As I said at the outset, I write only to pose the issue. I do not know what the answer to the question is.

Indeed, the issue becomes murkier when we return to the first stage of rent-seeking discussed above. If there is a lot to be gained from controlling government, as in the second case above where rents are converted to transfers by political actors, then perhaps a lot is spent at the first stage of the contest to control the government. Alternatively, where there is not much to be made through monopoly creation, little effort may be expended to capture the state. Of course, this is all quite *ad hoc*. For example, the divine right of monarchs with clearly defined rules of royal succession leads to a fairly low-cost means of transferring control of the state, even though the state may be fairly effective at using monopolies as a source of revenue (Ekelund and Tollison, 1981).

One can thus find odd combinations of first- and second-stage incentives. Majoritarian democracy, for example, appears to give away regulatory rents through in-kind auctions, which maximizes the incentive to create monopolies at the second stage, while allowing maximal dissipation to acquire legislative majorities at the first stage. One, almost perversely, gets lots of Tullock and Harberger waste in such a case. The point is that rent-seeking takes place within a given political order and that this order impacts on the character and amount of rent-seeking that we subsequently observe. This is really a problem of constitutional political economy. (Buchanan, 1980a). Of course, the control of rent-seeking is not the only objective in designing or evaluating a state, but the issue clearly deserves to be on the menu of relevant considerations.

13.9   Positive Economics and Rent-Seeking

There is a positive economics of rent-seeking which, if I were to do justice to it, would take another chapter. Briefly, the literature which expounds it is driven by the idea that much of government activity can be explained in wealth-transfer terms. That is, government is about taking wealth from some people ('suppliers' of wealth transfers) and giving it to other people ('demanders' of wealth transfers), or put into the terms of this chapter, about rent-protection and rent-seeking.[8]

Most people are taken aback at such a starkly simple (and cynical) view of government. They wonder, well surely government is about something more than organized, legitimized theft? Surely government is about Truth, Beauty, Justice, the American Way, and the production of Public Goods?

And, of course, the rent-seeking theory has answers to these types of questions. Yes, government does produce things in the rent-seeking theory of the state, but these are mere by-products of the fundamental transfers at stake. We thus get our national defense, roads, schools, and so on as an unintended consequence of the competition for wealth-transfers. As stated at the start of the chapter, government is not free, and rent-seeking is the cost of government.

But more importantly, and more scientifically, the rent-seeking theory of government is an *empirical* theory. Not only is it on the front page of the newspapers every day, but there is scholarly empirical support for the theory which is strong and growing. This cannot be said about any other theory of government (such as the public-interest theory) of which I am aware. And it is this scientific hallmark (the testability) of the rent-seeking theory, which will make it harder and harder to avoid as the best available rational choice explanation of government (median-voter models to the contrary notwithstanding).

I shall cease and desist from reviewing positive developments in rent-seeking theory for want of time and space. Suffice it to say that there is a growing literature in this area, ranging from legislatures and legislators (McCormick and Tollison, 1981), to pressure groups (Becker, 1983), to regulation (Stigler, 1971; Peltzman, 1975), to the independent judiciary (Landes and Posner, 1975), to monarchies (Ekelund and Tollison, 1982), and so on, to virtually all aspects of government behavior. Perhaps another time I shall write a paper about this literature. The reader should be aware, however, that the statements in this section are not idle boasts. There is an important empirical theory of government extant, and it is the rent-seeking theory.

---

[8] This is meant to be simplified. Obviously, individuals belong to many different groups, sometimes as rent-protectors, sometimes as rent-seekers, and sometimes as quiescent rent-"suppliers" (why spend a dollar to save a dime?).

13.10   Conclusion: What hath Tullock Wrought?

The theory of rent-seeking is here to stay. As I have observed in another context (Tollison, 1982), the most interesting thing about Tullock's ingenious insight is how simply he put it. Like Coase, he communicated his vision in terms that every lay economist could follow. This is a criterion by which greatness in science is measured. In economics, the Tullocks of our profession are more indispensable than ever. To wit, the scarcest thing in any science is a good idea, clearly communicated.

References

Anderson, G. M. and Brown, P. J. (1985) 'Heir pollution: a note on Buchanan's "Laws of Succession" and Tullock's "Blind Spot." *International Review of Law and Economics*, 5, June, pp. 15–24.

Baysinger, B. and Tollison, R. D. (1980) 'Evaluating the social costs of monopoly and regulation', *Atlantic Economic Journal*, 8, December, pp. 22–6.

Becker, G. S. (1983) 'A theory of competition among pressure groups for political influence', *Quarterly Journal of Economics*, XCVII, August, pp. 371–400.

Bhagwati, J. N. Brecher, R. A. and Srinivasan, T. N. (1984) 'DUP activities and economic theory', in D. C. Colander, (ed.) *Neoclassical Political Economy*. Cambridge: Ballinger, pp. 17–32.

Buchanan, J. M. 'Reform in the rent-seeking society'; in J. M. Buchanan, R. D. Tollison, and G. Tullock, (1980a) (eds) *Toward a Theory of the Rent-Seeking Society*. College Station: Texas A & M University Press, pp. 359-67.

Buchanan, J. M. (1980b) 'Rent seeking and profit seeking', in J. M. Buchanan, R.D. Tollison, and G. Tullock, (eds) *Toward a Theory of the Rent-Seeking Society*. College Station: Texas A & M University Press, pp. 3–15.

Buchanan, J. M. (1983) 'Rent-seeking, noncompensated transfers, and laws of succession', *Journal of Law and Economics*, 26, April, pp. 71-86.

Comanor, W. S. and Smiley, R. H. (1975) 'Monopoly and the distribution of wealth', *Quarterly Journal of Economics*, 89, May, pp. 177–94.

Corcoran, W. J. (1984) 'Long-run equilibrium and total expenditures in rent-seeking', *Public Choice*, 43, 1, pp. 89–94.

DiLorenzo, T. J. (1984) 'The domain of rent-seeking behavior: private or public choice', *International Review of Law and Economics*, 4, December, pp. 131–5.

Ekelund, R. B. and Tollison, R. D. (1981) *Mercantilism as a Rent-Seeking Society*. College Station: Texas A & M University Press.

Fisher, F. M. (1985) 'The social costs of monopoly and regulation: Posner reconsidered', *Journal of Political Economy*, 93, April, pp. 410–16.

Harberger, A. C. (1984) 'Monopoly and resource allocation', *American Economic Review*, 44, May, pp. 77–87.

Higgins, R., Shughart, W. F. and Tollison, R. D. (1985) 'Free entry and efficient rent-seeking', *Public Choice*, forthcoming.

Higgins, R. and Tollison, R. D. (1985) 'Life among the triangles and trapezoids: notes on the theory of rent-seeking', unpublished ms.

Hillman, A. L. and Katz, E. (1984) 'Risk-averse rent-seekers and the social cost of monopoly power', *Economic Journal*, 94, March, pp. 104-10.

Kreuger, A. O. (1974) "The political economy of the rent-seeking society", *American Economic Review*, 64, June, pp. 291-303.

Landes, W. M. and Posner, R. A. (1975) 'The independent judiciary in an interest-group perspective', *Journal of Law and Economics* 18, December, pp. 875-901.

Lee, D. R. and Tollison, R. D. (1985) 'Optimal taxation in a rent-seeking environment', unpublished ms.

McCormick, R. E., Shughart, W. F. and Tollison, R. D. (1984) 'The disinterest in deregulation', *American Economic Review*, December, pp. 1075-79.

McCormick, R. E. and Tollison, R. D. (1981) *Politicians, Legislation and the Economy: An Inquiry into the Interest-Group Theory of Government*. Boston: Martinus Nijhoff.

Mundell, R. A. (1962) Review of L. H. Janssen, 'Free trade, protection and customs unions', *American Economic Review*, 52, June, p. 622.

North, D. (1984) 'Three approaches to the study of institutions', in D. C. Colander, (ed.) *Neoclassical Political Economy*. Cambridge: Ballinger, pp. 33-40.

Peltzman, S. (1976) 'Toward a more general theory of regulation', *Journal of Law and Economics*, 2, August, pp. 211-40.

Posner, R. A. (1975) 'The social costs of monopoly and regulation', *Journal of Political Economy*, 83, August, pp. 807-27.

Rogerson, W. P. (1982) 'The social costs of monopoly and regulation: a game-theoretic analysis', *Bell Journal of Economics*, 13, Autumn, pp. 391-401.

Stigler, G. J. (1971) 'The theory of economic regulation', *Bell Journal of Economics and Management Science*, 2, Spring, pp. 3-21.

Tollison, R. D. 'Rent seeking: a survey', *Kyklos*, 35, (fasc. 4), pp. 575-602.

Tullock, G. (1967) 'The welfare costs of tariffs, monopolies, and theft', *Western Economic Journal*, 5, June, pp. 224-32.

Tullock, G. (1980a) 'Efficient rent-seeking', in J. M. Buchanan, R. D. Tollison and G. Tullock, (eds) *Toward a Theory of the Rent-Seeking Society*. College Station: Texas A & M University Press, pp. 97-112.

Tullock, G. (1980b) 'Rent-seeking as a negative-sum game', in J. M. Buchanan, R. D. Tollison and G. Tullock, (eds.) *Toward a Theory of the Rent-Seeking Society*. College Station: Texas A & M University Press, pp. 16-36.

Tullock, G. (1985) 'Back to the bog', *Public Choice*, 46, 3, pp. 259-64.

14

Rent-Seeking is Here to Stay

MICHAEL A. CREW

14.1 Introduction

The fundamental insights provided by Tullock (1967) and Tullock (1975) are the foundation for my remarks on rent-seeking and regulation. Both of these papers are little gems. Both are economical in words, and yet clear and concise in expressing fundamental ideas.

The 1967 paper, admirably summarized by Tollison in chapter 13, makes the important point that the welfare losses from monopoly, taxes, tariffs and theft may be greater than the familiar Marshallian triangle, ABC in Tollison's figure 13.1, and could be equal to as much as the larger trapezoid P_mP_cBA. The rectangle ACP_cP_{cm} is equal to economists' usual measure of monopoly profits. Tullock's insight was to look beyond traditional neoclassical economics which assumed that monopoly rents are guaranteed by entry barriers, and to question the nature of the entry barriers. Where the entry barriers are the result of a grant of monopoly by the state the prospect of monopoly rents would entice individuals to invest resources to obtain a share of such monopoly rents. In the limit, rent-seekers would compete away the rectangle of monopoly rents making the welfare loss equal to the trapezoid. This is a significant insight making it crystal clear that the welfare losses from monopoly may be much greater than previously agrued. Similar considerations would apply to regulation, to the extent that it creates artificial scarcity.

Tullock's argument that, as a result of rent-seeking, the welfare losses from monopoly and regulation are considerably greater than previously recognized, is now widely accepted. Posner (1975) used this reasoning to argue that regulated monopoly caused much greater welfare losses than the benefits of price control it was intended to provide. Given this, it is paradoxical that regulation and monopoly still amount to a substantial part of the US economy. If nobody gained rents from regulated monopoly and if consumers were exploited, it would be an unmitigated disaster and there would be no obvious incentive to retain it. Its survival thus seems somewhat paradoxical. I would like to give some attention to this paradox which has also been addressed by McCormick, et al. (1984) in the context of a 'Disinterest in Deregulation'.

14.2 A Paradoxical Aspect of Rent-Seeking and Monopoly

Tullock (1975) has shown that it is the initial rent-seekers who benefit from a regulation or grant of a monopoly. Let us review his example of taxi cab medallions. When the restriction on the number of cabs in New York was first introduced the initial owners received rents. These rents were quickly capitalized; a medallion now sells for over $100,000. Those who purchase medallions do not obtain rents. Their payment for the medallion reflects the up-front value of the rents. Thus the gain in this case from abolishing the monopoly is close to the Marshallian triangle. The loss to the medallion owners is considerable. Abolition of regulation would to them be akin to the confiscation of their property, worse than if the cabs themselves were seized. They have every incentive to try to protect their property. As Tullock himself noted, "It is hard to recommend any positive action to deal with this kind of situation." (1975, p. 677.) He suggests we try to avoid such traps in the future.

One possible way out of the trap, the phasing-in of deregulation, while on the face of it promising, is fraught with problems. Suppose that New York announces a phased deregulation of taxi cabs. The immediate effect is an outcry amongst cab owners. They begin to lobby the mayor and the council, and law suits are initiated. The value of the medallion falls by the present value of the reduced profits expected from increased entry plus the extra cost medallion owners incur to protect themselves from the deregulation and to reverse it. The effect has been to increase welfare losses. The medallion owners are now expending resources to protect their interest, which they previously were not. Moreover, the value of their property has declined just as if it had been confiscated. Tullock is right to warn us to beware of the transitional gains trap.

Tullock's insight on the transitional gains trap and the taxi cab example, however, provides a means of analyzing the circumstances under which deregulation of monopoly is likely or not to succeed. In the example we can distinguish between two kinds of rent-seeking expenditures. First there are up-front expenditures by the original owners of the medallions. Presumably these were less than the value of the medallion. These are sunk and do not continue to show up as a welfare loss. (They do not enter in the rectangle at all.) In addition there are the on-going expenditures needed to keep the monopoly. Unlike the former these are continuing welfare losses. At the limit they could be equal to the whole rectangle, in which case the value of the medallion would be zero. The lesson seems to be that if government is going to allow a monopoly it has to protect that monopoly so strongly that the existing owner has no incentive to expend resources on preserving it and entrants have no incentive to invest resources in obtaining entry.

Traditionally public utilities have presumably been operated in this manner. A franchise was guaranteed by the state in return for which the company gave up its rights to set prices to a regulatory commission. The monopoly provided some benefits perhaps in terms of scale and scope economies. However, the attraction of the potential rents makes it worthwhile for utilities to invest in rent-seeking on an on-going basis, not primarily to protect themselves from the threat of entry, but to increase prices. Similarly labor unions of regulated companies are likely to be able to get some of the rents of the monopoly in terms of higher wages or less efficient operation. Since commission regulation operates on a cost-plus basis the company is going to be able to recover such extra costs.

The moral of the story is that competition amongst rent-seekers will out somehow. If an invulnerable regulated monopoly is created, rent-seekers will expend resources to influence regulators to obtain potential rents. Of course the more successful they are the smaller the dissipation of the rents and the smaller the welfare losses. With utility regulation there may have been, at least until recently, a sharing of the rents that did not fully dissipate the rectangle. The rents may have been shared by an implicit coalition consisting of managers, regulators and labor.

Historically such coalitions, like a cartel, may contain the seeds of their own destruction. For example, one of the parties may seek a larger share, or technological change may occur making the benefits from the natural monopoly less significant. The result may be that all the rents are dissipated. When this happens, when the rectangle has been eaten up by rent-seekers, as Crew and Rowley (1986) have argued, deregulation may be sought as offering more potential benefits than the regulated monopoly. Where the alternative in mind consists of an essentially unregulated oligopoly the potential gains do not seem to be any less attractive than the highly regulated markets that had previously prevailed. Moreover, if, as generally believed, the regulated monopoly was paying above market wages and was subject to inefficient work rules by the unions, as their share of the rents, the prospect of getting wage costs lowered tends to weaken the coalition of management and labor. Thus for deregulation to be attractive, it seems necessary that almost all the rents must be dissipated on an on-going basis.

In telecommunications, while such forces were at work, it is arguable that the major changes in technology associated with optics and computers were the driving force that upset the equilibrium. Given the political clout of the Bell system, it is surprising that the divestiture took place. However, perhaps here also the rents were dissipated and the prospect of a dominant oligopoly appealed to AT and T, especially if such a market structure potentially allowed it to enter into new ventures forbidden before divestiture.

14.3 Some Implications of Tullock's Contributions on Rent-Seeking

The implications of Tullock's contribution are clear in principle. The details, however, are more difficult, as the following concluding remarks illustrate.

1 It is tempting to say that institutions should be designed to take account of the dangers of rent-seeking. By the process of regulating, society creates a potential for rent-seeking. In designing regulatory institutions attempts should be made to ascertain whether the welfare losses from the opportunities to rent-seek will swamp the intended benefits from the regulation. Exactly how to do this is a problem. In attempting to control existing forms of rent-seeking new rent-seeking opportunities will be created. Rent-seekers always have the last say.
2 Just as, traditionally, economists have been concerned with monopoly and abuse of market power in product markets, they now need to reflect on the consequences of the market situations facing rent-seekers. There may be barriers to entry. For example, the lawyer domination of the regulatory process may sufficiently restrict entry so that rents remain. This results in fewer welfare losses from rent-seeking. On the other hand, perfect competition between rent-seekers will eventually dissipate all rents and set in motion the decay of the monopoly, at least in the case of on-going rent-seeking. However, some rents may be capitalized, and there may be a trap along the lines of Tullock's transitional gains trap, in which case competition amongst rent-seekers will not have the effect of promoting deregulation of the monopoly.

Tullock has given us a gold mine in rent-seeking analysis and it will be many years before it is exhausted. Tollison's conclusion that 'the scarcest thing in science is a good idea' is especially true today, when the economics profession seems to be preoccupied with policy-irrelevant technique. This is aimed, not at making economics accessible to more people, as Tullock has done with his path-breaking ideas, but at making it a discipline restricted to technicians who, unlike Tullock, have no natural grasp of economics. We need more ideas from Tullock-like individuals, and they must be marketed to a reluctant profession. Rent-seeking is one such idea whose time has come.

References

Crew, Michael A. and Rowley, Charles K. (1986) 'Deregulation as an instrument of industrial policy', *Journal of Institutional and Theoretical Economics*, **142**, March.

McCormick, R. E., Shughart, William E. and Tollison, Robert D. (1984) 'The disinterest in deregulation', *American Economic Review*, **74**, December, pp. 1075–9.

Posner, Richard A. (1975) 'The social costs of monopoly and regulation', *Journal of Political Economy*, **83**, August, pp. 807–27.

Tullock, Gordon (1967) 'The welfare cost of tariffs, monopolies and theft', *Western Economic Journal*, **5**, June, pp. 224–32.

Tullock, Gordon (1975) 'The transitional gains trap', *Bell Journal of Economics*, **8**, pp. 671–8.

15

Rent-Seeking and the New Institutional Economics

DOUGLASS C. NORTH

15.1 Introduction

The major insight of the rent-seeking literature was to extend economic analysis into the black box of political structure and institutions. It has directed political economists to ask questions about the resources that are devoted to political activity and their consequence for economic performance. All of this is to the good and has led to a great deal of pioneering work.

The foremost deficiency of the rent-seeking literature is that the term 'rent-seeking' implies something special about human behavior, rather than something special about the institutional framework. But given maximizing behavior by the actors, the institutions are so structured that they raise the rate of return to rent-seeking relative to 'productive activity'. Thus the emphasis should not be on the unique behavioral pattern of actors, but on the institutional structure that makes such activity profitable.

The second deficiency is that it does not make clear exactly what the measure of inefficiency is. Is it a world of zero transactions costs, in which case it is not a terribly interesting measure, or is it a world in which the alternative model is a competitive equilibrium? But surely the reason we do not have a competitive equilibrium has something to do with the institutional structure that emerged either as a consequence of differential influence among the players in the game, or perhaps as a consequence of assymetrical information. The counterfactual, therefore, is to imply a restructured system in which the political pressures and asymmetrical information characteristics are absent. In the real world of positive transaction costs measuring inefficiency has a large arbitrary component.

15.2   Some Reflections on Tollison on Rent-Seeking

I would like to concentrate the rest of my comments on sections 13.8 and
13.9 of Robert Tollison's chapter. In section 13.9, Tollison implies that the
rent-seeking framework can be a theory of government, and indeed it has
been so employed by Tollison and others. I think this is unfortunate, because
by looking at government as a gigantic process of income redistribution and
legalized theft, we have been largely diverted from our exploring, in an
analytical and non-pejorative fashion, the political process.

How do we explain the rise of the Western World or, alternatively, explain
the poor performance of Third World countries? In the case of the former, a
political structure somehow evolved that provided incentives for economic
growth. In the case of the latter, it is obvious that the political structure that
exists is one that provides disincentives for productive economic activity.
Now I suspect that Tollison would say that a simple maximizing model of
rent-seekers can be used to explain completely the rise of the Western
world, and indeed the book *Mercantilism as a Rent-Seeking Society* by Ekelund
and Tollison does just that. While I like the book and have admiration for its
contents, I am not altogether a believer, and indeed I rather suspect that
Tullock himself would raise questions about it. There is simply more to the
whole process of economic development and performance of economies
than can be adequately dealt with in the kind of interest-group models from
which the rent-seeking literature stems. It is not just that ideas matter.
Everybody except the most hide-bound neoclassical economist surely
recognizes that. Rather, the interplay between institutions and the
opportunities they afford for ideas to matter, and the way institutions evolve
are all a part of the complex set of issues that we would like to understand
when looking at economic growth or the performance of economies.

The observable dimensions of institutions are the contracts (implicit or
explicit) made between parties at all levels of political and economic
exchange: constitutions; statute law; common law; and contracts involving
economic exchange, such as those involving market exchange, firms, trade
unions, etc. The response of actors to rules, however, will result in a more or
less elaborate structure of informal procedures and norms of behavior which
are determined by the structure and effectiveness of enforcement and by the
strength of the set of preferences individuals hold. Let me briefly elaborate.
The more costly it is to measure the attributes of goods and services involved
in exchange or the performance of agents, the more likely that enforcement
will be imperfect, particularly since third parties enforcing rules are
themselves agents of principals. Accordingly, the actual informal structure
that will result will take into account the effectiveness of enforcement by
attempting to structure contracts in ways that minimize the dissipation of
rent at difficult to measure margins of enforcement. In addition, however,

the attitudes of the parties to the rules in terms of their fairness or justice will (given the costliness of measuring performance) influence the costs of contracting. Ideological conviction is the premium individuals are willing to incur not to free-ride (the price of one's convictions). While the strength of convictions varies with the issues and the individual, the premium is surely negatively sloped; that is, the higher the costs one incurs, the less does ideological conviction matter. Therefore the actual choices individuals make are derivatives of rules, of the costliness of measuring performance, of enforcement characteristics, and of the strength of ideological conviction.

Now ideally what we would like to understand about the way in which the games are played is the interplay between these parts. But clearly one thing stands out and that is that there is substantial slack in the system for ideas to matter. Not only is this slack sometimes created deliberately, that is, the agent is deliberately given latitude to express his or her convictions at little or no cost, but there are also many occasions when the agents have little in the way of interest-group pressures on them, and we do observe historically occasions when slack appears to be an accidental by-product of intended policies of the participants. Now, if there is slack in the system, then preferences or ideology matter.

Another feature about institutions about which we know very little is one concerned with the institutional evolution. Institutions evolve incrementally out of previous sets of institutions, and the way in which the institutions are modified in subsequent generations is a reflection not only of the past performance characteristics of institutions, but also how, in the perception of the players, those performance characteristics carry over in the context of new problems and policies. But the important point is that institutions do evolve in such a way as to have a substantial amount of non-reversibility in the process, so that divergence of institutions at some time may lead to radically different patterns of development. Look at the contrast, for example, between the evolution of the Spanish settlements in the New World in the sixteenth, seventeenth and eighteenth centuries and their consequences for nineteenth and twentieth- century Latin American countries; and the English settlements in the new world, where the free settlers themselves constituted the majority of the existing population.

Let me illustrate the point I am making with respect to the English case. I have little quarrel with the Ekelund Tollison story about the relationship between the Crown and Parliament in, seventeenth-century England. Indeed, to quote Ekelund and Tollison (p. 64):

In a crucial reassertion of rights, Parliament blocked once and for all the despotism of monarchy and established fundamental constitutional rights and the power of Parliament. Among these was the passage in 1640 of a statute putting an end to all but one of the exceptions of the Statute of 1624.

The story they tell is essentially an interest-group modeling of the struggle between the Crown and Parliament, which ends with the supremacy of Parliament. The right of the parliamentary players to gain the same kind of monopoly privileges that the Crown had, turned out to be unenforceable and too costly to be able to enact. But more was going on than that. The judicial protection of property rights, religious tolerance, the rights of political expression, prevention of arbitrary imprisonment, etc., which in the first instance probably were advanced because groups feared that they themselves might be in the minority, subsequently took on an ideological caste and helped define future choice sets of the players. Ekelund and Tollison make noises in this direction (p. 65):

We do not assert moreover that the public interest, whatever this may have been in these times, played no role in the classic decision by which the common law courts transferred monopoly granting power to Parliament.

Now let us move on more than a century to that critical year in American economic history, 1787, when two fundamental documents, the Constitution and the Northwest Ordinance, were being devised. The heritage of seventeenth-century English policy is everywhere evident in the institutional structure: in the specification of fee simple ownership of land, which is first written into the Northwest Ordinance; and in the set of political policies of territorial governance and in the protection of individual rights, which are first incorporated in a number of the colonial charters, and then specified in the provisions of the Northwest Ordinance and, later, in the first ten amendments to the Bill of Rights. When we look at the subsequent provisions of the Constitution, we may bow in the direction of Charles Beard, but Madison and others were concerned with the viability of the structure in a way that transcended many of the immediate interests that he and others might have had.

While the specific provisions of the Constitution and the Northwest Ordinance can, in part at least, be traced to log-rolling decisions on the part of participants, the overall framework is one that reflected the lessons that had been learned over the previous century with respect to the development of a long-run viable political-economic system. Moreover, let me remind you that the way the game is played is a composite of rules, enforcement characteristics and the strength of preferences (ideology if you will). Clearly rules are an *insufficient* basis for understanding the American political-economic system. The viability of the system from 1787 to today has been fundamentally influenced by the strength of the heritage of ideas which helped to define and limit choices. We are a long way from being able to understand the interaction between interest-group behavior and the importance of ideas, but certainly when we do we shall be able to have much more insight into the relationship between the polity and the economy than we can derive from the rent-seeking model.

References

Ekelund, R. B. and Tollison, R. D. (1981) *Mercantilism as a Rent-Seeking Society*. College Station: Texas A & M University Press.

VI

The Law

16

Public Choice and the Law: The Paradox of Tullock

CHARLES J. GOETZ[1]

16.1 Introduction

Those who know Gordon Tullock personally realize how dearly he loves a good argument. Nowhere is this more evident than in his legal writings.

As one of Tullock's students, admirers and intellectual debtors, I have reason to ponder whether my present career is not fate's whimsical way of balancing the interdisciplinary trade accounts: Gordon, the economics professor wholly without economics training, helps train a law professor entirely innocent of legal education. Perhaps with especial appropriateness, therefore, the duty falls to me to comment on the Tullockian legal scholarship. I deliberately undertake this task with at least three self-imposed handicaps.

First, insofar as possible, these comments will attempt to reflect the (sometimes crabbed) perspective of my adopted discipline, the law. I come to praise Tullock but also to represent faithfully, albeit with affection, the mixed reaction he has provoked. I come even to argue with him a bit.

Second, rather than succumbing to the temptation of discussing work that – although quite plainly important and law-related – is 'mainly economics',[2] my focus will be on only such of Tullock's scholarship that falls within the narrower bounds of traditional legal areas such as evidence, procedure and the role of the courts.

Third, I shall accept with reluctance but candor the onus of attempting to explain an ironic reality: that, notwithstanding its frequent power and imagination, Tullock's scholarship has been far less influential in his disciplinary 'homeland' of law than in the sweeping path of his veritable intellectual army of occupation through the camps of economics and politics.

---

[1] Joseph M. Hartfield Professor of Law, University of Virginia.
[2] In this category I place Tullock's work on the economics of crime and punishment, such as 'An economic approach to crime', *Social Science Quarterly*, 50, 1969, p. 59; and 'Does punishment deter crime?' *The Public Interest*, 36, 1974, p. 103.

To the best of my knowledge, Gordon's work has never been cited by a court,[3] and scholarly citations of him within law are also relatively sparse. I seek to explain the reasons, both good and bad, why this has happened and why it is unfortunate.

Let us be clear on several things at the outset. One is that lack of heavy impact on a particular audience, such as the legal profession, is not an indictment of the quality of the work itself. The vagaries of intellectual 'fashion', timing, stylistic idiosyncrasies, the peculiar capacities and hallowed conventions of the audience itself, and just plain 'luck' all affect even presumably sophisticated scholarly audiences in ways that intellectuals are reluctant to admit. I suggest below that there are aspects of Tullock's style that, quite apart from any issues of substance, are uncongenial to legal scholars. Moreover, the substance itself is inherently nettlesome to lawyers. Still, when the brilliance of a message does not fully shine through, one can find in the causes lessons that we – both as scholar-authors and scholar-audience – might profitably ponder. To an extent that the reader may ultimately judge for himself, both Tullock and the lawyers can arguably be held at some fault.

Second, 'success' is discussed here under an exceptionally difficult relative standard. In the absolute sense, most full-time members of selective law faculties would do well to exchange their reputations as legal writers for that of Gordon Tullock. That does not diminish the obvious relative disparity between his superstar status in other fields and his considerably more modest success in law.

16.2 Salesmanship in the Market of Legal Ideas

What makes economic analysis 'sell' to lawyers? A persuasive case might be made that the most successful – from the point of view of audience acceptance and influence – law and economics scholarship has been of the explanatory or rationalizing type. For instance, the Posnerian 'efficiency of the common law' thesis has the attraction of explaining the existing legal rule structure in a principled way;[4] it purports to articulate the common-sense

---

[3] This statement is based on a search of the Westlaw database since 1965.

[4] See generally Posner, *Economic Analysis of Law*. But perhaps the most succinct statement of this 'hidden agenda' explanation is:

The rules assigning property rights and determining liability, the procedures for resolving legal disputes, the constraints on law enforcers, methods of computing damages and determining the availability of injunctive relief – these and other important elements of the legal system can best be understood as attempts, though rarely acknowledged as such, to promote an efficient allocation of resources.

Source: Posner, 'The economic approach to law' *Texas Law Review*, 53, 1975, pp. 757, 764.

mechanics of the otherwise difficult-to-understand arrangements that we see in the world around us. Much the same thing might be asserted about, for instance, Tullock's best and most influential contributions to public choice economics, where we learned to see familiar institutions with new and more understanding eyes. While this new vision sometimes did uncover warts, my own impression at least was that the analysis tended to be almost comfortingly 'conservative' in that it made sense out of seemingly peculiar institutions such as supermajorities, log-rolling, bicameral legislatures, etc.

Herein lies at least one striking difference of substance between Tullock's mainstream economics work and his legal writings. In law, it is difficult to find any existing institution – at least of the Anglo-American legal system – about which his analysis gives solace and comfort. Indeed, his major work, *The Logic of the Law*,[5] might more descriptively be titled as dealing with the folly of the law. For instance, he harshly critiques such basic institutions as evidence law,[6] the adversary system,[7] and the process of deriving precedents.[8] As recast in the ideal Tullockian mold, there would not be much left of the corpus of conventional legal procedure.[9] Perhaps even more painful to legal academics is the notion that their emphasis on cases where the law is doubtful is 'overdone' even if not actually irrational.[10] The merits of Tullock's positions on certain issues are discussed briefly below. Suffice it to say that, whatever their underlying validity, many of his views on law can be labeled as far more reformist, 'radical', or anti-conventional than those of his other writings. While a more dispassionate reader might not view Tullock as a loose-cannon iconoclast, this is precisely the alarmed reaction of the legal establishment.[11] His legal writing is not only provocative in the best sense, but it is also provoking.

When its result is an intellectually bitter pill, the analysis itself not unnaturally falls under hostile scrutiny. To an economist, Tullock's analytics may seem quite straightforward, indeed often admirably clear and simple. To most lawyers, especially a decade ago, his relatively simple formal

---

[5] Basic Books, 1971. This is his earliest and by far his best known work among academic lawyers of my acquaintance.

[6] See, for example, *The Logic of the Law*, pp. 93–104.

[7] Ibid., pp. 84–92.

[8] Supreme Court precedents are alluded to only briefly in *The Logic of the Law*, pp. 11–12, 38, but this sacred cow is confronted squarely in a recent piece by Good and Tullock, 'Judicial errors and a proposal for reform,' *Journal Legal Studies*, 13, 1984, p. 289.

[9] While *The Logic of the Law* touches on a number of areas of procedure, this is the main theme of *Trials on Trial: The Pure Theory of Legal Procedure*, Columbia University Press, 1980.

[10] *Trials on Trial*, p. 3.

[11] Among my colleagues on the University of Virginia Law Faculty, perhaps Gordon Tullock's biggest fan is Jeffrey O'Connell. There may be significance in the fact that O'Connell himself carries impeccable credentials as a radical institutional reformer, having been a key promoter of no-fault legislation and other imaginative but unconventional approaches to the settlement of tort claims. O'Connell's favorite Tullock work is 'Negligence again', *International Review of Law and Economics*, 1, 1981, p. 51.

economics – graphs, algebraic symbols with subscripts and superscripts, game matrices etc – are nonetheless heavy going. Also, even we economists understand full well how the critical linchpin of a model is often buried in an apparently innocuous assumption. Lawyers are by training, and perhaps by disposition, inclined to be cynics about *any* form or argumentation. Perhaps partially due to the adversarial tradition that Tullock criticizes, lawyers have a proper visceral wariness about being done in by clever sleight-of-hand. This suspicion comes into full flower when unfamiliar modes of economic reasoning are used to tell them something that they do not want to hear.[12]

Part of the problem, then, is inherent in the nature of the message itself, and part in the incapacity of the audience to appreciate and assess the cross-disciplinary language. But Tullock is perhaps chargeable with not attentively playing by the lawyers' rules of the game: although a lawyer, he does not write like one.[13] The contemporaneous work of Richard Posner, for example, has been more fully recognized than Tullock's, partially because it is much less reformist in tone but also because he is scrupulous to get the little things right: the footnote references, the accuracy of the legal examples. Posner gives us the 'feel' of traditional legal scholarship. Gordon Tullock is flip and irreverent, footnote-phobic and – dare I say it? – sometimes just plain wrong in his recollection or characterization of little illustrative legal points.

Little mistakes can be important out of all proportion to their magnitude. There is in trial advocacy the concept of 'infection' of the strong part of a case by a weak part. A lawyer looking for a good excuse not to buy Tullock's message finds it when he stumbles on the tiny flaws: 'Not a careful fellow. If he's wrong about this, heaven only knows what's wrong with this other stuff that I do not understand.' Case closed; *both* parties lose.

Some intellectually difficult ideas contain their own unsquelchable seeds of success. Thus, in addition to ivory tower conceptual appeal, there is another basis on which economic analysis of law sometimes commands acceptance in the legal community: it occasionally yields insights that are potentially result-affecting practical arguments. The most obvious example of this is the acceptance in courts, law schools and legal scholarship of the dramatic utility of economic arguments in antitrust cases,[14] but applications

[12] In a similar vein, I remember an undergraduate student of Gordon's at Virginia Tech many years ago telling me that 'I couldn't find any holes in any of his arguments, but . . . somehow I have the feeling he put one over on me.' Tullock is such an obviously clever debater that it sometimes engenders wonder whether he won on the merits or just on the sheer power of argumentation.

[13] One may ask: 'Why should he have to write within their rules?' And the answer is 'He need not – unless he wants them to pay serious attention to him.'

[14] 'Probably the single most important factor affecting antitrust analysis has been the introduction and application of economics into anti-trust law'. Sullivan and Hovenkamp, *Antitrust Law Policy and Procedure*, 1984, p. 1.

abound in almost all areas of the law.[15] Ideas that can be reduced to practice by even an intrepid few will not be long ignored for, however unpalatable and initially inaccessible they are, tangible rewards beckon those who recognize and put them to use.

Militating against this avenue of idea-propagation is the fact that the legal writings of Gordon Tullock do not fall within this forensic-application genre. Almost without exception, they are not designed as ammunition for the advocate but, rather, suggestions for reform of the *institutions* of law itself. To the extent that he does not capture the interest of the legal intelligentsia, Tullock's alternative clientele must be the policy-maker, for his topical focus tends to cut him off from the practitioner. Indeed, the policy-maker audience must perforce be a powerful, high-level one, since the proposed institutional changes are mostly sweeping ones, not small steps on the road to utopia that can be implemented on an incremental basis.

In sum, the widespread appreciation of Tullock's scholarship in legal circles has been handicapped by a number of factors that do not bear directly on its underlying merits. Some of these factors were inherent in the methodology and the subject matter, others in the (culpable? avoidable?) personal and professional idiosyncrasies of both the author and the audience. It advances our understanding of this chunk of intellectual history if we acknowledge such factors with candor.

16.3 Tullock at War with Himself?

We turn now to the content of Tullock's legal analysis. Although his several books and many shorter works cannot be summarized in any detail, I shall focus on a few topics that (1) are recurrent themes running through his work, and (2) are, in my view, interesting because they present some surprises, and even possible conceptual discord, when compared with the thrust of the main body of his non-legal work.

A dominant theme of Tullock's legal work is what he terms Anglo-American procedure. He is certainly in respectable intellectual company when he attacks the adversary system[16] or prefers continental inquisitorial procedures.[17] But there is not necessarily comfort to be taken from this

[15] I at least hope to have exemplified many of these in my casebook, *Law and Economics*, 1984.

[16] See, for example, Jerome Frank, *Courts on Trial: Myth and Reality in American Justice*, 1949; Brazil, 'The adversary character of civil discovery: a critique and proposals for change *Vanderbilt Law Review*, 31, 1978, p. 1295; Rhode, 'ethical perspectives on legal practice', *Stanford Law Review*, 37, 1985, p. 589.

[17] See, for example, Langbein, 'The German advantage in civil procedure', *University of Chicago Law Review*, 52, 1985, pp. 823, 866: 'Nothing but inertia and vested interests justify the waste and distortion of adversary fact-gathering. The success of German civil procedure stands as an enduring reproach to those who say that we must continue to suffer adversary tricksters in the proof of fact.'

company. Although perhaps a somewhat maverick group, the anti-adversarial school of legal writers is of that awkward size where it is too large to retain novelty value and too small to be highly influential. Tullock does clothe some of the arguments of this school in the new garb of economic analysis, but one can question to what extent his economic tools can fairly be credited with breaking significant new ground in the debate.

More interesting to me, though, is how his procedural analysis exemplifies another issue: I am not sure that he applies the particular economic tools or winds up on the side of the debate that one would predict by inference from and extension of his other work. Showing that an adversary system is superior to an inquisitorial system is an 'easy kill' at the theoretical level. Still, the debate can arguably be analogized in many ways to that of the 1950s between the central-planner government-interventionists v. the free marketeers. The Public Choice analysts made a magnificent contribution when they examined 'anatomy of government' failure in a manner similar to that of market failure. A key element in that movement was coldly realistic analysis of the motivations that actuated non-market decision-makers such as politicians and bureaucrats. Those familiar with that literature will surely concede that it would no longer be appropriate to conceive of the debate in terms of the simplistic comparisons of yesteryear when wasteful markets were compared with the works of omnicompetent philosopher-kings.

Does Tullock's legal work fit the pattern of his own past? Let us set ourselves a problem. Suppose that we, purged of knowledge of Gordon's subsequent legal writings, were to be moved back to 1971, immediately prior to publication of *The Logic of the Law*. Our assigned mission would be to predict, from that juncture in time, the type of analyses that Tullock might produce on legal matters in general, but on the relative merits of the adversarial and inquisitorial systems in particular. You may wish to pause here and supply your own predictions. Among mine would be the following:

1   Tullock will conceptualize judges as bureaucrats along the lines of his *The Politics of Bureaucracy* (1965) and will emphasize the difficulty in making their reward structure congruent with the social interest as generally conceived.
2   He will have a visceral distrust of (inquisitorial or any other) judges, recognizing the decision-making power that can be exercised under the guise of fact-gathering, interpretation or procedural operations.
3   He will have, if anything, more sympathy than the conventional wisdom for highly motivated adversaries whose selection and performance is monitored by a market system. He will remind us with words to the effect that 'the sometimes counteractive competition of very *interested* persons (adversaries) may nonetheless produce more net output than a coordinated effort by less interested persons (inquisitors).'

4 Especially considering his biological interests[18], he will highlight certain Darwinian-type survival characteristics of legal rules that make the observed rules likely to be efficient.

(5) He will re-examine and challenge certain facile assumptions about the goals of legal process and the capabilities of its participants. For instance, he might question whether the system's objective really is 'truth' or whether judges have more expertise than the advocates that argue before them.

6 He will apply log-rolling and agenda-control analyses to the deliberations of appellate panels and regulatory agencies.

7 He will advocate optional dispute-resolution systems chosen by the parties.

Although intended to be merely illustrative rather than exhaustive, this list is not, I submit, implausible. What, then, is the score? Prediction 7 would be right on the mark, especially as understood to encompass arbitration agreements. The seemingly quite natural voting model applications of prediction 6 were mysteriously absent from the literature until published relatively recently – by others.[19] Consideration of prediction 5 will be implicit in much of what is said in both this and the following section, but the verdict is mixed.

In my own view at least, the record on prediction 1 through 4 is somewhat unexpected. As indicated in 16.2 above, Tullock himself has little good to say about existing Anglo-American legal institutions. Other writers did apply the survival theory analogue to argue that observed legal institutions are likely to have efficient properties.[20] But his stance on judges is at least equally odd. *Trials on Trial* devotes an entire chapter to 'The Motivation of Judges'[21] part of which is allegedly in response to the 'disinterested' judge argument. That chapter acknowledges the incentive problems, correctly discusses their mitigation in the special case of paid arbitrators, and gives little cheer as to motivating state-provided judges under either an adversarial system or a Continental-type system.

What is concluded from this? Tullock grudgingly concedes it to be 'at least

[18] For example, 'An application of economics in biology', *Toward Liberty*, II, 1971, pp. 375–91; 'Biological externalities' *Journal of Theoretical Biology*, 33, 1971, p. 565; 'The Coal Tit as a careful shopper', *The American Naturalist*, 105, 1971, p. 77.

[19] Easterbrook, 'Ways of criticizing the courts', *Harvard Law Review*, 95, 1982, p. 802; Levine and Plott, 'Agenda influence and its implications', *Virginia Law Review*, 63, 1977, p. 561; Spitzer, 'Multicriteria choice processes: an application of public choice theory to Bakke, the FCC, and the courts', *Yale Law Journal*, 88, 1979, p. 717. See also the casebook problems on these topics in Goetz, *Law and Economics*.

[20] See, for example, Rubin, 'Why is the common law efficient?', *Journal Legal Studies*, 6, 1977, p. 51; Priest, 'The common law process and the selection of efficient rules', *Journal Legal Studies*, 6, 1977, p. 65.

[21] Chapter 8, pp. 119–34.

conceivable' that undermotivation of the (more functionally important) judges in an inquisitorial system will possibly overbalance the over-investment of resources by adversaries, but then goes on to rely on the superior theoretical properties of the inquisitorial model.[22] My eyebrows are raised not because he is wrong, but because he seems to resolve doubtful institutional cases in law in a different way than he would be expected to in the choice between high transaction-cost markets and dubiously motivated bureaucratic planner-coordinators.

In fact Tullock's discussion of the market-like reward system for arbitrator expertise invites a similar acknowledgement about the provision of expertise by adversaries. My own experience with litigation is a somewhat biased sample in that it involves cases calling for unusual types of litigation expertise such as economic or statistical analysis. These cases – antitrust, employment discrimination, etc. – tend to produce a specialized bar with respect not only to the legal but also the cross-disciplinary skills involved. These specialist-advocates really do know how to present the facts favorable to their own case in a very superior way. In principle, I suppose that it would be possible to have as rich an array of inquisitor-judges as those generated in the market for professional adversaries, but a theoretical case might be made here that the adversary market is a critical ingredient in the proper conduct of highly complex cases.

I abandon the present exercise at this juncture in the hope that my point has been made intelligibly even if not extensively: not only does Tullock's legal work omit many of the expected outcomes; but some of it has what paradoxically might be regarded as a certain affirmatively un-Tullockian flavor.

16.4   The Familiar Tullock

A more familiar Tullock is apparent when he addresses other areas of law. Although he views the topics through his own distinctive procedural lens, his position on judicial lawmaking[23] and interpretation[24] is restrictive and predictable in terms of his overall perspective. His writings on constitutional review are literally vintage Tullock for those who remember it being delivered orally before ever it was committed to paper.

I shall defer to Warren Schwartz for further comment on criminal law but, here again, Tullock's conclusions are the ones we might expect within the framework of his overall methodological and ideological thrust.

[22] Ibid., p. 99.
[23] 'Courts as legislatures' in Robert Cunningham (ed.) *Liberty and the Rule of Law*, 1979; and *Trials on Trial*, chapter 12.
[24] *Trials on Trial*, chapter 10.

16.5 Over-Challenging and Under-Challenging

As suggested both explicitly and implicitly above, Gordon Tullock really is a great debater and loves an argument, perhaps too much for his own good. He can be both under- and over- critical in regard to procedural rules for reasons that almost seem to have as much to do with the spirit of the game as with his own analysis.

An example may be helpful. From his 1971 book, one would pardonably gain the impression that the rules of evidence are one of the silliest collections of regulations known to mankind. As an unblushing economic systematizer and rationalizer, I would be prepared, instead, to defend the opposite proposition: that the modern rules of evidence are – with a few exceptions – a remarkably coherent and rational construct, eminently suited to explanation in terms of economic cost-benefit analysis. By contrast, the *Trials* book nine years later actually recognizes this. Albeit backhandedly, it supplies one of the more lucid and persuasive explanations of the evidence rules in precisely the language of cost-benefit trade-offs, thus providing the kind of systematizing or rationalizing function described as both beneficial and eminently "saleable" in section 16.2.

But Tullock's personal bottom line does not change as he avers that he 'does not think that [the rules] have very much' sense.[25] Tullock has a strong prejudice against exclusionary evidence rules and his earlier position was, in effect, that more evidence is always better than less evidence. He may be able to point to *some* rulings that do not make sense, but I feel that a neutral reading of his own analysis suggests that adversaries frequently need be limited by such rules. Tullock perhaps needs to let his analysis qualify his preconceptions more effectively.

Elsewhere I think that Tullock is not challenging enough of underlying assumptions. This concern may arise at an almost metaphysical level. Much of his work analyzes institutions on the assumption that a desideratum of the legal process is truth or the minimization of error. The more I come to know law, the more impressed I am with the infinite malleability of truth, even with respect to inquiry about fact rather than law. Indeed, my colleague Stephen Saltzburg argues that the description of the American adversary system as a search for truth is a fundamental misconception.[26]

16.6 Conclusion

It will be clear from all that was said above that I see Tullock as having made

[25] *Trials on Trial*, p. 155.
[26] Saltzburg, 'Lawyers, clients, and the adversary system', *Mercer Law Review*, 37, 1986, pp. 647, 654.

some grave tactical errors in the tone and format of a large part of his otherwise insightful and pathbreaking legal writing. In re-reading much of this work, I was surprised at how it could be at one and the same time so instructive and stimulating and yet often ultimately unpersuasive or annoying. Its contentiousness challenges the reader to wriggle on the hook rather than to be reeled in willingly, to poke for weaknesses and identify overstatements that, alas, are sometimes there to uncover. As do we all, Tullock has certain hobby-horse topics that he likes to ride and sometimes becomes self-indulgent about his own personal predispositions.

For these and the variety of reasons suggested above, Tullock's reach toward a legal audience has too often fallen short, notwithstanding the rewarding quality of many of his insights to one who is patient. But many of his actual and potential readers have been unable or unwilling to separate the proverbial wheat from the chaff. There is a personal cost to Tullock himself for this. In particular, he deserves far greater recognition as one of the founding figures in the law and economics nexus on the same level as, for instance, Calabresi, Coase and Posner. While there are those who know to place his name in that company, this is not the popular view. Such under-appreciation, therefore, implicates another cost to the world of ideas in the form of a missing readership that could have been beneficially influenced.

But part of Tullock's genius is that he thinks big and he thinks aggressively. His failed launches of interplanetary rocket probes fall short and hit the moon while most of the rest of us try only to light, at best, perfect roman candles. And yet another part of Gordon's genius is the confidence that he is right in all of those arguments he has. And maybe he is. Well, if he is not always right, at least he is always interesting.

17

Tullock and the Inefficiency of the Common Law

SUSAN ROSE-ACKERMAN

17.1 Introduction

Gordon Tullock has avoided falling between the two stools of law and economics by the simple expedient of placing a board of his own devising between them. Unfortunately, however, the stools are rather high so that when Gordon sits on his board, his feet do not quite touch the ground. But before we conclude that he looks a bit ridiculous sitting like that and lecturing us, it is well to listen to what he has to say. As Charles Goetz has pointed out, (Chapter 16) Tullock likes to shock and what better way to shock lawyers than by both using economic jargon *and* restricting the use of footnotes to homely references to casual conversations and reminiscences about one's years in China and at law school? Conversely, how better to shock economists than by an eccentric choice of research topics considered with polemical flourishes but with few of the mathematical tools of modern economic theory? Surely the lawyers are not troubled by the polemics, nor the economists by the jargon, but each has something to feel uneasy about. While Tullock has found a way of avoiding an awkward fall, he has not been easily accepted by either of the fields he seeks to unite.

But let us leave surface impressions aside – Tullock sitting on his board, his eyes glinting as he talks – and consider Professor Tullock's message. One reason Tullock has not been central to the field of law and economics is that he has been ahead of his time. The lawyers and economists who sought to broaden the field beyond a concern for antitrust and regulation focused on the substantive doctrines of tort, contract and property law and argued over their efficiency. One group, represented by Richard Posner and others at the University of Chicago, argues that the common law both is and ought to be efficient (Posner, 1986). Others, led by Guido Calabresi (1970) and others at Yale and elsewhere, argue that courts ought to take efficiency as one of their goals but that considerations of fairness and distributive justice also should be of central concern. These scholars also challenge the Chicagoans' positive, empirical claim that the common law is, in fact, efficient.

17.2 Tullock as a New England Liberal

Tullock has not contributed much to the first part of the dispute over the content of substantive rules such as the use of strict liability versus negligence in tort law or the use of expectation versus reliance measures of damages in contract. However, when the Yale school of law and economics takes on the Chicagoans' positive claims, they have an unlikely ally in Gordon Tullock – an ally whom they have not recognized as such because of his generally conservative positions on substantive issues. Yet Tullock's long-standing interest in procedure and in the interaction between courts and private arrangements is central to any effective critique of Chicago law and economics. A major weakness of that line of research is the lack of a strong positive theory of the operation of the legal system that would explain why doctrinal outcomes should be efficient. While this weakness has been recognized, the attempts to remedy it have not been convincing even to the authors of the principal articles.[1] But one salutory effect of these attempts is an increased interest in the economic analysis of the legal system itself. And here is where Tullock's work can provide a foundation. Professor Tullock's ideal legal procedure is one which resolves particular disputes cheaply and accurately. He recognizes the trade-off between cost and correct decisions but argues that our existing system is poorly set up to resolve this trade-off effectively. His view of the courts is expressed in his stylized model where Mr Right and Mr Wrong are the names of the parties. His idea is that if the facts were known, then Mr Right, who has the law on his side, will win. His main argument is that an adversarial system wastes resources as each side spends money and tries to counteract the spending of the other. Common law courts, as presently organized, are a very poor way to resolve disputes. An arrangement like the continental system which gives more power to the judge to manage the proceedings would be better (Tullock, 1980; 1984).

Unlike recent doctrinal work in law and economics, Tullock does not analyze situations where the law is unclear so that the court's decision will have precedential value. Nevertheless, this analysis can be turned into a critique of the Chicago school view of common law courts which emphasizes the development of efficient legal rules through case-by-case adjudication. This can be done by observing, first, that most cases are of the routine sort that Tullock analyzes, and second, that even for those that are not, existing

---

[1] The original articles are Priest (1977) and Rubin (1977). The authors' more skeptical recent views are in Priest (1980); Priest and Klein (1984); and Rubin (1983, pp. 13–35).

procedures are not well designed to facilitate the efficient evolution of doctrine because of the high cost of suits and the biases of the evidence and the arguments.

Tullock's analysis of accident law provides another distinct argument which undermines strong Chicagoan claims about the efficacy of tort law and is quite complementary to Calabresi's analysis. As Tullock points out, the existence of an insurance system with rates that poorly reflect people's behavior can undermine whatever incentives are built into liability rules. He then goes on to argue that even if insurance were unavailable for automobile accidents, tort liability for an occasional disaster is inferior to increased enforcement of speeding laws with high fines levied on violators. This system would, he believes, be both a cheaper and more effective deterrent (Tullock, 1971, p. 109).

He is also skeptical of the use of court decisions to produce an efficient law of contracts. In one of his few observations on the substance of contract (another is his demonstration that the legal prohibition against selling oneself into slavery is a good idea, Tullock, 1971, pp. 53-54, Tullock asserts that judge-made law does not contain the optimal amount of detail (1971, p. 48):

Under the Common Law, each case that reaches an appellate court adds an additional bit of detail into the law. There is no effort on the part of anyone to decide how detailed the law should be. The result is a situation in which the person more learned in the law has the distinct advantage over the person less learned. In particular, it gives a major advantage to the lawyers. It is also helpful to the ego of the judges who are permitted to make the law for future contracts. Nevertheless, it cannot be said that it works any vast amount of harm. Substituting flipping coins for the details of out present interpretative law would be somewhat more efficient, but the difference would be minimal.

Thus Tullock does not argue that existing rules are perverse but rather that they are largely irrelevant and are produced by a needlessly expensive process. Later in the same volume (p. 208), however, he makes a somewhat stronger claim:

There is, however, no reason why individual courts trying individual cases should be the authority that supplements the inadequate legislature. The French administrative court that produces an authoritative interpretation of the law in general terms rather than with respect to individual cases does as well. Thus, we could have the law itself and a gloss on it made by a selected group of judges. It would not be necessary to wade through thousands and thousands of judicial decisions in order to determine the rights of a party to a dispute.

The final substantive area I consider is Tullock's analysis of the criminal law. Some of it is, rather surprisingly, in the mainstream of law and economics work and Tullock's position is thus not that of prescient outsider but of a person who along with Gary Becker (1968) and George Stigler (1970) helped to revive the utilitarian analysis of crime and law enforcement. The idea that those who consider breaking a criminal law are economic actors balancing the expected costs of detection and punishment against the benefits of the crime is still a shocking idea to some people; but it has considerable empirical validity, at least for crimes against property (Tullock, 1971, pp. 211–27).

Nevertheless, Tullock's main concern here is once again with procedural matters, that is, the costs of detecting and punishing crimes. He wants to introduce more market tests into the systems. He would pay people who are subsequently exonerated the opportunity cost to them of pre-trial detention. He would like the police to pay people in return for searches of their homes and encourage the payment of those willing to supply evidence or tips especially if these can be checked against other information. He is also a persistent advocate of polygraph tests and a critic of the jury (Tullock, 1984). However, he recognizes the limitations of fines as punishments for crimes and would use prisons as job training centers (Tullock, 1971, Part III).

17.3 Conclusions

Finally, a word about Tullockian ethics. He claims to avoid ethics and use only utilitarian considerations (Tullock, 1971, p. 253). But this is disingenuous. Utilitarianism *is* an ethical theory with its own familiar strengths and weaknesses.[2] In fact, Tullock's own ethical values pervade his writing. For example, he argues that theft and violence should be illegal on the ground that most people believe that the costs outweigh the benefits. Crimes are only to be distinguished from torts or contract breaches because of the qualms of conscience that some people feel and because of the cost and difficulty of catching people. The benefits to the thief or bully are counted positively in the social calculus but are outweighed by the costs imposed on others. This fundamental ethical premise, made persuasive to the reader by beginning with traffic violations and tax avoidance (Tullock, 1971, chapter 8), is not examined critically. Yet it is the basis on which his analysis rests and it cannot be made innocuous by labeling it non-ethical. In some of his analyses, Tullock's utilitarian perspective produces relatively uncontroversial proposals to save resources, but in a range of other situations, especially in the discussion of criminal law, Tullock's ethical presuppositions should be clearly recognized for their quite controversial implications.

[2] See e.g. Ackerman (1980) and Rawls (1971).

References

Ackerman, Bruce (1980) *Social Justice in the Liberal State*. New Haven, Conn: Yale University Press.

Becker, Gary (1968) 'Crime and punishment: an economic approach', *Journal Political Economy*, 76, January/February, pp. 169–217.

Calabresi, Guido (1970) *The Cost of Accidents*. New Haven, Conn: Yale University Press.

Posner, Richard (1986) *Economic Analysis of Law*. 3rd edn, Boston: Little, Brown.

Priest, George L. (1977) 'The common law process and the selection of efficient rules'. *Journal Legal Studies*, 6, pp. 65–82.

Priest, George L. (1980) 'Selective characteristics of litigation', *Journal Legal Studies*, 9, March, pp. 399–421.

Priest, George L. and Klein, Benjamin (1984) 'The selection of disputes for litigation', *Journal Legal Studies*, 13, January, pp. 1–55.

Rawls, John (1971) *A Theory of Justice*. Cambridge, Mass: Harvard University Press.

Rubin, Paul H. (1977) 'Why is the common law efficient?', *Journal Legal Studies*, 6, pp. 51–63.

Rubin, Paul H. (1983) *Business Firms and the Common Law: The Evolution of Efficient Rules*. New York: Praeger.

Stigler, George (1970) 'The optimum enforcement of laws', *Journal Political Economy*, 78, May/June, pp. 526–36.

Tullock, Gordon (1971) *The Logic of the Law*. New York: Basic Books.

Tullock, Gordon (1980) *Trials on Trial: The Pure Theory of Legal Procedure*. New York: Columbia Unversity Press.

Tullock, Gordon (1984) 'Why I Prefer Napoleon', Paper presented at a Conference on New Directions in Law and Economics, sponsored by Columbia University Law School's Center for Law and Economic Studies, New York, November.

18

The Logic of the Law Revisited
WARREN F. SCHWARTZ

18.1 Introduction

My route to this conference has been marked by a series of events which seem to defy easy generalization but somehow convey an important message. I first encountered Gordon Tullock in a shower room in a dormitory at the University of Rochester when I was a member of Henry Manne's first class of law professors learning economics. I (accurately) warned Gordon that if he turned on the hot water in any but very small quantities he would be badly burned. Tullock (somewhat later) expressed his gratitude by inviting me to give a paper at the Public Choice Center. There I met Charles Goetz whom I immediately recognized as someone who belonged in a law school. This was later arranged and Goetz and I began teaching each other law and economics. Now, in the present paper, I am provided the opportunity to comment on Goetz commenting on Tullock.

What appears to be strangely prophetic about all this is that, as I now recognize, the economics which Goetz quite naturally brought to bear when analyzing legal problems was in large measure shaped by the ideas of Gordon Tullock. Indeed, more generally, Tullock's seminal work in public choice theory, indirectly through his influence on other economists like Goetz, and more directly, as legal scholars have become familiar with it, has had an enormous impact on legal thought.

I was reminded of all this when I read in Goetz (Chapter 16) the erroneous predictions that might have been made in 1971, just before the *Logic of the Law* appeared, of the themes which Tullock would develop in his writings about law. What is remarkable is that these ideas, and many others which derive from public choice theory, have indeed been influential among legal scholars but that, as Goetz correctly observes, Tullock, himself has only to a limited degree grounded his writings on law upon his work in economics which has so influenced legal scholars.

One issue may serve to illustrate this point. Tullock has written both about appellate review and the desirability of jury trials. An important characteristic which is shared by appellate tribunals and juries is that they involve decision-making in non-market settings. With respect to appellate tribunals (and administrative agencies), moreover, the interaction is iterative, extending to all the cases which will be decided and the range of administrative and personnel matters which must be addressed by any functioning institution.

One would expect all of this to be grist for Tullock's theoretical mill. How useful and provocative it would have been for him to have suggested, for example, that a responsible appellate judge should trade votes across cases to maximize the value of the votes he has to cast.

Tullock, however, in analyzing the functioning of juries and appellate tribunals, does not focus on issues of this kind, which seem so naturally to flow from his theoretical work in economics. I believe that this surprising discontinuity between Tullock's theoretical writings in economics and his analyses of legal issues is remarkably general.

18.2   The Importance of Public Choice

This brings me to the point that I have been trying to find a graceful way to make. The *Logic of the Law*, Tullock's most ambitious writing focusing directly on the legal system, is both a less successful book and, I speculate, a less influential one, precisely because the analysis does not proceed as a systematic application of economic theory.

Public choice theory provides the most useful set of organizing principles for analyzing legal issues of which I am aware. The necessity *ex ante* to confront the tendency to opportunism *ex post* is the essential insight for understanding a vast array of social organizations ranging from the simple bilateral contract to the modern corporation to the institutions of government. Moreover, the means for enforcing the legal obligations associated with these organizations provided by the state or private parties are themselves responses to the pervasive problem of opportunism. Seeing all of these phenomena as efforts to achieve cooperation so that gains of trade can be realized renders the inquiry coherent.

When I read the *Logic of the Law* recently I found myself performing an experiment similar to that of Goetz. I wondered what, in 1971, the person who had been so influential in developing the ideas that had come to constitute my own 'logic of the law' would offer as his own theoretical foundation. My surprise parallels Goetz's erroneous prediction of how Tullock would apply his theoretical insights to legal issues.

This is not to say that the insights of public choice theory are wholly absent from the book. Indeed, the treatment of contract and procedure implicitly applies many of them. What is, however, not offered, is the

systematic development of the normative and positive issues which characterizes Tullock's work in economics.

I can only speculate why Tullock chose to lay down his economist's hat
(not entirely, of course) when he put on his legal one. He seemed to believe,
in writing the *Logic of the Law*, that the legal system is characterized by large,
easily detectable and correctable errors which only had to be pointed out for
the proposed reforms to command universal assent. This may have been in
part intended as a 'put on' to enrage and get the attention of the lawyers. But
I am afraid as I read the *Logic of the Law* that Tullock, to a considerable
extent, really believed this. With all respect I suggest he was mistaken.

I do not know Tullock's current views on the difficulties of devising and
implementing fundamental institutional changes. I suspect, however, that he
himself would regard many of the 'easy kills' as less easy and less clearly kills
than they are portrayed in the *Logic of the Law*.

18.3   Conclusions

So I will conclude with an invitation on behalf of my fellow legal scholars.
Gordon Tullock, write us another *Logic of the Law*, building systematically
and explicitly on your seminal theoretical work. My only reservation about
the value of this enterprise is that in large measure we have already
discovered and been greatly influenced by your economic insights in
formulating our ôwn theoretical framework for analyzing legal issues. But I
would be very surprised if we have not missed some very fruitful applications
which would occur to you in discharging the assignment.

VII

The Reform of Institutions

19

Why Some Welfare-State Redistribution to the Poor is a Great Idea

MANCUR OLSON

19.1 Introduction

Everyday observation suggests that most people readily reveal their sympathy for those in trouble and are by no means reticent in recounting their contributions to charity and other altruistic acts. Some even appear ostentatiously to display their empathy with those who are suffering and may also advertize or exaggerate what they have selflessly done for others.

According to the account I have heard from those who know him best (and to some extent my own observations), the man honored in this volume, by contrast, appears to go to unusual lengths to conceal his considerable sympathy for the losers in life's struggles and to hide his many acts of generosity. Indeed, if my observations are representative, Gordon Tullock even appears during arguments to revel in rejecting many of the common-place concerns for those at the bottom of the heap (at least when they are expressed by those of left-liberal ideology) and to ridicule many moralistic or altruistic efforts to help the poor (especially if welfare-state programs are involved).

When someone of substantial sympathy and unusual generosity deni-grates, in political or ideological arguments, many of the most familiar manifestations of sympathy and generosity, we have at least a bit of a paradox. When the person in question is such an insightful and incisive scholar as Gordon Tullock, the paradox becomes all the more interesting. Conceivably one way to resolve the paradox would be to focus on the fun that many of us get from shocking the bourgeois, or shocking whatever audience we prefer to shock; it might be argued that Gordon Tullock loves to shock his audiences (and that my essay in this volume tries to honor him by

I am thankful to Charles C. Brown, Norbert Hornstein and Ellika Olson for helpful criticisms and ideas, and to the Thyssen Stiftung for support of my research.

following his example). Another way to deal with the paradox would be to look at the grave deficiencies of many of the existing welfare-state programs and to show how many of them are not rational mechanisms for serving the humane objectives they are supposed to serve. Yet another way of dealing with the paradox would be to look at the familiar ideologies that play such a large role in the debates of our time, and to ask whether they are quite sufficient to do justice to the personal choices and the detailed scholarship of their leading spokesmen.

Without pretending it is the whole story, I shall restrict myself to the last of these three ways of looking at the subject. This third, ideological aspect of the matter is a natural one for me to deal with in this volume. Presumably one role I am expected to play in this book is to demonstrate the considerable diversity among the economists and others who especially value Gordon Tullock's science and scholarship. There are indeed a great many people of many different disciplines and point of view who are exceptionally impressed by Gordon Tullock's vast work, and I am happy to offer myself as one small piece of evidence of the number and variety of his admirers.

But everyone who knows both Gordon Tullock's work and my own will know that it would be futile to attempt to conceal the great differences in some of our conclusions about politics and public policy. Though the two of us have always agreed about the importance of using the economist's methods of thought to analyze political and social life (and agreed on this at a time when only a handful of people thought this was an appropriate thing to do), we have not had the same views about many matters of ideology and politics.

Indeed, since Gordon Tullock has been such a very large part of the 'Virginia School', I can go further and apply my argument to the Virginia School as a whole. I have enormous admiration for the Virginia School and emphasize its prominent role among those who pioneered the use of the economist's methods for the study of politics. More than a decade and a half ago my colleague Christopher Clague and I thought this work was so important that we used it as the star example of the insights that could be found in the (then) dissenting schools of economics, in our article on 'Dissent in Economics'.[1] In the process, my friends in the Virginia School tell me, we were the first to use the phrase 'Virginia School'. I take some pride in the long-standing extent of my recognition of the importance of the work of James Buchanan and Gordon Tullock and their colleagues in the Virginia School.

This long-standing admiration of Gordon Tullock and his colleagues in the Virginia School does, I think, give me a special license to raise questions about how successful Tullock and the Virginia School have been in

[1] *Social Research*, 1971, pp. 751–76.

separating their methodological innovations and other scientific advances, which every informed and fair-minded economist irrespective of ideology must respect, from right-wing and classical-liberal ideology. The casual reader of some of the work of Gordon Tullock and his colleagues should certainly be forgiven for concluding that the Virginia School's scholarship suggested that the welfare state was undesirable. He could also reasonably draw the impression that this School provided a rationale for a conservative or classical-liberal view of the world and even for some measure of support for conservative political leaders such as Ronald Reagan and Barry Goldwater. Though the intellectual contributions of Gordon Tullock and the Virginia School are undoubtedly scientific and scholarly contributions that social scientists of all persuasions should cherish, the leaders of the Virginia School have devoted relatively little resources to distinguishing these contributions from conservative or classical-liberal ideology, and have at times at least come very close to arguing that their discoveries do indeed strengthen the case for the classical-liberal ideology and certain conservative political agendas.

In my opinion, the value of the scientific contributions of Gordon Tullock and his colleagues in the Virginia School is obscured when it is treated as a part of or a justification for any right-wing ideology. As I have been arguing for some time in 'Ideology and economic growth'[2] and other essays, neither the left-wing nor the right-wing ideology is sufficient to guide societies through the problems of the day. An attachment to either of these ideologies makes us overlook some overwhelmingly important matters that both ideologies ignore. Though each of the familiar ideologies contains some elements of truth, they more often obscure than illuminate the problems that modern societies face. And each of these ideologies taken alone also leads, as others have argued earlier, to a view of reality that is incomplete and unbalanced.

I shall endeavor in this essay, which is dramatically different from some of my other articles opposing each of the familiar ideologies, to show the losses that occur when we look at the welfare state exclusively from one or the other of the familiar ideologies. I shall endeavor to develop a different (and I hope slightly less ideological) way of discussing programs designed to transfer resources to the poor. The method I shall use is essentially the same procedure that Gordon Tullock and the rest of the Virginia School have also been using. It involves applying the economist's familiar tools of thought in contexts and in ways in which an earlier generation of economists would have said took one outside of the discipline.

---

[2] Charles R. Hulten and Isabel V. Sawhill, eds, *The Legacy of Reaganomics: Prospects for Long-Term Growth*, Washington, DC: The Urban Institute, 1984, pp. 229–52.

19.2   The Fundamental Debate

Every possible general answer has already been given to the question of how much should be transferred to the poor. Some people have readily accepted (or even celebrated) great inequalities in the distribution of income and want no transfers at all to the poor. Others have advocated a completely equal distribution of income and whatever transfers to low-income people are needed to achieve this. Many prefer one alternative or another between these extremes, and the intermediate levels of transfers that have been recommended are so varied and numerous that almost every general level of transfers must have been advocated. Thus the answer that this essay will give to the question at issue is bound to be unoriginal; it will be found to lack detail as well.

The purpose, as I have indicated, is rather to develop a way of thinking about this question that makes it possible for empirical research and logical demonstration to play a somewhat larger role, and for ideological judgments to play a somewhat smaller role, than in prior approaches. To be sure, it is not possible with any type of empirical research or logical demonstration to resolve all disagreements about the distribution of income, but it is possible to resolve some of them and to narrow the domain in which we must rely on purely subjective judgments.

It would surely be useful to reduce the range and degree of disagreement about how much should be transferred to the poor. The debate about this question has gone on for centuries, if not for millennia. On one side, many emphasize the misfortunes and deprivations the poor endure and the moral appeal of compassionate public policies. On the other side, many call attention to the role that improvidence and indolence play in accounting for poverty and the extent to which programs to aid those of slender means impair the incentives to work and to save.

Since this debate has gone on so very long without any sign of consensus, and apparently even without narrowing of the range of disagreement, there is some presumption that the issue has not been debated and researched in the best way. Generally, when there is no narrowing or diminution of disagreement, there is also little or no intellectual progress. The emergence of areas of consensus, by contrast, usually signifies compelling results. This has certainly been the case in the physical and natural sciences. It has also been true, I believe, in my discipline of economics; the study of the business cycle and macroeconomics generally is sharply divided between contending schools, presumably because there are obvious shortcomings in each school's theory. Yet at the same time there is something like consensus about how individual markets work and about microeconomic theory in general, presumably because the explanations microeconomic theory offers are compelling to competent researchers of all complexions.

Possibly the debate about the distribution of income is entirely different from the disputes in the areas where intellectual progress tends to resolve disagreements. Some would say that the debate about the distribution of income cannot even be narrowed by intellectual progress because it centers on an enduring conflict of interest between those of higher and those of lower incomes, and that so long as human nature remains unchanged, each side is bound to argue that it should have a larger slice of the social pie. But conflicts of interest cannot be the only source of the problem. People often disagree about the distribution of incomes even in foreign societies in which they have no personal stake, and the views that they have on the inequality of the income distribution in their own societies are by no means perfectly correlated with their personal income levels, so ideology and moral tastes clearly play a role. If, however, the distribution of income is a matter of moral taste, this is also discouraging, since there is no way to show which side is right in disputes about matters of taste.

Conflicts of interest and differences of taste certainly are a part of the problem, but they are a smaller part of the problem than might be supposed; we shall see that there are neglected common interests that can generate agreement, and that observation of individual choices reveals that there are also pertinent tastes or preferences that are common to quite different ideological groups that are assumed to have totally different tastes about this issue. It turns out that the same source of energy that has generated so much heat can also give us light.

19.3 Expected Utility Analysis: Von Neumann/Morgenstern to Friedman/Savage

We can obtain a deeper understanding of public policies about poverty and income distribution, and also transcend to some extent the unending and unproductive debate between the secular religions of the Right and the Left, if we look at the satisfaction or 'utility' that people of different income levels get from their incomes and from marginal increases in their levels of consumption. We must look, in other words, at the urgency, intensity, or importance of the desire or need for additional consumption at different levels of consumption or income. At first it may seem that this is such a simple and obvious matter that it needs no attention. Is it not obvious that the poor need additional income more than the rich and that the poor would therefore obviously get more satisfaction out of a given absolute increase in consumption than would the rich? The issue, however, is not quite so simple. We cannot look into anyone's head and see how intensely he or she suffers because of a low level of consumption, or how intensely he or she desires a higher income. How, then, can we verify any assertion that this or that category of persons will get more satisfaction or utility out of a given increase in consumption? There is no completely objective or regularly reliable way of making what economists call 'interpersonal comparisons of utility'. It is not immediately obvious just how a researcher can even begin to get a handle on the question of how important additional income is to people at different levels of income or consumption.

There was an opening for a scholarly or scientific way of doing research on this problem in John von Neumann's and Oskar Morgenstern's classic book *The Theory of Games and Economic Behavior*. That book, though it focused on other matters, introduced the notion that we could get an idea how much a given gain in consumption or income would matter to an individual by asking how much he or she would pay for a given probability of obtaining some larger sum. We could, for example, ask how much an individual would pay for a one-in-ten chance of getting a thousand dollars. Obviously, the arithmetic expectation or 'expected value' of this gamble is the product of one-tenth times a thousand dollars, or one hundred dollars. If a very large number of such gambles were offered, each for a hundred dollars, the amount paid out to winners in the aggregate would, of course, tend to equal the total amount paid for the gambles.

But we cannot conclude from this that every individual would necessarily be willing to pay exactly a hundred dollars for a one-in-ten chance of getting a thousand dollars. An individual might be willing to pay no more than, say, eighty dollars for a gamble with an expected value of a hundred dollars. This would be rational if the individual believed that each of the dollars he would gain if he won the gamble would be worth less to him than each of the hundred dollars he would lose if the gamble were unsuccessful. This person would have a 'diminishing marginal utility of income' – he or she would expect more utility per dollar of consumption at the pre-gamble level of income than would be obtained at the higher level of consumption he or she would have if the gamble were successful. If, on the other hand, the individual were willing to pay, say, $110 for a one-in-ten chance on a thousand dollars, this would make sense only if the utility per dollar from the thousand dollars he might win was greater than the utility per dollar of each of the 110 dollars he was willing to pay for the gamble. This person would have a 'rising marginal utility of income'. Obviously, if the person were willing to pay up to $100 but no more for the gamble, then this would suggest that dollars ventured on the gamble were worth exactly as much as any that were won in the gamble: the utility of consumption or income rises in a straight line with income.

Some four years after von Neumann's and Morgenstern's book was published, two other researchers applied their procedure to everyday observation of behavior and, in an article entitled 'The utility analysis of choices involving risk',[3] drew some influential conclusions about the value or utility individuals would get from given increases in income or consumption. The two researchers were Milton Friedman, the Nobel-Laureate economist, and Leonard Savage, a distinguished statistician.

Friedman and Savage pointed out that individuals reveal something about the utility or satisfaction they derive (or lose) from given increases (or decreases) in income when they buy insurance, and also when they gamble in lotteries and casinos. In other words, they used the von Neumann – Morgenstern approach to analyze the behavior observed in real life.

Consider, first, what we do when we buy, for example, fire insurance: we do not give up money and get something *different* in exchange for it, as we do when we spend money in a store. We get nothing back at all, unless the unusual contingency against which we have insured occurs – and then we are likely to get back much more money than we paid out in premiums. In other words, insurance is trading a small amount of money for some probability of getting a larger sum, should the specified contingency occur – or trading the certainty of losing a modest amount of money in premiums for what is normally a small chance that we will get a large amount of money back. But the amount that, as purchasers of insurances, we in the aggregate pay in premiums normally greatly exceeds the amount that we – again, in the aggregate – get back in settlement of claims. As we know, the insurance company has expenses and it was set up to make a profit. Accordingly, the premiums we pay to an insurance company are normally less than the amount we would get in claims multiplied by the probability that we would have a claim; that is, the 'expected monetary value' or 'mathematical expectation' of what the individual will receive from the insurance company is normally less than the amount he or she puts in.

But if this is so, why do we buy insurance at all? The money we receive if our house burns down means more to us than money does when we have not had any such misfortune. So of course the answer to our question is that the insurance companies pay us money at a time when it is especially useful to us. And it is especially useful then because, for most of us, our house is a large part of our total wealth, so that if it burns down, we are made very much poorer, and we believe that when we are poorer, money will be worth much more to us – that is, we will 'need' it more.

It is convenient here, as so often in economics, to use the language of utilitarianism, although in our context, using the word 'utility' does not in general mean that we have to accept the controversial features of the philosophy of utilitarianism. From the foregoing, we can see that usually we

---

[3] *Journal of Political Economy*, **56**, August 1948, pp. 179-304. *See also* Milton Friedman, 'Choice, chance, and the personal distribution of income', *Journal of Political Economy*, **61**, August 1953, pp. 277–90.

get more utility per dollar after a catastrophe that leaves us much poorer than we do in normal times. Though we generally get less money, or expected value in money, out of insurance companies than we pay into them, we anticipate greater expected *utility* from the possible insurance payouts to us than the utility lost from the money paid out in premiums. In other words, the great number of 'utils' we would get from any dollars the insurance company paid to satisfy our claims, times the normally small probability that we will actually have a claim, yields a product greater than that of the number of utils lost because we had to reduce our consumption marginally to pay the premium. The expected value in dollars of our transaction with the insurance company is negative, but the expected value in utility is positive for any rational purchaser of insurance.

This simple logic is quite relevant to the distribution of income and the question of whether the government ought to protect people against poverty. Suppose that what holds true for the individual, when he considers the circumstances in which he might be poor and compares them with his normal circumstances, also holds true for comparisons between people of normal or high incomes and people of low incomes. Friedman and Savage do not by any means make this supposition, but we shall see later that there is a compelling justification for something very like it. On this supposition, we already have a possible rationale for public programs to aid the poor. Whatever individuals may say about the income distribution when they rehash the familiar ideological debates, their impartial and considered behavior in purchasing insurance for themselves and their families contains at the least a hint that probably low-income people on average get more utility or satisfaction out of marginal increments in income than middle- or upper- income people do. Low-income people presumably usually get more 'bang for the buck' out of a given increment of income than do those who have substantially higher incomes.

There is, to put it mildly, much more to the matter (such as the impact of programs to aid the poor on the incentives to work and to save), and it is too early for any conclusions whatever. Yet we seem to have stumbled upon at least a possible argument for a more egalitarian distribution of income, and this is by no means the sort of thing one expects to find every day in writings in which Milton Friedman has had a hand.

There is, to be sure, another part of the Friedman-Savage argument, and it is a very interesting one. Insurance is not the only activity in which people give up money, not for some different good, but in return for some probability of getting back a larger sum. Gambling also has this same property, and Friedman and Savage correctly observed that many people not only buy insurance but also gamble. If we buy a ticket for the Irish Sweepstakes, we give up a small amount of money to pay the lottery ticket and get in return a minute probability that we will win the grand sum. We also know, or ought to know, that the government of Ireland would not have established the Sweepstakes if there were not something in it for the Irish. And there is a very great deal in it for them: they pay the winner much, much less than the sum they collect from selling tickets. So it is essentially with all gambling; the total payouts are usually very much smaller than the total paid in. Yet gambling, Friedman and Savage pointed out, is commonplace.

By now, you can undoubtedly see it coming. Friedman and Savage emphasize that widespread gambling implies that, for a great many people, a dollar at their present level of income is believed to generate *less* utility or satisfaction for them than the average dollar of extra income they would have if they obtained a much *higher* income by winning a gamble. Though the expected return in dollars of most gambles is less than the amount ventured, the expected value of the gamble in terms of utility must be positive or else the person would not have gambled. Using the logic offered to explain the purchase of insurance, Friedman and Savage conclude that (at least for the many people who gamble) the utility per dollar of consumption or income would be greater at the high income levels they would be at if they won the gamble than it is at the level of consumption and income they are at when they decide to make the gamble. That in turn implies that the marginal utility of consumption rises for people who gamble as consumption levels rise; satisfaction or utility rises in greater proportion than income and consumption do.

If, as Friedman and Savage observe, most people buy insurance and also gamble, then we should, they say, infer that most people are at intermediate or middle-income levels that are inefficient in generating utility. The decision to gamble implies that the utility loss from the sums ventured is less than the expected utility gain, and with the actuarily unfair odds that normally prevail in gambling, this in turn implies that utility per dollar from the amount won must be appreciably greater than the utility per dollar of the amount ventured. After a sufficiently big gamble the individual will be at a level of consumption that is efficient in generating utility; the person will either have won the gamble and be at the high level of consumption that is ostensibly efficient in generating utility per dollar, or have lost, in which case total utility is lower than before the gamble but the person is at a consumption level that is efficient in generating utility per dollar of consumption. At the efficient levels of consumption that occur after the win or the loss at gambling, it pays to buy insurance to protect oneself against contingencies that would leave one at consumption levels that generated less utility per dollar.

What, then, would be the implication of this for the appropriate distribution of income? If again we make the (still provisional) assumption that, on average, people in different income classes have much the same inherent capacities to enjoy consumption, then we get the conclusion that society would get more kick out of the national income if it had a distribution of income with relatively more people at high incomes and relatively more people at low incomes and relatively fewer with middle incomes. An egalitarian distribution of income would tend to put a larger proportion of society in the intermediate income levels and could reduce the total satisfaction obtained from the society's income. An unequal distribution of income, quite apart from any gain from the incentives it might provide, could have the further advantage of generating more utility out of a given income.[4]

For most of us, there is something profoundly counter-intuitive about this last result. We shall see later that Friedman and Savage made some serious logical mistakes. Yet I urge the reader not to dismiss their argument out of hand, because it is an indispensable step toward a better understanding of appropriate public policies toward poverty and income redistribution. Despite its counter-intuitive character and the strong ideological motives for attacking it, the Friedman-Savage argument stood entirely undamaged for more than thirty years; all the efforts to refute it failed, and in ways that any competent judge would have to agree were failures.

19.4   The Impact of Rawls

Before going on to the shortcomings and, as I should like to think, the surprises that are hidden beneath the surface of the Friedman-Savage argument, it is necessary to turn to the work of another leading thinker, the philosopher John Rawls.[5] There is an important relationship between Rawl's theory of justice and the strengths and shortcomings of the Friedman-Savage argument that, so far as I know, has been totally neglected.

Rawls showed that, to some extent, we could get away from the biases arising from ideology and from conflicts of interest when debating moral questions if we could think about these questions behind a 'veil of ignorance, we could try to think of the possibility that we might be in any category of humanity – that we might enter the world healthy or unhealthy, able or dull, rich or poor, and so on. Given a veil of ingnorance, we can possible an instructive type of 'thought experiment'. Behind the veil of ignorance, we could try to think of the possiblity that we might be in any category of humanity – that we might enter the world healthy or unhealthy, able or dull, rich or poor, and so on. Given a veil of ignorance, we can

---

[4] This requires the same supposition set out in the last paragraph of section 19.2 of the text, and Friedman and Savage do not make this assumption in their joint article. Milton Friedman's further argument in 'Choice, chance, and the personal distribution of income' (see Note 1) does, however, at least come very close to leaving the impression that a given national income would generate more utility if it were unequally distributed. Later parts of this paper will show that the supposition at issue is approximately correct.

[5] *A Theory of Justice*. Cambridge, Mass.: Harvard University Press, 1971.

abstract from the particular characteristics we have that give us vested interests on one side or another of a moral issue.

If we can abstract from any knowledge we have of our personal stake, then we have an incentive or reason to choose moral rules that are, in some sense, socially rational or efficient, and which take account of the interests of all the people; if we could be any one of the people in a society, our prospects are better if that society has moral rules that make it function well and that take account of the interests of people in all kinds of circumstances. In so describing Rawl's veil of ignorance I may be offering a slightly personal interpretation not precisely the same as Rawls's, but in a very general way my interpretation should be acceptable; as Rawls put it, his 'contract doctrine. . . conceives of moral philosophy as part of the theory of rational choice.'[6]

In my opinion, Rawls has introduced an exceptionally valuable type of thinking. The moment we look at moral questions as part of the theory of rational choice, we can see the possibility of focusing on rational arrangements for furthering our common interests, and here we can hope to achieve some agreement. As I argued at the beginning of this essay, this is not something we can reasonably hope for when the focus is on conflicts of interest or disputes about taste. As I see it, the veil of ignorance need not always be a hypothetical state, but may also fit certain real-life situations to a degree. This can perhaps be seen by considering how two people may easily be able to agree before starting a trip by car how they will handle expenses in the event of a breakdown, yet disagree heatedly about how to do this if there has been no agreement in advance. The same logic is sometimes evident when the participants in a meeting agree, before they know how any debates and votes will turn out, or perhaps even before they know what disputes will arise, on some relatively efficient procedures for the meeting, such as Robert's Rules of Order.

This example should remind us that there is a very important parallel to Rawls's veil of ignorance in the work that our honoree, Gordon Tullock, has co-authored with James Buchanan on *The Calculus of Consent*.[7] The 'constitutional' context, as Buchanan and Tullock first explained, is one in which the parties have relatively little information about how general rules will bear on their particular situations over a long run that is imperfectly known, so the parties in a constitutional context have some incentive to seek efficient or rational constitutional rules. Though I have elsewhere argued that the practical force of this consideration is sometimes overestimated in debates about some proposed amendments to the United States constitution, I believe that this insight into the incentives in the constitutional context is quite profound. My general point in this essay about the

---

[6] Ibid., p. 172.
[7] Ann Arbor, Michigan: University of Michigan, 1962.

importance of distinguishing science and scholarship from ideology is supported by the fact that much the same insight was independently derived by Rawls and by Buchanan and Tullock, even though they appeared to start from vastly different ideological positions.

The first principle that Rawls drew from reasoning behind a veil of ignorance is that a society that gives every individual as much liberty as possible, so long as the individual does not infringe upon the like liberties of others, is morally desirable. We can immediately see the attractions of this principle when we suppose we do not know whether we are going to want this life-style or that, be lovers of socialist realism or of abstract art, or know whether we will have much of a role in establishing any rules that needlessly constrain individual liberty. A society that has a large degree of freedom must surely be a more appealing prospect than a society that would gratuitously outlaw what we might want to do or especially constrain a minority or weaker group of which we might be a part. It seems to me important that this commonplace conclusion is obtained by ordinary principles of rational and even self-interested decision-making, and differs from other rational decisions essentially in the supposition that there is no knowledge of any conditions that might give the decision-maker a particular interest that is not shared by the others in the society in question.

The second principle that Rawls derived with the aid of the veil of ignorance specified what inequalities were morally justifiable, but this part of his argument has apparently not impressed readers nearly so much as his intellectual method. Indeed, it does not, in contrast to his conclusion about liberty, appear to have attracted any widespread agreement. Rawls's second, or 'maximin', principle is that no inequality is morally justified unless that inequality makes the worst-off person in the society better off. He supports this principle by pointing out that an individual behind the veil of ignorance would rationally take account of the possibility that he might be the worst-off person in society, and that in a matter of such importance it is appropriate to avoid risks and to assume that one's worst enemy was to determine one's place in society. Of course, it would be irrational, even if one would be the worst-off person in society, to prohibit any inequalities that would make one better off, so Rawls thereby derives the conclusion that any inequalities that help the worst-off are morally-justified.

19.5   The Principle of Maximin

A great many critics have argued that Rawls's second principle has a number of implications that show that it is profoundly flawed. For one thing, the principle, even though its exclusive focus on the worst-off is exceptionally egalitarian, utterly neglects the interests of many of the poor. Suppose the great majority of the poor are not quite as desperate as the very poorest, and that we can, without hurting the very poorest, greatly ease the plight of the second-poorest class at little cost to society. Should this not be done? Possibly the operation of the maximin principle would eventually operate to raise the standard of living of the second-poorest class, because the help it mandates for the poorest class might raise it to same level as those who had been second-poorest, and thereafter help this class too on the grounds it was now in the worst-off category. But there is nothing in the logic of the matter to keep those differences in income (or, more precisely, in what Rawls calls 'primary goods') near the bottom of the social scale from being a crucial part of the just society's system of incentives, and thus justified as in the interest of the very poorest.

Suppose for concreteness that the second-poorest class is composed of totally unskilled workers, whereas the poorest are paralyzed and unable to work. It is easily possible that a system which eliminated all incentive for unskilled workers to work, by giving non-workers the same income as workers, would reduce the society's income and the level of provision to the worst-off. Schemes may be suggested that would lessen this problem; I have in other contexts argued myself that plans of public assistance to low-income people which distinguished among recipients according to their ability to work were probably preferable to a simple negative income tax. But this does not solve the problem that Rawls's maximin principle does not give us any reason whatever to take account of the interests of those who were not quite at the bottom; it does not provide any justification for efforts to aid the second-poorest, even if this could be done without any loss to others.

It is by no means just a theoretical possibility that the second-poorest could be helped without cost to the rest of society. Indeed, the importance of this possibility is suggested by Rawls's first or liberal principle. If all individuals should be given the maximum liberty consistent with a like liberty for others, then the second-poorest could under this principle easily make a deal with someone of higher income that made them both better off and hurt no one else; this kind of thing happens every day when low-income people accept jobs that leave both them and their employers better off. Thus Rawls's two principles are not consistent with each other. Others have suggested that this problem could be solved by introducing a lexicographical ordering of the two principles wherein the liberal principle would always come first and the maximin principle would be invoked only after all mutually advantageous transactions (or, more precisely, all those without non-pecuniary external diseconomies) had taken place. But this does not answer the charge that Rawls's maximin principle takes no account of the interests of those who are just above the worst-off, and Rawls's fundamental insight does not in any case really call for a maximin principle rescued by a lexicographical ordering.

This is evident the moment we note that the somewhat bizarre implications of Rawls's maximin principle arise because, in deriving this principle, Rawls did not remain faithful to what, at least in my interpretation, is his fundamental and precious insight. Much of the appeal of Rawls's overall theory of 'justice as fairness' derives from its potential to convert apparently arbitrary disputes about conflicts of interests and differences in moral taste into soluble problems of rational decision-making under uncertainty. Rawls's first or liberal principle, for example, can be derived without departing from ordinary procedures for decision- making under uncertainty. The essence of the matter is evident when we realize that *taking all the possibilities into account* behind the veil of ignorance argues in favor of the principle that individuals ought to be allowed all liberty consistent with a like liberty for others. If one took account only of the possibility that one would be the only person in the society that had a certain preference or circumstance, so that one was a 'minority of one', then that would entail a principle that one was free to do what one wanted to do provided that no one else wanted to do it. But clearly it is rational behind the veil of ignorance to take account of the possibility that one might have a preference or circumstance that one shared with a minority, or even with all, of the population.

It is similarly rational to take account of the possibility that one could, in the world for which moral rules are being made, have any one of the conceivably important preference orderings or situations. Thus taking all the possibilities into account (or at least all those of any importance) calls only for those constraints on individual liberty that protect the legitimate liberties of others. Of course, the problems involved in determining exactly which individual liberties infringe on the liberties of others is, in certain cases, a complex and controversial matter. But these complexities and controversies do not alter the point that rational decision-making under uncertainty requires taking at least all the significant possibilities into account.

The strange implications of Rawls's maximin principle arise precisely because, in deriving this principle, Rawls did not take all significant possibilities into account. Rawls's maximin principle can be derived behind the veil of ignorance by taking into account exclusively the possibility that one will be the very poorest person in the society. Obviously, it is also possible that one might be the richest person in society, or the second-poorest, not to mention some in-between level of income. To get the maximin principle behind the veil of ignorance is like concluding that one should never leave the house on grounds that one might be struck by lightning, and ignoring completely the possibility that if one left the house one might instead stumble on a fortune, or fall in love, or have an ordinary day. Such a preoccupation is bizarre.

Naturally, a thinker as subtle and careful as Rawls offers many interesting arguments in favor of his maximin principle. His objections to taking all of the significant possibilities into account are notably evident in his section 28, on 'Some difficulties with the average principle'. One of the things Rawls does in this section is object to the procedure of assuming, on grounds of the principle of insufficient reason, that it is equally likely that one will be any one of the people or in any one of the income or primary goods levels of the society; the percentage of people in the society that will be in each category is, Rawls assumes, unknown behind the veil of ignorance, and there is accordingly no good reason to suppose that all possibilities are equally likely. Rawls claims that his position is

'. . . plausible in view of the fundamental importance of the original agreement and the desire to have one's decision appear responsible to one's descendants who will be affected by it. We are more reluctant to take great risks for them than for ourselves; and we are willing to do so only when there is no way to avoid these uncertainties, or when the probable gains, as estimated by objective information, are so large that it would appear to them irresponsible to have refused the chance offered even though accepting it should actually turn out badly'.[8]

Unfortunately for Rawls's maximin principle, there is no amount of risk aversion that will make the focus on the worst possible outcome generally the best solution. Suppose, not implausibly, that there are many people in the society who will be very near the bottom and only one who is worst-off. Then choosing the maximin principle, in addition to ignoring the possibility that the outcome would be average or better than average, also leaves one with no insurance at all against the many possibilities that are very bad even if not the worst possible. Even on Rawls's own assumptions about the decision-making behind the veil of ignorance, the focus on the worst-off is like buying a fire insurance policy for one's house that pays nothing at all when one's house burns down unless one also received the most serious possible burns in the fire, or like a life insurance policy on one's life that pays nothing to one's children unless, say, one's grandchildren happen to die at the same time.

19.6 The Relevance of Expected Utility Maximization

Normally, in economics, statistical decision-theory, and in applied work, rational decision-making under uncertainty is taken to be the maximization of 'expected utility'. That is what the individuals considered in von Neumann's and Morgenstern's *Theory of Games*, and Friedman's and Savage's gamblers and purchasers of insurance, were taken to be doing. It is probably unfortunate that economists and decision-theorists have kept on

[8] *A Theory of Justice*, p. 169.

using the word 'utility', inherited from their utilitarian forbears, in their analyses of rational choice, for this suggests a logically necessary connection with utilitarian philosophy that is not there. To the economist and the statistical decision-theorist, people tend to choose what they prefer, and if an individual gets more of whatever he wants, he has a higher level of 'welfare' or 'utility'. There is nothing in this that entails that one must, in the manner of the nineteenth-century utilitarian philosophers, necessarily advocate the goal of maximizing total social utility.

The idea that rational decision-making maximizes an individual's utility subject to the constraints given by his income and other limitations does not by itself entail any recommendation about whether a society should strive to maximize total utility or the average utility of the people in it. The statement that an individual has an increase in 'utility' is simply a shorthand for saying that that individual has attained his given objectives, whatever they happen to be, to a greater extent than before.

To say that rational decision-making maximizes 'expected utility' says little more than that decision-makers take *all* of their objectives, material and intangible, selfish and altruistic, into account; that so far as they are able they also take *all* of the possible outcomes of an uncertain situation into account; and that in addition they use whatever objective information or subjective judgments they have about the likelihood of the possible outcomes in estimating the probability of each of the contingencies. Then they choose what, all things considered, seems to them the best option.

Rational decision-making does *not* normally involve choosing the outcome with the highest expected *monetary* value, for this (as we learned from von Neumann and Morgenstern) neglects the different amounts of welfare or utility that a dollar will bring at each different level of consumption. If we decided to maximize expected monetary values, we would then, after we had made what appeared to be our optimum choice, have to think again about whether it really was the best choice considering the risks involved and our attitudes toward them. With standard rational decision-making under uncertainty it is expected utility that is maximized, so risks and our evaluations of their impact on our welfare are taken fully into account from the start.

Apparently the main attraction of the veil of ignorance, both to Rawls and to most of the legions of scholars he has influenced, is that it makes it possible to deal with long-intractable moral questions within the general framework of rational decision-making. Why, then, has not everyone who has used the justice-as-fairness approach assumed expected utility maximization behind the veil of ignorance? The whole spirit of expected utility maximization is in keeping with the derivation of Rawls's first or libertarian principle. But it is dramatically at variance with his focus, in deriving the maximin principle, exclusively on the possibility that one would be the worst-off. In his own formulation, Rawls seems almost to go out of his way to specify the *details* of the veil of ignorance in such a way as to rule out expected utility maximization.

Why have not Rawls's many followers and critics developed his insights in what, according to the argument here, is the only natural and proper way? Undoubtedly, some have done so, at least to some extent. John Harsanyi, who earlier worked out something analogous to Rawls's veil of ignorance,[9] has consistently assumed utility maximizing decisions. But why has not almost everyone done this? Why, when so many intelligent people have taken Rawls so very seriously, have so few been faithful (when considering the morality of institutions for determining the income distribution) to what seems to be his fundamental insight, of putting moral issues in a context which helps us resolve them in terms of valid principle of rational decision-making under uncertainty?

One remote possibility is that investigators were influenced by some experiments and opinion surveys, mainly relating to relatively uncommon situations, that suggest that most people do not, in certain types of situations, make consistent or rational choices, as they would do if they always successfully sought to maximize expected utility.[10] But the explanatory power of the hypothesis of expected utility maximization is so far ahead of any alternative theory that it is even hard to say what the leading alternative is.[11] And observed departures from rationality in some situations are not in any case relevant for prescriptive or philosophical inquiries, such as Rawls's or the one underway here.

19.7   The Error of Friedman/Savage

Just possibly the reason that so many people have avoided rational decision-making behind the veil of ignorance is that the logical implications of doing this, given the Friedman-Savage results, are (for most people) counter-intuitive and even shocking. When one uses a correct method of making decisions under uncertainty behind a properly specified veil of ignorance,

---

[9] 'Cardinal utility in economics and the theory of risk-taking', and 'cardinal welfare, individualistic ethics, and interpersonal comparisons of utility', in the *Journal of Political Economy*, **61**, pp. 434–5; and **63**, pp. 309–21.

[10] For a survey that gives considerable emphasis to these experiments and studies, see Paul J.H. Schoemaker, 'The Expected Utility Model', *Journal of Economic Literature*, **20**, June 1982, pp. 529–83.

[11] Some of the examples or experiments that appear to raise questions about the prevalence or appeal of expected utility maximization called into question the 'independence axiom'. For a demonstration that this axiom is not generally necessary to expected utility maximization see Mark Machina, 'Expected utility analysis without the independence axiom', *Econometrica*, **50**(2), March 1982, pp. 277–323.

and does this in the way that takes account of and accepts the well-known Friedman-Savage argument, one is *forced logically to come to the conclusion that social arrangements that generate inequalities of income far greater than those we have now are morally desirable, and would be morally desirable quite apart from any incentives for work and saving that they provide.*

The Friedman-Savage observation that most people both gamble and buy insurance appears to demonstrate that, even if we assume a fixed national income, a distribution of income with relatively few at middle-income levels, but many more poor and many more rich, would generate the most utility. Thus the normal and correct rational decision-making would appear to lead people behind any reasonably specified veil of ignorance to choose social institutions that would strive to *increase* inequalities in income, and would do so quite apart from any need for the incentives to work and to save that these inequalities provide. Maybe, in some subconscious way, the Friedman-Savage result may have kept Rawls's readers, or – no one can be sure – conceivably even Rawls himself, from using a natural and correct method of decision-making behind the veil of ignorance.

If those who read Rawls's book, in the decade or so after it first came out and was getting the most attention, had asked what were the implications of expected utility maximization behind a veil of ignorance, they would have had to deal with the implications of Friedman's and Savage's finding. And, unless they could have disproved the Friedman-Savage results, or introduced some very special and extremely dubious auxiliary assumptions, they would have had no choice but to conclude that the Rawlsian method suggests that the moral goal should be greater inequality of income. Whether it is historically accurate or not, it is interesting and intellectually useful to imagine that the unattractiveness of the result one gets by combining the veil of ignorance with the Friedman-Savage finding tended to keep many of Rawls's readers from using the veil of ignorance in an appropriate way.

In any case, we have a serious dilemma. If we use the Friedman-Savage finding, we get the strange result that we ought to have highly unequal incomes, whether any improvement in incentives flows from the inequality or not. On the other hand, if we follow Rawls, we end up with the invalid focus on the worst-off. Is there any escape from this dilemma?

Happily there is, at least as I see the matter. The escape from and resolution of this dilemma arose serendipitously. Two colleagues, Martin J. Bailey and Paul Wonnacott, and I happened to discover a compelling (and, so far as I know, undisputed) refutation of one part of the Friedman-Savage argument. It will turn out, as I shall soon attempt to show, that this discovery also lets us use Rawls's insights in a new and more convincing way.

The Friedman-Savage argument about gambling is not only counter-intuitive, but also demonstrably wrong, or wrong in ways that all competent parties of whatever ideology will concede. Unfortunately, the logical demonstration of the error in this argument is inevitably fairly technical, (see Bailey-Olson-Wonnacott 1980).[12] It is easy, though, to convey a sense of the flavor of the Friedman-Savage mistake. Suppose it were true that at very high levels of consumption or income we got a tremendous bang for the buck, and that at very low levels we also got a tremendous amount of utility per dollar. To shift to the efficient levels of consumption, we would not have to gamble; we could accomplish this by borrowing and lending. We could, for example, live for a time at the low levels of consumption that bring a high amount of utility per dollar and thereby save a lot of money. With these savings, we could live it up later, consuming at the high level of consumption that, by assumption, is also efficient in generating utility per dollar. Alternatively, we could borrow and live high-on-the-hog now and live at a low level of consumption later.

Bailey and Wonnacott and I have shown that, in almost all circumstances, borrowing and lending to obtain alternate high and low levels of consumption dominates, that is, by all criteria is superior to Friedman-Savage gambles. It would require a long detour to prove why this is so,[13] but in essence it is because our 'rate of time preference' is usually not equal to the interest rate, so saving or alternatively dissaving is, in the assumed conditions, bound to provide a gain. In addition, borrowing and lending are not usually taxed at such high rates as is legalized gambling.

But do most people save in a Spartan fashion and consume very little in order to live high-on-the-hog later, or spend wildly out of borrowing and drop to low levels of consumption later? These are by no means the most common types of behavior. Rather, people borrow and lend to *even out* their level of consumption. This suggests that the level of utility per dollar of income or consumption diminishes as consumption rises. If alternately high and low levels of consumption generated the most utility from a given permanent income, why would people strive to even out their level of consumption?

Another problem with the Friedman-Savage gambling argument is that is entails only a single – and very large – gamble, one that would result in the gambler being at one or the other of the efficient levels of consumption. In fact, we observe that most people who gamble do so repeatedly. Repeated fair gambles tend to leave a person at the same level of consumption he or she started with, and repeated unfair gambles will make one poorer. Thus, for these reasons and partly for others, we can be sure that most gambling is not motivated by the Friedman-Savage logic, but is rather due to a taste for adventure or a failure to know or comprehend the odds.

[12] 'The marginal utility of income does not increase: borrowing, lending, and Friedman-Savage gambles', *American Economic Review*, June 1980.
[13] See Mancur Olson and Martin J. Bailey, 'Positive time preference', *Journal of Political Economy*, 89(1), 1981, pp. 1–25.

Interestingly, the man in whose honor this volume has been written has been among the most emphatic on the role of adventure as a motive for gambling. In a paper that has not, so far as I know, been published, Gordon Tullock showed the strength of the demand for adventure by citing, among other things, the sums many people pay at amusement parks for rides designed to terrify and to convey the impression that the rider is taking a large or adventurous risk.

In summary, the Friedman-Savage argument about insurance holds, but their argument about gambling does not. The demand for insurance, the absence of the type of gamble that the Friedman-Savage utility function would call for, and the observed tendency to even out consumption suggest that there is a diminishing marginal utility of consumption and income. This matter is, to be sure, not nearly so simple as I have just made it out to be, but the technical complexities have been fully dealt with elsewhere[14].

19.8 The Case for Income Equalization

Thus the same method Friedman and Savage used, when corrected for logical errors, would seem to provide a strong case for limiting the degree of inequality in the distribution of income. But there is a gap in my analysis thus far that, unless it can be filled in, keeps us from being able to draw any such conclusion. The aforementioned observations on purchases of insurance and on the tendency for people to even out their levels of consumption over time indicate that, the higher the level of consumption an individual already has, the smaller the increment in satisfaction that a given increment in consumption will bring. But a diminishing marginal utility of consumption and income for a given individual does not by itself entail that a poor individual will necessarily get more utility from an extra dollar of consumption than a rich person. The fact that rich Smith and poor Jones both have a diminishing marginal utility of consumption or income does not make it certain that a shift of one dollar from Smith to Jones will increase total utility: Smith might get so much more satisfaction out of each dollar of consumption than Jones at each income level that he would get more utility from a marginal dollar than Jones even when he is rich and Jones is poor.

Here we must remember that the disputes about how much should be transferred to the poor are almost always about *general* policies or programs for low-income people. This is appropriate. No major group is advocating that some civil servant or government agency should examine each individual in the country, and then decide, without reference to any rule or standard, whether he should give or receive a transfer and how large such a transfer should be. The developed democracies, at least, are loath to give any official

---

[14] In the Bailey, Olson, and Wonnacott, and Olson and Bailey papers cited above.

or bureaucracy such power, and it is easy to see how such power could corrupt the democratic process. Programs of income transfers to low-income people in the developed democracies, at least, come under the 'rule of law'. In practice, officials and bureaucracies are given powers to determine such matters as whether a given recipient of public assistance is able to work or not, or how the tax laws apply in a particular case, but if an official or agency departs too far from the general laws of the land the matter may be appealed to independent court systems that are designed to uphold the general laws. Thus the practical problem that is at issue and is the subject of ideological debate is the nature of the general legislation that guides transfer to low-income people and how much money should be devoted to these programs.

This means that there is no need, for the present purposes, to deal with certain special cases. The problem of individuals who are regularly morose or depressed, irrespective of their levels of consumption, is an important problem, but it is mainly a problem for psychological or biochemical research, and does not have much to do with the case for or against income transfer programs. Similarly, the hypothetical individuals so often mentioned by critics of a certain type of utilitarianism ('act' utilitarianism), who might be fantastically efficient at converting consumption into utility, need not trouble us here.

If some group were to advocate a government program designed to allocate transfers and taxes to individuals, according as some official or agency deemed them to be efficient or inefficient producers of utility, then that group would have to confront at least the hypothetical possibility that its program could make some exceptional individuals very rich and others very poor, according as these individuals were deemed to be exceptionally efficient or exceptionally inefficient converters of consumption into utility.

But there is no need to answer any such question when considering general programs of transfers to low income people. The concern here, as in Rawls's book, is with the basic institutions or legislation that influence the broad outlines of the income distribution. So far as I am aware, no one suggests that any broad income class is made up mainly of people who are either morose or fantastically efficient at converting consumption into utility.

Since the concern here is with broad classes rather than exceptional individuals, we might fill in the aforementioned gap in the argument by pointing out that there is some basis for the claim that, in many cases, we can and do make rough interpersonal comparisons of utility that appear to generate consensus. These rough interpersonal comparisons suggest that people in different income classes are, in most cases, broadly similar in their need for income and in the satisfactions they get from it. Everyday language tells us that wealthy people tend to be 'well-off' and that there is reason to be concerned about the 'well being' of the poor. Indeed, even with respect to individuals there are sometimes interpersonal comparisons that generate consensus. If someone were being tortured, it would sound very strange and pedantic indeed to say that we could not know whether he was suffering because that would require an interpersonal comparison.[15] There is sometimes also general agreement that so-and-so is generally miserable, and (as IMD Little has pointed out[16]) this would not occur unless different people were drawing the same conclusions from their interpersonal comparisons.

There is, as this paper pointed out earlier, no infallible or totally objective method of making interpersonal comparisons. Thus we can well imagine that an actor of genius might totally mislead others about the extent to which his level of utility changed with his consumption levels. But surely no broad income class could be made up mainly of actors of genius, or of people who for any reason were so different from the rest of us that we could not even get rough and ready insights into their levels of welfare. Thus the gap in the argument here could be filled in by concluding that surely people in different income classes are at least broadly similar in their needs for and gains from extra consumption. It follows, then, that the foregoing evidence that an individual values extra income more when his income is low than when it is high also applies, at least in a statistical sense, to the different individuals in different income classes.

There is, however, no need to assume that we can make any interpersonal comparisons at all. My overall argument holds even if there is no information whatever about any differences in the heights of the marginal utility of income schedules of different individuals. All that is required is that there be a diminishing marginal utility of income or consumption. This point was demonstrated long ago by Abba Lerner[17] and has since been proven more elegantly by Amartya Sen and by others.[18] Perhaps because Friedman and Savage appeared to show, not very long after Lerner published his demonstration, that there was often an increasing marginal utility of income, Lerner's result is not as well known as it should be.[19]

[15] See I. Waldner, 'The empirical meaningfulness of interpersonal comparisons of welfare', *Journal of Philosophy*, 69, 1972.

[16] I.M.D. Little, *A Critique of Welfare Economics*, 2nd ed, London: Oxford University Press, 1957. On this general issue I have profited greatly from reading Amartya Sen, 'Interpersonal comparisons of welfare', and other essays in Sen's collection of essays entitled *Choice, Welfare, and Measurement*, Oxford: Basil Blackwell, 1982; and Cambridge, Mass.: Institute of Technology Press, 1982.

[17] Abba Lerner, *The Economics of Control*, New York: Macmillan, 1944, chapter 3, 'The optimum division of income', pp. 23–40.

[18] See Sen's 'On ignorance and equal distribution', *American Economic Review*, 63, December, 1973, pp. 1022–4, and in *Choice, Welfare, and Measurement*, cited above. See also Milton Friedman, 'Lerner on the economics of control', *Journal of Political Economy*, 55, 1947, pp. 405–16, and reprinted in Friedman's *Essays in Positive Economics*, Chicago: University of Chicago Press, 1953, pp. 301–19.

[19] I am thankful to a student participant in the Yale Legal Studies seminar in 1983 for calling Lerner's work on this to my attention.

The insight behind Lerner's demonstration is beautifully simple. Suppose the total social income is fixed at a level of, say 100, and that this social income is given by the total length of the horizontal axis in Figure 19.1 below. If individual *A* gets all of the social income we are at the extreme right of the figure, and the amount of income going to *B* increases as we move to the left from this point. Suppose we can make no interpersonal comparisons whatever and it is as likely that *A* has a higher marginal utility of consumption schedule than *B* as it is that *B* has a higher one than *A*. Assume we start at an equal distribution of 50 for each, and change to an unequal distribution of income that favors *A*. If the marginal utility of consumption schedules that are unknown to observers happen to be as they are drawn in this illustration, the gain in utility to *A* will be smaller than the loss in utility to *B*, and total social utility will have diminished by the amount in the area *G*. If, on the other hand, the income distribution had been tilted by a like amount in favor of *B*, the gain in social utility would have been only *H*, which is smaller than *G*. The downward slope of the marginal utility of consumption schedule that has been established is sufficient to show that an equal distribution of a fixed social income maximizes the expected value of total social utility. Thus interpersonal comparisons are not required for the argument that is offered here (see figure 19.1).

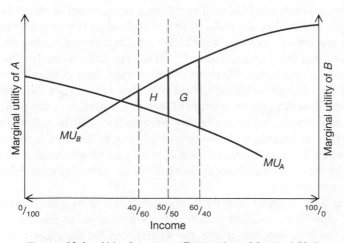

Figure 19.1 Abba Lerner on Diminishing Marginal Utility

Though the results that have been developed so far in this paper are of consequence even when taken by themselves, they have particularly satisfying implications in a Rawlsian framework. I argued that the general appeal of Rawls's argument was that it put questions of morals and the distribution of income in the context of the theory of rational choice under uncertainty, and thereby helped us bypass or abstract from certain conflicts of interest and of tastes. But Rawls's focus exclusively on the worst-off did not meet even the rudimentary requirement of rational choice that all possibilities should be taken into account, and for this and other reasons it fell far short of the expected utility maximization that rational decision-making under uncertainty requires. This in turn explained why Rawls's maximin principle had some strange and unappealing features, like the tendency to neglect the interests of those who were not quite in as bad a situation as the worst-off.

Though a veil of ingnorance cannot serve its function unless it abstracts from information that would give a decision-maker a personal bias, it is made more useful if it does not throw away relevant information about people or societies in general. In Rawls's particular formulation of the veil of ignorance, decision-makers had to know that incentives could have an influence on the level of national output, for they would not otherwise have agreed to allow those inequalities that made the worst-off better off. Decision-makers making rational decisions behind the veil of ignorance should similarly be allowed to know Lerner's result and to be aware that the marginal utility of consumption decreases with consumption.

Since reasoning behind the veil of ignorance should above all be completely impartial and without bias toward any individual or group, such a veil is not properly used unless it begins with the assumption that it is *equally likely* the individual be any of the people in the society to which the reasoning behind this veil of ignorance would apply. If it is assumed behind the veil of ignorance that the decision-maker would be, say, twice as likely to be a man as a woman, or (worse still) certain to be a man, then obviously reasoning behind the veil will be biased toward rules that favor males. Note that this requirement is not chosen because of lack of knowledge or the principle of insufficient reason, but rather on the grounds that it is the *only* assumption that is fully in keeping with the proper purpose of a veil of ingnorance: to help us reach fair and rational decisions on ethical questions that are not biased by the accidents of history that have given each of us a special position and therefore a bias.

Rawls goes to some lengths to argue that the 'principle of insufficient reason' does not provide a sufficient basis for the assumption that one is equally likely to have any role in the society; but his argument here, in my opinion, is profoundly erroneous. The need for this assumption is not due to any *lack* of knowledge – the whole idea is to abstract from or avoid having certain information that would give one's decisions a bias – but rather to the very purpose a veil of ignorance should have: to avoid the partiality that arises from those personal interests one has that give one a conflict of interest with others in the society, and this purpose is served beautifully by the assumption that it is equally likely that one will be any of the people in the society in question.[20]

Since the decision-maker behind the veil of ignorance is supposed to be rational, he maximizes expected utility. We know from our initial account of the von Neumann-Morgenstern insight that maximizing expected monetary values would be wrong because it would ignore risk and could not explain why we do things like buy insurance. But when we maximize expected utility we take full and complete account of risk: all the disadvantages of a 'risky' alternative are embodied in the adjustment we make, because of the diminishing marginal utility of consumption, for the disproportionate value of more consumption when we are badly off, and in the estimates of the probabilities that each contingency will occur. Profound as Rawls's book is, it seems to me to fail to take proper account of this elemental property of the treatment of risk in rational decision-making under uncertainty.

A rational decision-maker behind the veil of ignorance will take into account the possibility that he might have any situation in the society; he must take into account not only the possibility he would be the poorest but also the possibility he would be the second-poorest, or the richest or anything in-between. But given the declining marginal utility of consumption, the poorer he turns out to be the more he would value each dollar he obtained. He would value the consumption he would have if he were the poorest very highly indeed, but he would also give his consumption a high value if he were the second-poorest. He would give a significant if lesser weight to the consumption he would have if he had a moderate income, and a smaller but still positive weight to his consumption if he turned out to be rich. He would be definitely egalitarian, but at the same time he would be humanistic, in that he would give some weight to gains in consumption for any human being. This implication is not only more widely acceptable than Rawls's minimax result, but it is also derived by a method more in keeping with what I have (like some others) taken to be Rawls's most important innovation.

If the Friedman-Savage result were correct, a valid procedure for decision-making behind the veil of ignorance would lead decision-makers to choose rules that would generate great inequalities. Because it is wrong, and because of Lerner's result, the decision-maker behind the veil of ignorance will in fact vote for an equal distribution of income if the size of the social income is fixed and all other things are equal; this will maximize his expected utility. This result, as it happens to turn out, is in an important sense no less egalitarian than Rawls's finding, but it is the result of observations of

[20] I discovered after drafting this argument that much the same argument was made long ago by John Harsanyi. See, for example, his 'Morality and the theory of rational behavior', in *Social Research*, 44(4), Winter 1977, reprinted in Amartya Sen and Bernard Williams, eds, *Utilitarianism and Beyond*, Cambridge: Cambridge University Press, 1982, pp. 301–62.

individual behavior toward risk and rational decision-making under uncertainty behind a perfectly impartial veil of ignorance, not an artefact of an inappropriate assumption that one should ignore all the world's possibilites except the one that one will be worse off than everyone else.

19.9   The Problem of Moral Hazard

So, if other things, and most notably the size of the social income, are equal, we know that egalitarian distributions of income will tend to generate more utility than inegalitarian ones. Though this is an important result, we know that other things are *not* equal. The decisive significance for public policy of the things that have been left aside can best be seen by returning to look at the same insurance markets that have already been so suggestive.

Suppose we consider what happens if we buy casualty insurance for our automobile, or for that matter most other kinds of insurance. In general, we cannot get one hundred per cent insurance; that is, we are not usually allowed to insure ourselves completely against all loss. Some amount of any loss from a collision is not covered. This uninsurable amount is sometimes larger than it appears to be, partly because premiums may automatically rise if one has a claim, and partly because we are almost never paid for the time we lose when we file a claim and have the needed repairs done. One part of the reason for the deductible amount is obviously to save administrative expenses, but this is definitely not the only reason. This is shown by many types of evidence, such as the prevalence of 'co-insurance', which makes the purchasers of many types of insurance (for example, some kinds of health insurance) pay a specified percentage of the loss on any claim. There is no reason to suppose that this normally saves administrative costs.

The main reason for co-insurance and one of the main reasons for deductibles is what in the literature on the insurance industry has been called 'moral hazard': the increase in the likelihood that the contingency insured against will occur because of the insurance. Why take as much trouble to avoid hitting the fire hydrant and bending the fender if the insurance company will pay all of the costs of fixing it? Why go to the trouble of making sure one chooses a hospital or physician that gives good value for money if the insurance companies bear all the cost? The importance of moral hazard is also shown by the easy availability of some kinds of insurance (such as insurance for farmers' crops or tornado insurance) where moral hazard is nil, and the special difficulty of buying insurance against cont ingencies where moral hazard is especially high: private companies are normally unlikely to offer unemployment insurance, partly because the likelihood that one will keep a job, or zealously seek another if it is lost, is influenced by whether the insurance company or the unemployed person bears the loss.

A private insurance company that would offer us insurance against unemployment has another problem as well. The people who are not planning either to work very hard or ardently to search for a new job if they become unemployed know that they have a greater likelihood of unemployment than others. The insurance company has no way to look into the heads of insurance applicants to see what the applicants' true intentions are and the applicants often have an incentive to conceal these true intentions; so there is an asymmetry in the availability of information between those who want insurance and those who sell it. The people who do not plan to work hard at jobs or at job-searching obviously have more incentive to try to buy unemployment insurance, at any given schedule of premiums and payout rates, than those who plan to go all-out to avoid unemployment. That means more payouts for the insurance company, and that in turn means higher premiums. This could make private unemployment insurance unattractive for those who will do everything possible to avoid unemployment, so the private insurance company is then left with an unrepresentative set of risks.

In the extreme this can mean no private insurance is available at all; indeed, private unemployment insurance has never been common, for this reason. The problem at issue is that of 'adverse risk selection' – the tendency for those who are more likely to have claims to want to purchase the insurance – and this in turn is due to an asymmetry of information that keeps the insurers from knowing as much as the applicant does about the likelihood he will have a claim and adjusting premiums accordingly.[21]

There is no way for a private insurance company to avoid this problem for a vast variety of contingencies, and as a result the market does not offer insurance against most of the risks of life. There is no way to buy insurance against poverty, or the failure of a marriage, for example.

For some other important risks there is what I like to call the problem of the 'impracticable sequence'. It is not possible, obviously, to buy insurance before one is born, and thereby to insure oneself against an unlucky draw in the lottery at birth which determines what health and abilities one will have, and even what quality of upbringing and size of bequest one will receive. Thus the market does not offer anything resembling insurance against the risks of birth, or to some extent even of childhood. Only multi-generational institutions are able to buy insurance in advance against bad draws in the lottery at an individual's birth.

---

[21] Any satisfactory explanation of the operation of markets is a rather long story. There is a substantial literature on this subject, only a small part of which I know. For example, see George Akerlof, 'The market for "lemons"', *Quarterly Journal of Economics*, 84, 1970, pp. 488–500; Michael Rothschild and Joseph Stiglitz, 'Equilibrium in competitive insurance markets', *Quarterly Journal of Economics*, 90, 1976, pp. 629–50; Mark V. Pauly, 'Overinsurance and the public provision of insurance', *Quarterly Journal of Economics*, 88, 1974, pp. 44–45; Michael Spence and Richard Zeckhauser, 'Insurance, information, and individual action,' *American Economic Review*, 61, 1971, pp. 380–7.

   A government can get around the problem of asymmetrical information
and the adverse risk selection that results from it by making insurance
compulsory and thus insuring everyone (or everyone in various objectively
defined categories). This is, of course, what many countries have been doing
in the case of unemployment insurance. Governments can also provide
insurance in cases where the sequence is impracticable for the individual,
such as protection against an inadequate endowment at birth, and since
governments also can often implement policies that will survive over many
generations, they are not constrained as separate individuals are to
considering only choices within a given generation. Governmental programs
to aid the mentally retarded, the mentally ill, and those with severe defects of
birth or upbringing can usefully be understood in this way.

   Indeed, the whole range of welfare-state or social insurance programs can
best be understood as manifestations of the imperfections or absence of an
insurance market, or the impossibility of the individual purchasing insurance
in advance of the adverse contingency. The welfare state is universal and
compulsory and can avoid adverse risk selection, and it can also provide the
insurance that the individual cannot purchase because of the impracticable
sequence.

   There is evidence in favor of this interpretation in that, at least in the most
prosperous and successful countries, governments usually do not provide
those types of insurance which the market provides relatively efficiently and
which the individual has the option of purchasing in advance. Governments
do not usually provide hail insurance or fire insurance, for example. With
these types of insurance the insurance company can have much the same
information as the buyers of insurance, so these is not much adverse risk
selection, and it is obviously possible to buy these kinds of insurance before
the adverse contingency occurs. Surely at least the wiser governments do not
provide these types of insurance because there is no need for the government to protect people against risks they can protect themselves against
through the market, and very often at a lower cost.

   There is further evidence in favor of the argument in this essay in the fact
that other institutions usually do offer some insurance against those
contingencies, such as poverty or misfortunes at birth, against which the
market offers the individual little or no opportunity to insure. In modern
developed countries a large part of this insurance is provided by the welfare
state, but some such insurance is also provided by the nuclear family. In
times past, and in some developing societies even today, these types of social
insurance are often provided by tribes, jatis or sub-castes, and extended
families. In these traditional social institutions there are various tribal or
familial obligations that are also more or less compulsory and thereby largely
avoid adverse risk selection, and the intimate and long-lasting social
relationships may also mean that there is little asymmetry of information.

Like governments, tribes and families are, of course, multi-generational institutions that are not constrained by the impracticable sequence.

In the light of the analysis offered in this essay, these practices of modern welfare-state governments and of traditional social institutions can also be normatively reasonable. The widespread purchase of insurance when this is provided efficiently by the market, the tendency to smooth out consumption over time, and the absence of the types of gambles that a Friedman-Savage utility function would call for, all show that there is a diminishing marginal utility of consumption. We saw, with the aid of Lerner's argument and a properly specified veil of ignorance, that when social income is fixed, rational decision-making leads to the choice of an egalitarian income distribution (as well as to the maximum liberty consistent with the liberty of others).

But what about moral hazard? This increase in the probability that the event insured against will occur is by no means eliminated by socialized insurance. A traditional tribe or extended family may sometimes be able to deal with this through close monitoring and intimate social control, but the large, modern welfare state has no such resources, and is very possibly not even as good as the private insurance market in dealing with moral hazard. We can see that if unemployment insurance replaces one hundred per cent of the income we lose when we quit, then we have no incentive to work. The familiar belief that an excessively generous welfare state weakens the incentive to work and to save is true. As anyone who has mastered the relevant literature knows, there are very many kinds of evidence that individuals are responsive to incentives. But the truth of this familiar belief is evident most directly by observing the insurance market once again, and noting the provisions for deductibles and co-insurance that insurance companies need to survive the competition of other insurance companies. The insurance market shows that protecting individuals against any adversity that can be influenced by an individual's behavior creates moral hazard. I have shown elsewhere,[22] that the distortions of incentives arising because of organized interest groups representing the non-poor are far more damaging to economic efficiency than are the programs of aid to the poor in the developed democracies today. The losses from these programs are nonetheless significant, and the losses from a welfare state that offered anything approaching one hundred per cent insurance would be unsustainable. No system of insurance, public or private, can ignore the reality that, if you insure too much, you subsidize and multiply the very adversities that inspired the demand for insurance.

---

[22] 'Supply-side economics, industrial policy and rational ignorance', in Claude E. Barfield and William A. Schambra, eds, *The Politics of Industrial Policy*, Washington and London: American Institute for Public Policy Research, 1986, pp. 245–69.

19.10   An Unoriginal Solution

Early on in this essay I indicated that it could not offer a new answer to the question about how much ought to be transferred to the poor, since about every broad answer to this question had already been given, and that the focus would be rather on the method by which the answer was derived. It is evident now that the answer I have provided is not only unoriginal, but also the most commonplace of all the answers to the question. It appears to be the answer that guides public policies not only in all of the developed democracies but in many primitive societies and in various families and other social institutions as well. The belief that the poor need additional consumption much more than the rich do and that it is morally desirable to have programs that transfer some resource to the poor, but that one must not make these programs so generous that poverty becomes more attractive than an earned income, is a belief so common that it is sometimes deemed to be only 'common sense'.

There are, of course, some who disagree with the 'common sense' view on the ground that there should normally be no transfers to the poor, and others who disagree on the ground that society can, at least in certain institutional contexts, get the output it needs without offering incentives that generate inequalities of income. Advocates of one or the other of these latter two positions are not necessarily wrong because they are in a minority or because their opponents claim the support of common sense – very often experience eventually shows that is was only a small minority that really had any common sense; that is why papers like this one are necessary. I am nonetheless pleased that there is so much concordance between common sense or opinion and the conclusions that I have reached with an uncommon combination of standard scientific procedures. As Thomas Huxley once said, 'science is ... nothing but trained and organized common sense, differing from the latter only as a veteran may differ from a raw recruit: and its methods from those of common sense only so far as the guardsman's cut and thrust differ from the manner in which the savage wields his club'.[23]

Neither common sense nor this paper provides the detail and the quantitative specificity that are needed to choose wise public programs to aid low-income people. It makes a great deal of difference just how programs of transfers to the poor are organized and just how generous or austere they are, and it would take a very long essay indeed to deal adequately with these matters. The way that we deal with these matters should, moreover, be influenced by new information as it becomes available. If more detailed research should show that the desire to insure against adversity, and the

[23] Thomas Huxley, *Weiner*, 1953, p. 130, quoted in Blaine Roberts and Bob R. Holdren, *Theory of Social Process*, Ames, Iowa: Iowa State University Press, 1972, p. 23.

costs (say, in the form of actuarily 'unfair' odds) that people are willing to pay for it are greater than previously supposed, then that would argue for somewhat more generous programs to aid low-income people than would otherwise have been appropriate. If, on the other hand, detailed research should show that the moral hazard or losses from impaired incentives that arise from private insurance and welfare-state insurance are larger than previously supposed, that would call for less generous programs than otherwise.

There are also other aspects of the question of how much should be given to the poor that this paper has not considered, but which should in practice be taken into account. There are even perfectly admissible (if somewhat untypical) value judgments that can be made that would, for those who shared these value judgments, call into question the pertinence of the approach I have offered; there is no suggestion here that this method involves no value judgments or ideology at all. The approach offered here is nonetheless much more open to objective research, constructive debate and open-minded reflection than are the familiar ideologies of the left and the right, which by now probably subtract more than they add to the quality of our thinking and policy choices.

19.11 Conclusions

If what has been said so far here is correct, much of Gordon Tullock's work can have a usefulness that many of his readers might never have expected. Some of his readers, and readers of works by others in the Virginia School, could certainly be excused for picking up the impression that this work demonstrates or claims to demonstrate that there should be no welfare-state policies. At the least, it may be said that the Virginia School has not devoted much effort to prevent this impression from being picked up. As I see it, the most notable contributions of Gordon Tullock and the Virginia School indicate that there is a variety of heretofore unsuspected ways in which everyday human motivations will keep political processes and government programs from working in a Pareto-efficient fashion, and will sometimes make some of these processes and programs work very badly indeed. How badly or how well the political and governmental mechanisms work will depend in part on how they are designed. As someone who (though not in the Virginia School) has done some work in the field of collective or public choice that has some of these same implications, I should not have to dwell on why I think work of this kind can be useful. It is undoubtedly important to note that political and governmental mechanisms, like other human institutions, will work imperfectly, and if the structure of incentives implicit in the design of the political and bureaucratic institutions is sufficiently perverse, these institutions will do a great deal of damage.

This is, of course, also true with respect to welfare-state institutions, though as I showed in the aforementioned article on 'Ideology and Economic Growth'[24] there are several reasons why distributional coalitions or special-interest groups will do significantly less damage to economic efficiency where programs for the poor are concerned than in most other areas. Thus, in calculating the costs of public programs to aid the poor, one must expect not only the moral-hazard losses inherent in most kinds of insurance, but also additional costs that arise from the imperfect workings of the welfare bureaucracies and the mistakes the political system will normally make when deciding on transfers to the poor.

The extent of these losses will be less if public policies and institutions to aid the poor are designed with the aid of the theory of collective choice, including that of the Virginia School in general and that of Gordon Tullock in particular. (In other words, the advocates of welfare-state transfers need to know the work of Gordon Tullock and the Virginia School just as much as others do.) With intelligent institutional designs, there will be less waste and the society will have more resources at its disposal. If the argument in this chapter is correct, the *same analysis of incentives and behavior that is the staple of public or collective choice* also shows that some of these resources ought to be devoted to transfers to the poor. For the man to whom this volume is dedicated, there is the further implication that all those generous acts need not be concealed, for such acts are nothing to be ashamed of!

---

[24] Charles R. Hulten and Isabelle Sawhill, eds, *The Legacy of Reaganomics* . . . , Washington, DC: The Urban Institute, 1984, pp. 229–52.

20

A Political Economy of Budget Deficits

MARGARET A. MONACO and
CHARLES K.ROWLEY

20.1 Introduction

For the classical economists, with only Malthus dissenting,[1] budget balance
was an uncontroversial issue in political economy. Consensus existed that
budgets should balance, not just taking one year with another, but more
generally, even across periods of recession and major war. Even the sinking
fund was viewed with suspicion[2] as a potential Trojan horse threatening the
existing balanced budget order, especially in Britain, emerging as the world's
richest nation as a consequence of the industrial revolution.

The classical economists (Rowley, 1987) were not driven, in their support
for balanced budgets, by contemporary efficiency objectives alone, at least in
the narrow ends-related sense emphasized by late twentieth-century welfare
economics.[3] The drive was as much libertarian in nature, and in particular,
was based on a fear that government, able to finance its growth by
deficit-financing, would over-extend its activities, thereby threatening or
destroying individual rights. Such governments would engage too easily, in
foreign wars, with the cost of such adventures borne by future taxpayers.[4]

Smith's views on balanced budgets were conditioned additionally by his
anti-mercantilist philosophy. The state, which had become the bulwark of a
far-ranging system of trading privileges, monopoly grants and tariffs, was

---

[1] Malthus (1798) was unconvinced by the market-clearing, equilibrating mechanisms of the
supply-driven classical model. He feared demand-deficiency and viewed deficit financing as a
not-outrageous preventive device.

[2] See Levy (1987, p. 99) Characteristically, Ricardo gave a crisp and to the point statement of
the issue: "The sinking fund", he wrote, "instead of diminishing the debt, greatly increased it".
This attribute of sinking funds, to provide an easy source of the funding of new government
expenditures, is a variation on an eighteenth and nineteenth-century classical economic theme
that debt financing of public expenditure was preferred by taxpayers to tax financing.

[3] On this see Coats (1971) especially p. 6.

[4] Adam Smith (1776) most particularly emphasized the imperialistic consequences of deficit
financing of wars.

viewed as grossly inefficient, transferring savings from merchants and industrialists, which it wasted in riotous consumption. This transfer was particularly damaging for a capital-poor economy, as England still was in the late eighteenth century. The requirement to balance the budget at least imposed a tax constraint on governments that otherwise might defer, even perhaps eventually default on, the costs implicit in their wasteful expenditures.[5]

Smith was also clearly aware of the burden of the debt issue which, much later in 1961, was to be ridiculed by Abba Lerner[6] and jettisoned by Keynesians, despite James Buchanan's spirited resuscitation of the notion in 1958. Smith's insight was that the bondholder underwent no sacrifice when the debt was created, but rather made money by lending it to the government. In thus recognizing the mutuality of advantage from voluntary exchange, Smith signaled an approach to public debt analysis which was later developed and extended by other classical economists. In essence, this insight placed a major burden of debt creation on future generations, even ignoring the diversion from capital creation to consumption on the expenditure side of the budget. In this contribution, Smith anticipated almost by two centuries the important public choice notion that the vote motive operates powerfully in favor of budget deficits in an unconstrained environment.[7] It is to this important issue and its implications for constitutional and/or legislative reform within the United States budgeting system that this chapter addresses itself.

20.2   The Burden of the Debt

When governments contemplate expenditure decisions, they are simultaneously confronted with a choice-influencing cost[8] of how to finance such outlays as may be endorsed – through taxation, money creation, debt issue or even outright default.

Under the regime of taxation, current spending is paid for by taxpayer citizens in the same time period. Resistance to taxes will tend to constrain the magnitude of expenditure decisions. This regime maximizes transparency in the budgeting process. Under the regime of money creation, which is open to the government or its agents in the absence of non-discretionary constraints, there is an implicit inflation tax imposed on all citizens some 18

---

[5] On this see Rowley (1987).

[6] Who dismissed the burden of the debt issue contemptuously with the statement: 'We owe it to ourselves' (Lerner 1961).

[7] Ricardo also was aware of default potential and was not at all an advocate of what is now referred to as the Ricardian equivalence theorem.

[8] On this see Buchanan (1969).

months to two years after the money creation. Although inflation is resented, the link between it and money creation is less transparent and those who are well informed can alleviate expected damage.[9] Under the regimes of debt creation and default, the apparent cost of the expenditure decision is postponed and may or may not be incurred by those who benefit from the expenditure decision, depending on their age and life expectancies together with the anticipated time-horizon of debt retirement and/or default.[10]

Adam Smith, as we have noted, was opposed to debt financing both because it crowded out more productive private expenditures in favor of less productive government expenditures and because it imposed a tax burden on future generations when they would be called upon to retire existing debt. David Ricardo, whilst agreeing with Smith about the crowding-out effect, denied the inevitability of the taxation burden imposed on future generations. In what is now referred to as the Ricardian Equivalence Theorem, Ricardo spelled out a list of stylized conditions under which taxation and government debt become equivalent in their economic effects.[11]

The following seven conditions are required for the theorem to hold:

1 the same level of expenditure will be made regardless of the method of finance;
2 the debt is expected to be retired via future taxes;
3 perfect capital markets exist;
4 lifetime earning prospects are known;
5 individuals act as if they expect to live forever;
6 individuals capitalize future taxes via savings when current debt is issued; and
7 all taxes are lump sum.

Ricardo was quite explicit in his own writings that these conditions failed to hold in the real world.

In 1974, in an influential paper, Robert Barro took up the argument based on this theorem. Arguing on the basis of Ricardo's assumptions, Barro suggested that individuals are benevolent toward future generations (their children) and do not wish to burden them with the cost of their own current consumption. Parents thus increase the bequests to their children by an amount sufficient to retire the public debt they have accumulated, thereby avoiding any burden on their descendants.[13]

---

[9] Under anticipated inflation almost everyone will protect themselves. Where inflation is unanticipated it is a tax on those who hold wealth denominated in nominal terms.

[10] On this, see Buchanan (1987).

[11] Ricardo did not believe that the conditions held in real world economies.

[12] See Brennan and Buchanan (1987).

[13] See Barro (1974, p. 1116)It was shown that households would act as though they were infinitely lived, and, hence, that: 'there would be no marginal net-wealth effect of government bonds, so long as there existed an operative chain of intergenerational transfers which connected current with future generations'.

This extension of Ricardo's theorem implies that as government spending increases, private saving follows suit by some present-value, determined in order to offset the implied tax on future generations, thus reducing if not entirely eliminating the crowding-out effect. In such circumstances, the primary concern of both Smith and Ricardo about deficit-financed expenditures is sharply reduced. Superficial econometric evidence, by Levis Kichin (1974) and others, which demonstrates a high positive correlation between the size of the United States federal deficit and the rate of private saving, does not refute Barro's hypothesis.[14] (But see Feldstein, 1976.)

Barro's theory, however, looks decidedly unconvincing within the context of the contemporary United States economy. Under the balanced budget constraint, it is true that taxpayers have incentives to become acquainted with their own taxation implications of alternative government expenditure proposals. Even so, such calculations cannot be precise *ex ante*, given the complexity of tax incidence analytics and the difficulty experienced both within Congress and the executive in correctly assessing the budgeting implications of specific expenditure/taxation regimes. Present value calculations, in such circumstances, assume an especially nebulous characteristic.

Once the prospect of unbalancing the budget is embraced, all credibility concerning Barro's theorem completely evaporates. The future taxation implications of current debt are simply non-forecastable, given the opportunities available to governments to default, if not overtly, then via the inflation tax. Even if debt retirement dates are definitive, and perceived so to be, capital markets are far from perfect with respect to individual taxpayers who cannot lend and borrow necessarily at the same interest rates as the government.[15] Indeed, liquidity-constrained taxpayers may gain access to credit in some instances only at rates of interest massively higher than the return on bonds, as credit card experience clearly demonstrates. In such circumstances, to talk about the equivalence between debt and taxes is misguided.

Barro's intergenerational model claims that individuals act as if they will live forever through their benevolence toward their offspring. Yet, within the contemporary United States, individuals are tending to marry later, if at all, one half of all marriages end in divorce, and many parents fail to make their court-mandated child-support payments even under the threat of imprisonment for contempt.[16] Since the overall birthrate is declining as well, there is a fundamental question-mark over the inter-generational linkages model.

---

[14] Econometric testing using current deficits ignores the impact of the inflation tax on the stock of real national debt. This may go far to explain the private saving phenomenon in the US.

[15] One wonders if Barro has ever attempted to borrow at interest rates available to government, save in the case of mortgage finance.

[16] To say nothing about the sizeable homosexual population in the US. Perhaps San Francisco is excluded from the model.

The portion of the population with, at best, a weak positive link or, more bleakly, with a strong negative link, is evidently increasing. There is no reason to believe that such a population can be relied upon to draw down its current consumption in order to make good in bequests the tax burden that it imposes on future generations.[17]

Even that population with a strong positive linkage may under-capitalize the future tax burden as a consequence of myopia and/or of fiscal illusion. In both cases, such under-capitalization, *ex ante*, will tend to raise the level of government expenditures, to increase the rate of debt accumulation and thus to accentuate the burden bequested to future generations. Of course, the incidence of myopia and/or of fiscal illusion is an empirical issue – and one that has been explored extensively in the rational expectations literature. We share Tobin's (1980) skepticism concerning the degree of far-sightedness that can be expected of the ordinary individual in society where the welfare of others is at stake.

20.3 A Public Choice Perspective

The 'new' welfare economics which emerged during the early 1950s, (Little, 1951) and which still dominates the economics profession, despite some rise in skepticism, envisages government as the impartial and omniscient servant of the public good always ready to rectify the failure of markets. Public choice, which emerged during the early 1960s and represents a growing challenge to the old orthodoxy, views all actors in the political process – voters, politicians, bureaucrats and special interests – as pursuing utility-maximizing personal goals subject to environmental constraints. In an ironic twist, therefore, public choice posits a theory of government failure and counterbalances that notion against the theory of market theory so extensively researched by advocates of the new welfare economics.

At its worst, in the public choice prespective, the political process is viewed as a transfer mechanism, (McCormick and Tollison, 1981) brokering wealth away from the less successful rent protectors, typically unable to organize themselves effectively for collective action, in favor of special interests capable of powerful rent-seeking activities. In return for such services, politicians receive votes or wealth contributions from those who participate in the rent-protection/rent-seeking exercise, whether success-fully or not. To a not insignificant extent, the resources dedicated to this process are shifted from potentially productive to evidently unproductive ends, and are wasted to individuals in society.

The public choice perspective offers an extremely powerful insight into

---

[17] Especially if the threat of nuclear annihilation exerts its intertemporal price.

the United States budget deficit problem as it has emerged and grown since 1960; (Buchanan and Wagner, 1977; Buchanan Burton and Wagner, 1978). Deficits arise, in this perspective, because politicians in Congress, and the President responding to executive pressure, find it to be in their respective self-interests to take the easy way out in budgetary politics. By generating tax cuts and spending increases through the budgetary process, in-period politicians enhance their prospects of political survival. Those who look to tax increases and expenditure reductions as a fulcrum for political advancement tend to find their vote base in decline and their wealth expectations in ruins.

The role of disappearing environmental constraints in shifting the United States economy in 1960 from a century of overall budget balance to over a quarter-century of escalating budget deficits is difficult to exaggerate (Buchanan, Rowley, Tollison, 1987). The first constraint to go was the Gold Exchange Standard, which was systematically weakened by the Federal Reserve System from the latter's inception in 1913 and which was repudiated by President Roosevelt in 1933 as part of the New Deal. With the demise of this constraint, politicians and their bureaucrats were freed to raid the printing press in order to defraud debt-holders via the inflation tax, and to indulge in budgetary profligation without confronting significant political costs.

Of course, the shift away from gold was a slow, albeit a continuous, process in post-New Deal America. Bretton Woods provided an intermediate, fixed exchange rate alternative which offered greater political discretion than was the case with gold, but which still constrained fiscal prodigality in the absence of devaluation default. By 1971, however, a decade of budget deficits, facilitated by a loosening monetary policy, brought retribution in terms of an international dollar surplus. The 1971 repudiation of the dollar's link with gold removed the last vestige of externally-imposed fiscal and monetary constraint.

The second constraint on fiscal prodigality to be slackened following the Second World War was the moral resistance, inculcated most notably during the Victorian era, against the burdening of future generations with a negative national debt bequest. The impact of two world wars, the holocaust in Europe, the atomic bomb destruction of entire populations in Japan, and mass murder in Russia as an instrument of Stalinist collectivization, undoubtedly exerted a powerful impulse in favor of myopic hedonism in the United States as elsewhere. The strengthening grip of relativist philosophy, associated with loosened sexual morality and the decline in the absolute values of the late Victorian period, also played a major role. First, the extended household concept was swept away. Then, even the nuclear household became vulnerable, and with it, the inter-generational linkage so central to Barro's analysis.

The third important constraint limiting deviations from the principle of budget balance, the notion that thrift was equally praiseworthy for government as it was for households, was swept away after 1945 by the writings of John Maynard Keynes and his disciples (Rowley, 1987). The so-called 'paradox of thrift' denied the link between household and governmental budgetary morals, as an apparent fallacy of composition. The concept of a 'burdenless debt' consigned classical fears of deficit financing to some 40 years of policy irrelevance. The emphasis placed on stabilization policy offered budget imbalance a central role in the political process. By 1960, United States institutions had adjusted to such messages and an era of unremitting budget deficits began to unfold.

20.4   The Relevance of Constitutional Economics

The public choice perspective, epitomized by spatial politics in the sense of Downs (1957), by interest groups in the sense of Olson (1965), by bureaucracy in the sense of Niskanen (1971), by rent-seekers in the sense of Tullock (1967) and by congressional policy brokering in the sense of Tullock, (1981) Crain and Tollison (1979), is pessimistic in the extreme. The perspective, full of insight as it is, is driven by the most despairing vision of mankind, in that wealth-maximizing agents universally and relentlessly engage in wealth destruction, locked, apparently inescapably, into a horrendous prisoners' dilemma.[18]

Yet, in this environment of despair, there remains hope for those who desire to combine wealth-achievement with a democratic political system which offers the minimal prerequisite for liberty.[19] Indeed, there is clear evidence in the high living standards enjoyed by most United States citizens that self-mutilation is bounded by the institutions of a free society. Constraints exist, and, for the most part, such constraints are man made. In the United States at least, constitutional economics offers a relevant insight into the mechanism of escape from the public choice prisoners' dilemma. *The Calculus of Consent* (Buchanan and Tullock, 1962) was the seminal text presented to the economics profession by Buchanan and Tullock as providing the logical foundations of constitutional democracy. An understanding of the essential message of this book is essential for a full appreciation of the case advanced in favor of the balanced budget amendment to the United States Constitution.

The Calculus, drawing on the explicit form of the United States Constit-

---

[18] For an excellent discussion of this prisoners dilemma within a constitutional perspective see Buchanan (1980).

[19] Buchanan (1986) led a spirited attack on dystopia and urged public choice analysts to search for institutional reforms designed to restore a constrained utopia.

ution, with its two-tiered layering of federal decision-making, distinguished sharply between the behavior of individuals within existing political markets delineated by constitutional rules, and the behavior of those same individuals in formulating or amending the constitutional rules themselves. Within the former environment, in the absence of externally imposed constraints, man is endlessly and myopically self-seeking. However, at the constitutional level, he is capable of rule selection on the basis of a much more far-sighted, if yet still solipsist, vision. The outcome of the tense struggle between these two forces itself determines the wealth-enhancing or wealth-destructive nature of any polity.[20]

Decision-making at the logically prior, higher constitutional level is viewed, within the framework of *The Calculus*, in essence as a social contract, forged consentaneously by all individuals in society. As such, it spells out the rules under which society will operate. It sets forth the form of government and the nature of the polity within which it operates; the vote mechanism both for constitutional amendments and for the lower level legislative bodies; the separation of powers between the executive, the legislature and the judiciary, and the nature of oversight of each part by the others; the relationships between the federal government and the individual states; and the rights of individuals with respect to government itself.

All such rules are relevant to any evaluation of the constitutional route to budgetary reform. Whether or not the original contract is truly consentaneous is debatable, though *The Calculus* suggests that such may well be the case.[21] The 1787 constitutional convention in the United States certainly reported *nemine contradicendi*, in large part as a consequence of vigorous log-rolling. It is doubtful, however, that its recommendations met with universal consent throughout the emergent nation.[22] Fundamentally, the Founding Fathers forced Americans to be free, by introducing vote mechanisms designed to minimize the joint cost of transactions and of external diseconomy, whilst providing additional safeguards against tyrannical majorities which not infrequently had induced migration from the European democracies.

At the highest level of decision-making, the vote mechanism is only infrequently relied upon, only rarely invoked.[23] Individuals thus are more concerned, at this level, to protect themselves from external costs imposed by others than to minimize the transaction costs of the vote mechanism. It is

---

[20] In essence, whether a political market will be governed by a beneficent invisible hand or by some potentially malevolent visible boot.

[21] On the relevence of rent-seeking for the consent calculus see Rowley in Rowley, Tollison and Tullock (1987).

[22] A number of representatives absented themselves from the convention when final voting occurred. The slave population evidently was not consulted.

[23] The convention route has not been utilized since 1787.

not surprising, within this context to find that the United States Constitution requires a substantive supra-majority vote (initially two-thirds, but ultimately three-quarters whichever route is used) for constitutional amendments. By requiring such a high degree of consent, decisions are rendered more difficult to achieve; but the potential cost to individuals from collective action is sharply reduced.

At the lower, operational, level of government, however, decisions necessarily must be easier to reach and also to undo. The transaction costs of decision-making here assume much greater significance. Moreover, the external costs of collective action, at this level of government, are constrained by the higher level constitutional constraints. Predictably, the vote requirement will be lower as a consequence of this shift in the balance of costs. A simple majority requirement is usual in such circumstances.[24] In the United States, the effective vote requirement is higher than this as a consequence of the bicameral legislature and the role of the presidential veto power. Fears of the tyrannical majority forced this outcome despite the added transaction costs that the supra-majority vote requirement inevitably imposes.

A public choice evaluation of the United States budget deficit problem and an appraisal of reform possibilities assumes quite different characteristics in the constitutional as contrasted with the legislative perspective. Important differences arise precisely because the vote mechanism differs with respect to those separate levels of collective decision-making. We now turn to a comparative public choice analysis of the balanced budget amendment to the United States Constitution and The Balanced Budget and Emergency Deficit Control Act of 1985[25] as the two most keenly debated methods of returning the United States economy to long-term budget balance.

20.5 The Constitutional Route to Budgetary Reform

The public choice analysis of the United States budget deficit phenomenon powerfully suggests that the legislative and executive branches of government are incapable of effective internal reform.[26] Deficit financing, especially when it has been operative over an extensive time period, has an overwhelmingly powerful political constituency which can be ignored without a real fear of political retribution only during periods of acknowledged national emergency. Neither politicians nor presidents have been

---

[24] *The Calculus of Consent* is silent on the size of the preferred lower level majority (or indeed minority) vote. All depends on the structure of the external cost and the decision cost functions, which will vary from society to society and within a society over time.

[25] Known popularly as the Gramm, Rudman, Hollings Act.

[26] On this see Buchanan, Rowley and Tollison (1987), chapter 1.

prepared to withstand such pressures since 1960 when the United States economy first moved into almost permanent deficit, despite continuing evidence that a substantial majority of the United States electorate favors a return to budget balance.

In this perspective, the budget reform initiative, even if it should emanate from the legislature, with or without executive support, will not be sustained through the many exigencies of the political market that offer special interests the opportunity to log-roll against its continued application. Binding constraints on budget deficits, however powerful the underlying vote motive in their favor, can only come from above. The issue of constitutional amendment, costly though that process is, cannot be avoided if the public choice insight is accepted (Rowley, 1987).

Article V of the United States Constitution offers two routes to constitutional amendment, one initiated by the Congress and the other by the States. The article reads as follows:

The Congress, whenever two-thirds of both Houses shall deem it necessary, shall propose Amendments to this Constitution, or, on the Application of the Legislatures of two-thirds of the several States, shall call a Convention for proposing Amendments, which in either case, shall be valid to all Intents and Purposes, as part of this Constitution, when ratified by the Legislatures of three-fourths of the several states, or by Conventions in three-fourths thereof, as the one or the other Mode of Ratification may be proposed by the Congress.

It is clear from the wording of this Article that the president plays no role whatsoever in the formal process of constitutional amendment. The legislatures, both at federal and at state levels, are empowered *exclusively* to initiate and to effect amendments subject, of course, to constitutional surveillance by the judiciary. Even so, the two routes to reform pose distinct problems from the viewpoint of public choice.

The Constitution has been amended only twenty-six times since 1787, ten of which concerned the Bill of Rights. In each case, the method employed was that of congressional initiative. Although several hundred resolutions have been submitted to Congress by the states, requesting national constitutional conventions, none has proved successful. For this reason, the convention route has been called 'a constitutional curiosity', or 'one of the best known dead letter clauses of the Federal Constitution'.

The congressional route to a balanced budget constitutional amendment is not an impossibility; but it is fraught with all the public choice problems outlined above. Why would Congress provide two-third majorities in both Houses for a permanent balanced budget constraint upon its fiscal discretion when it cannot muster the simple majority necessary for balancing the budget in a single year of economic boom? Only an extremely determined president, in the first half of the first term, favored by majority representation in both Houses, would have any realistic chance of log-rolling such an outcome. No such president has emerged since the 1960 political market adjustment in favor of deficit financing in the United States.[27]

Even if a balanced budget amendment were to be brought before Congress under such favorable conditions, it could not possibly be evaluated within that context as a limited proposal. Special interests, potentially damaged by the amendment, would log-roll their favored policies in return for equivalent support elsewhere. School prayer and anti-abortion amendments to the United States Constitution are predictable outcomes, to say nothing of specific self-serving legislative provisions. In such circumstances, the wording of a balanced budget amendment predictably would be loose, reflecting log-rolled opportunities for special interests to escape the full force of its implementation. At best, each house of the Congress would provide a lame amendment, mutilated further in conference discussions designed to reconcile the divergent interests of the separate Houses.

Of course, Congress is not immune to the threat of the alternative amendment route, in the conduct of its own business. Upon occasion, Congress has amended the Constitution in order to avoid the convention alternative. For example, the Bill of Rights was introduced by a reluctant Congress in 1789 in response to convention petitions by Virginia and New York. Similarly, the seventeenth amendment, which provides for the direct election of senators, was driven through a reluctant Senate in response to a spate of state petitions that otherwise would have activated the convention mechanism.

Thus, although the convention route is yet unused, it has exerted influence over the constitutional amendment process.[28] In the case of budget balance, it may well be activated directly by state petitions. In such circumstances, the rules governing the convention assume important public choice dimensions. The rules essentially must be inferred from the Constitution itself, since the United States is a government of delegated powers, possessing no authority save that conferred upon it by the Constitution. This is especially important since the convention was viewed as a method of bypassing a hostile Congress. Unfortunately, Article V is less than explicit concerning the rules that govern a constitutional convention and thereby offers opportunities for congressional interference that only the United States Supreme Court could nullify.

Congress clearly must call a convention where the conditions defined by

[27] President Reagan, who has maintained a consistent rhetoric in favor of budget balance has equally consistently preserved large budget deficits as a means of retarding the expenditure appetite of the US Congress.
[28] Congressional amendments to the constitution not untypically have occurred under the shadow of the convention threat.

Article V are satisfied. If it failed to do so, the United States Supreme Court would be pitted against the legislature, however reluctant the Court might be to accept justiciability; and the United States Constitution would be in extreme jeopardy. Inevitably, however, Congress possesses discretionary power in determining whether or not the conditions of Article V have been met. Predictably, it would utilize this discretion to its own perceived advantage.

First, the Constitution is silent concerning the relevant time span over which state applications may be regarded as jointly relevant. By narrowing rather than widening this time span, Congress legitimately might rule out a convention even when two-thirds of the states have so petitioned. In guidelines yet not enacted, Congress has discussed seven years as the outer limit for jointly evaluated state petitions. In the event that two additional states should choose to join the 32 that have already petitioned for a balanced budget convention, the time limit defined by Congress would play a quite definitive role. The concept of contemporaneity thus exerts a powerful influence in the amendment process.

Second, the Constitution is silent concerning the criteria whereby state petitions should be bundled together by Congress in determining whether or not the two-third criterion has been satisfied. Should all state petitions, irrespective of interest, be so bundled? Or should only those petitions of similar nature be jointly considered? And if the latter, should Congress be the ultimate adjudicator? Or is this an issue of justiciability ultimately vested in the United States Supreme Court? Bills not yet enacted would allow the bundling of only closely related state petitions.

Third, and closely related, is the issue as to whether a convention must be open, or can be limited to the single issue on which the states have petitioned. This is an issue of substance from the public choice perspective. If the convention must be limited, the balanced budget amendment would be debated as a single issue. In such circumstances, log-rolling is impossible and the one-man, one-vote principle would effectively apply. Should the convention be open, however, as was the case in 1787, log-rolling would dominate and special interests well might overwhelm the underlying two-third majority on the specific balanced budget issue. The scaremongers among the constitutional lawyers most opposed to the Article V convention route raise the specter of a return to slavery, or even the assumption by the convention of sovereign rights, as occurred essentially in 1787. Fortunately, it is not in the congressional interest to allow an unlimited convention; and the limited convention, therefore, is the predicatable public choice outcome.

Fourth is the undecided issue of the procedural rules that would govern the convention in its deliberations. The Constitution once again is silent on this issue. The 1787 convention adopted its own rules of internal procedure, essentially relying on a simple majority vote and a quorum requirement of seven states. Inevitably, the delegates sought for supra-majoity agreement wherever possible, in order to enhance the probability that the Constitution would be ratified. They achieved unanimity among those signing the final proposal, though several delegates absented themselves from that meeting.

Predictably, Congress might attempt to influence rule selection in the late twentieth-century environment. Bills on this issue have sought to impose a requirement that three-fifths of the delegates must vote for rules for such rules to be effective. They have sought also to impose a requirement that two-thirds of the delegates must vote in favor of an amendment for that amendment to be proposed for ratification. In our view, such enactments, if effected, would be unconstitutional. The ratification rules themselves protect the consensus thrust of the ArticleV amendment process.

Fifth, and finally, the Constitution is silent on the precise mechanism of the ratification process, for proposals emanating from the constitutional convention. Article V indeed requires that proposed amendments submitted by a convention to Congress must be ratified by legislatures or conventions of three-fourths of the states in order to become effective. Important additional issues are not dealt with by the Constitution.

First, there is no guidance concerning the relationship between the original convention issue(s) and the actual amendments that might be proposed by a constitutional convention. Bills before Congress, if enacted, would attempt to regulate the convention by blocking the submission of amendments that lay outside the terms of the initial convention resolution. Whether or not such legislation is constitutional is an unresolved issue largely dependent upon the Supreme Court's interpretation of the justiciability of political issues.

Second, there is no provision concerning a time limit for ratifying constitutional amendments proposed by a convention. Nor is there an indication of who might set such a limit. Most constitutional lawyers expect Congress to fill this void. One Bill, before the House of Representatives, would provide a standard seven-year limit. Another, before the Senate, would permit the convention to set the limit, failing which the Senate would act, albeit constrained to a minimum time limit of four years.

Finally, it remains an open question whether the states are free to rescind their ratifications prior to the overall satisfying of the Article V condition. Probably they would not be allowed to do so. At state level, Congress has consistently denied the right to rescind, and the Supreme Court has deferred to Congress on this political issue. In any event, if ratification was by convention, rescission would be impossible once the convention had been dissolved.

In the event that all the above-mentioned difficulties can be overcome, and a suitable amendment passed, the enforcement mechanism itself at present does not exist. If Congress and the president should fail to secure a constitutionally-mandated budget balance, what action, if any, would the Supreme Court take? Is it realistic to anticipate the impeachment of a president and 535 elected politicians for failure to satisfy the Constitution? Or would the Supreme Court opt for survival and deem the issue to be non-justiciable, thereby avoiding an explicit constitutional crisis?

The convention route to constitutional reform, inevitably, is clouded by considerable uncertainty following two centuries of non-utilization and as a consequence of an absence of detailed constitutional guidelines. Even if it were to be activated, a balanced budget amendment, finally ratified and implemented, might well take until the early years of the twenty-first century. In the interim, nominal debt would continue to rise, and the specter of default, either implicitly via a combination of domestic inflation and exchange rate depreciation, or explicitly via repudiation, would continue to haunt the United States political economy. It is not surprising, in such circumstances, that pressure has mounted for straightforward legislative measures to remove the deficit phenomenon.

20.6   The Legislative Route to Budgetary Reform

Scholars critical of the balanced budget amendment proposal, for example James J. Kilpatrick (1986), often naively suggest that the appropriate solution is to elect 'responsible people'. Public choice has long disposed with this notion as a failure to comprehend the nature of spatial politics. Politicians who attempt to win elections in order to carry out their preferred policies are unlikely to be successful unless such policies coincide with the preferences of some decisive set of the electorate.[29] In the absence of binding constraints, public choice suggests that politicians who actively work to balance the budget – as distinct from those who act to widen the deficit whilst employing a balanced budget rhetoric – are unlikely to be electorally popular in the short run.

In principle, of course, Congress possesses the legislative authority to balance the budget, either by lowering appropriations, or by raising taxes, or by some combination of both measures. Even the presidential veto may be overridden by a two-third majority vote of each house. The Supreme Court could only intrude on such legislation if its constitutionality were to be subjected to challenge. In practice, however, procedures are more complex and even the separation of powers is not as distinct as the Founding Fathers might have supposed.

The executive branch, as personified by the president, can usually exert

[29] Or unless they are successful via entrepreneurship in reshaping voter preferences to conform with their own policy preferences.

powerful pressures upon individual members of the legislature – pressures which well may prove decisive on specific issues of legislation. Congressmen not infrequently are obligated to the president for electoral success, or may look for presidential support in up-coming elections. They are also aware of the influence of presidential rhetoric in adjusting electoral opinions on specific policy issues. In such circumstances, a popular president can dictate the congressional agenda and massage the legislative product. A veto threat offers additional log-rolling opportunities to a determined executive branch.

Congress itself differs from the conventional parliament evident in the European democracies in that party discipline is far less pronounced. In essence, this makes for a pluralist rather than a majoritarian system of government, in which elected representatives are much more vulnerable to special-interest group pressures and in which log-rolling and vote trading exist in much more explicit form. The systematic weakening of party leadership control over committee chairmanship, the loosening of seniority rules, and the mushrooming of the subcommittee system, since 1970, have further accentuated pluralism. The dramatic increase in the number of and outlays by political action committees over the past decade witnesses to the lobbying advantages offered via a decentralized Congress. In combination, these developments have exacerbated the United States budget deficit problem, by ensuring that all attempts within Congress to consolidate a central budget have been doomed to fail.

20.7 The Balanced Budget and Emergency Deficit Control Act 1985

The 1985 Act, more popularly known as the Gramm-Rudman-Hollings Act, was borne out of despair via a Congress out of time with its budget and fearing an adverse vote reaction to a \$2 trillion public debt. It was legislated with the support of congressmen opposed to its central provisions who were stalling for time, trusting that the Act would be ignored, would be reversed or would be found to be unconstitutional. It was signed into law by an other-issues-preoccupied president who was ultimately committed to maintaining and/or to advancing real outlays on defense and social security, the two largest items of federal expenditure, whilst simultaneously holding down tax rates in a slowly growing economy. This was no clarion call for a counter-revolution in United States budgetary politics.

The 1985 Act is fundamentally suspect on constitutional grounds since the 1985 Congress was concerned to bind the legislation of future Congresses, something which the Constitution prohibits. Certainly, any future Congress is free to overturn the Act by simple majority vote of both Houses supported by the presidential signature or by a two-third majority override of a presidential veto (even perhaps without the override if constitutional challenges succeed). Such is the flimsy protection provided by a legislative constraint, in stark contrast to the constitutional constraint.

In addition, however, the 1985 Act was quite clearly unconstitutional (Witt 1986) with respect to its sequester clauses, a fact confirmed by the 1986 judgment of the United States Supreme Court. The Act provided that the Comptroller General should activate automatic across-the-board expenditure cuts if the budget forecasts of the Office of Management and Budget and the Congressional Budget Office, as arbitrated by the General Accounting Office, failed to achieve the deficit reduction targets of the Act. The Comptroller General is an appointee of Congress, and his intervention via the sequester route evidently infringed the separation of powers so carefully built into the United States Constitution. That Congress and the president failed to recognize this infringement in 1985 demonstrates the carelessness with respect to the Constitution which has been a hallmark of the Reagan administration. That remedial legislation will not succeed is a predictable outcome of legislative politics.

The entire sequester process thus has been removed, leaving only a vulnerable fall-back position for the 1985 Act. The budget reports of the OMB and the CBO now must be submitted to a special joint committee of Congress which must report to both Houses within five days in the format of a joint resolution. This joint resolution is considered under special rules, and, if passed, and signed by the president, it serves as the basis for a constitutionally acceptable sequestration order. Self-evidently, in the absence of initial compliance with the deficit reduction targets of the 1985 Act, the vote motive is back in place. The ultimate sequestration constraint does not exist. Both the president and the 1986 Congress appeared to be undisturbed by this return to them of discretionary power in budgetary politics.

20.8 Loopholes in the Legislative Route to Budgetary Reform

In the absence of any history within the United States of a constitutional or legislative balanced budget constraint at the federal level of government, research into the actual behavior of government when confronted with such constraints has proceeded instead at the state level (Rowley, Shughart and Tollison, 1987). Care must be exercised in extrapolating from states to federal governments, since the budgets of the former are very much smaller, and since the states are not responsible for defense and social security outlays which constitute the major problem for budget balance at the federal level. Equally important, the states do not possess the default options available to the federal government, most notably with respect to the latter's readier access to the printing press. Yet some parallels may usefully be drawn.

Empirical analysis[30] clearly indicates that constitutional debt limits and budget-balance requirements do not reduce borrowing to zero. For example, West Virginia, constitutionally proscribed from debt accumulation and constrained to budget balance, borrowed $68 million during 1982. Multiple regression analysis confirms, however, that deficit financing can be constrained constitutionally to approximately one half of that predicted in the absence of such constraints. In contrast, legislative constraints appear to exert an insignificant effect.

Moreover, published statistics on the states' budgets predictably are distorted by the existence of budget-balance constraints. Research by Bennett and DiLorenzo (1983) indicates that when state expenditures are capped, either constitutionally or legislatively, politicians and state agencies redefine favored projects into off-budget categories and fund them via off-budget enterprises. Off-budget enterprises (OBEs), which take the organizational form of authorities, districts, commissions and agencies, finance their activities through bonds which are issued without voter approval. When revenues fail to finance such bond issues, the ensuing shortfall is met from the state budget. Such bonds are issued without state guarantees, and typically carry higher interest rate burdens.

Similar off-budget activities already exist at the federal level of government, as Bennett and DiLorenzo indicate. Among the federal OBEs are the Federal National Mortgage Association, the Federal Home Loan Bank, the Farm Credit Administration, and the Student Loan Marketing Association. A large portion of the loans and bonds issued through these agencies is purchased by the Federal Financing Bank (FFB), which is a part of the Treasury Department. Yet such borrowings do not appear in the Treasury's budget as expenditures or outlays. Perversely, when such loans are repaid, this is treated as a reduction in outstanding expenditures. It is noteworthy that much of the federal government's off-budget activity has occurred since 1974 when the Budget Control Act focused public attention on the nature and the size of the federal budget. Gramm-Rudman-Hollings attempted to counter such developments by tightening the definition of OBE activities. Whether such a tightening will be sustained once public asset sales no longer serve as a convenient political loophole for achieving deficit reduction targets remains to be seen.

---

[30] See Rowley, Shughart and Tollison (1987). Regression analysis clearly delineated interest groups and public sector employees as the two major determinants of deficit financing at state levels. Constitutional constraints typically halved the deficit that otherwise would have been predicted.

20.9   Conclusions

The route to United States budgetary reform at the present time is clouded with uncertainties and obstructed by the many-faceted objectives of special interest groups spawned by a pluralist polity which caters for a society increasingly involved in wealth transfers rather than in wealth creation. The issue of budget balance itself is controversial even among fiscal conservatives, given the 'supply side' view that tax reductions may usefully create deficits which in turn constrain the size of the federal government. Supply siders like Stockman and monetarists like Milton Friedman have forcefully argued, for example, that budget balance without expenditure limitations would render fiscal conservatives the tax collectors for a colossal welfare state.

For those who are concerned to achieve balance, and to protect the future generations from coercive transfers of wealth, public choice offers pessimistic insights, as this paper attempts to show. Despite the pessimism of the public choice story, however, we should like to conclude on a more optimistic note. The self-interest axiom which drives public choice analysis is powerful; undoubtedly it is for the most part dominant in political markets. It is not, however, the only force at work. Altruism may be only a small part of most individuals' motivation, but it evidently exists, as private charity demonstrates. Altruism harnessed to high quality political entrepreneurship can be an overwhelming force in specific areas of policy, as the recent tax reform revolution has shown. Perhaps budget balance in the post-tax reform era will attract a comparable entrepreneurial talent. Gordon Tullock is one of the few public choice scholars who would share such optimism. It is fitting therefore to end a book dedicated to the work of so fine a scholar with a conclusion derived from his own 'law' concerning human behavior which distinguishes him from the vast majority of his profession.

References

Barro, Robert J. (1974) 'Are government bonds net wealth?', *Journal of Political Economy*, **82**, November/December.

Barro, Robert J. (1976) 'Reply to Feldstein and Buchanan', *Journal of Political Economy*, **84**, April.

Bennett, James T. and DiLorenzo, T. (1983) *Underground Government: The off-Budget Public Sector*. Cato Institute.

Brennan, Geofrey and Buchanan, James M. (1980) 'The logic of the Ricardian equivalence theorem', *Finanzarchiv*, **38**, 1.

Buchanan, James M. (1958) *Public Principles of Public Debt*, Homewood, Ill.: Irwin.

Buchanan, James M. and Tullock, Gordon (1969) *The Calculus of Consent: Logical Foundations of Constitutional Democracy*, Ann Arbor: University of Michigan Press.

Buchanan, James M. and Wagner, Richard E. (1977) *Democracy in Deficit, The Political Legacy of Lord Keynes*. New York: Academic Press.

Buchanan, James M., Burton, J. and Wagner, R. E. (1978) 'The consequences of Mr. Keynes', Institute of Economic Affairs, Hobart Paper 78.

Crain, W. Mark (1987) 'Legislatures and the durability of deficits', in J.M. Buchanan, C.K. Rowley, and R.D. Tollison, (eds) *Deficits*. Chapter 15, Oxford: Blackwell.

Feldstein, Martin (1976a) 'Perceived wealth in bonds and social security: a comment', *Journal of Political Economy*, **84**, April.

Feldstein, Martin (1976b) 'Social security and private savings: international evidence in an extended life-cycle model', in M. Feldstein and R. Inman (eds) *The Economics of Public Services*.

Kichin, Levis (1974) 'Are future taxes anticipated by consumers?', *Journal of Money, Credit and Banking*, **27**, August.

Lerner, A.P. (1961) 'The burden of the debt', *Review of Economics and Statistics*, **43**, pp. 139–41.

McCormick, Robert E. and Tollison, Robert D. (1981) *Politicians, Legislation, and the Economy: An Inquiry into the Interest Group Theory of Government*. Boston: Martinus Nijhoff.

O'Driscoll, J. and Rizzo, Gerald P. (1977) 'The Ricardian nonequivalence theorem', *Journal of Political Economy*, **85**, pp. 207–10.

Little, T.D. (1951) *A Critique of Welfare Economics*. Oxford: Oxford University Press.

Padover, Saul K. (1983) *The Living Constitution*. New American Library.

Peterson, Paul E. (1985–6) 'The new politics of deficits', *Political Science Quarterly*, Winter.

Rowley, Charles K. (1987a) 'Classical political economy and the debt issue', in J.M. Buchanan, C.K. Rowley and R.D. Tollison (eds) *Deficits*, Oxford: Basil Blackwell.

Rowley, Charles K. (1987b) 'John Maynard Keynes and the attack on classical political economy', in *Deficits*.

Rowley, Charles K. (1987c) 'The legacy of Keynes: from the general theory to generalized budget deficits', in *Deficits*.

Rowley, Charles K. (1987d) 'The calculus of consent'. Chapter 5 of this book.

Rowley, Charles K. (1987e) 'The constitutional route to effective budgetary reform', in *Deficits*.

Rowley, Charles K. and Elgin, Robert, (1985) 'Towards a theory of bureaucratic behavior', in D. Greenaway and G. K. Shaw, (eds) *Public Choice, Public Finance, Public Policy*, Oxford: Basil Blackwell.

Rowley, Charles K., Shughart, William F. and Tollison, Robert D. (1987) 'Interest groups and the deficit', in *Deficits*.

Schick, Allen (1986) *Crisis in the Budget Process, Exercising Political Choice*. American Enterprise Institute.

Schick, Allen (ed.) (1983) *Making Economic Policy in Congress*. American Enterprise Institute Studies in Political and Social Processes.

Shepsle, Kenneth A. and Weingast, Barry R. (1981) 'Structure-induced equilibrium and legislative choice', *Public Choice*, 37, 3.

Tobin, J. (1980) *Asset Accumulation and Economic Activity*. Oxford: Basil Blackwell.

Tullock, Gordon (1981) 'Why so much stability?', *Public Choice*, 37, 2.

Witt, Elder (1986) 'High court re-examines separation of powers', *Congressional Quarterly*, 19 April.

APPENDIX

The Scholarship of Gordon Tullock 1954 Through 1986

Books Authored and Co-authored

The Calculus of Consent: Logical Foundations of a Constitutional Democracy (with James M. Buchanan). Ann Arbor: University of Michigan Press, 1962; Paperback, 1965; Spanish Translation, 1980; Japanese Translation, 1980.

The Politics of Bureaucracy. Washington DC: Public Affairs Press, 1965; Paperback, 1975.

The Organization of Inquiry. Durham, NC: Duke University Press, 1965.

Toward a Mathematics of Politics. Ann Arbor: University of Michigan Press, 1967; Paperback, 1972.

Private Wants, Public Means: An Economic Analysis of the Desirable Scope of Government. New York: Basic Books, 1970; Spanish Translation, 1979; Japanese Translation, 1984. *The Logic of the Law.* New York: Basic Books 1971.

The Social Dilemma: The Economics of War and Revolution. Blacksburg, Center for Study of Public Choice, 1974; Japanese Translation, 1979.

The New World of Economics: Explorations into the Human Experience (with Richard B. McKenzie). Homewood, Ill.: Irwin, 1975; 2nd edn, 1978; 3rd edn, 1980; 4th edn, 1984; Spanish Translation, 1980; Japanese Translation, 1981; German Translation, 1984.

Modern Political Economy: An Introduction to Economics (with Richard B. McKenzie). New York: McGraw-Hill, 1978.

Trials on Trial: The Pure Theory of Legal Procedure. New York: Columbia University Press, 1980.

The Economics of Income Redistribution. Hingham, Mass.: Kluwer-Nijhoff Publishing, 1983; second Printing, 1984.

Books Edited

A Practical Guide for the Ambitious Politician Columbia, SC: University of South Caroina Press, 1961.

Public Choice (since 1968). This journal was initially entitled *Papers on Non-Market Decision-Making,* 1966–68.

Explorations in the Theory of Anarchy Blacksburg, VA: Center for Study of Public Choice, 1972.

Further Explorations in the Theory of Anarchy, Blacksburg, VA: Center for Study of Public Choice, 1974.

Frontiers of Economics. Blacksburg, VA: Center for Study of Public Choice; Vol. I, 1975; Vol. II, 1976; Vol. III, 1980.

Public Choice in New Orleans. Blacksburg, VA: Center for Study of Public Choice, 1980.

Towards A Theory of the Rent-Seeking Society jointly edited with James M. Buchanan and Robert D. Tollison. Texas A & M University Press, 1981.

Toward a Science of Politics: Papers in Honor of Duncan Black. Blacksburg, VA: Center for Study of Public Choice, 1981.

The Simons' Syllabus, Henry Calvert Simons Fairfax, Virginia Center for Study of Public Choice, George Mason University, 1983.

The Political Economy of Rent-Seeking (jointly edited with Charles K. Rowley and Robert D. Tollison) Bingham Massachussetts: Martinus Nijhoff, 1987.

Monographs and Occasional Papers

The Sources of Union Gains. Research monograph, Thomas Jefferson Center for Political Economy, University of Virginia, 1959.

The Fisheries: Some Radical Proposals. Essays in Economics, Bureau of Business and Economic Research, University of South Carolina, February 1962.

Entrepreneurial Politics. Research monograph no. 5, Thomas Jefferson Center for Political Economy, University of Virginia, February, 1962.

Fragments for a Theory of International Politics. Research monograph No. 8, Thomas Jefferson Center for Political Economy, University of Virginia, 1964.

Colloquium on the Welfare State (Papers read in a debate between Charles Frankel of Columbia University and the author arranged by the Department of Philosophy, Pennsylvania State University). Occasional Paper No. 2, Thomas Jefferson Center for Political Economy, University of Virginia, December 1965.

A Model of Social Interaction. Monograph, Virginia Polytechnic Institute and State University, November, 1968.

The Vote Motive, with a British commentary by Morris Perlman. London: Institute of Economic Affairs, Hobart Paperback No. 9, 1976; Spanish Translation, 1980, Madrid; Spain: Espasa Calpe, Translated by Maria Jesus Blanco; French Translation, *Le Marche Politique*, 1978, Paris, France: Association Pour L'Economie Des Institutions.

Svenskarna Och Deras Fonder: En Analys av LO-SAPs Forslag. Timbro; Utgiven av Forlags AB Timbro, Stockholm: KREAB, Kreativ Information AB, 1978.

Welfare for the Well to Do, Dallas: The Fisher Institute, 1983.

Reprinted Excerpts from *The Calculus of Consent*

'The Search for a Majority Rule', in Bean and Buchner (eds) *Readings on American*

Government Concepts in Context (p. 241ff), pp. 327–34. 'The Orthodox Model of Majority Rule', in A. J. Robinson and James Cutt (eds) *Public Finance in Canada: Selected Readings*, Toronto: Methuen Publications, 1968, pp. 60–73 (from appendix).

'The Costs of Decision Making', in Bruce M. Russett (ed.) *Economic Theories of International Politics*, Chicago: Markham Publishing Co., 1968, pp. 455–71 (from Chapter 8, pp. 97–115).

'The Calculus of Consent', in Stewart Macauley and Lawrence M. Friedman (eds) *Law and the Behavioral Sciences*, Indianapoli: Bobbs-Merrill, 1969, pp. 56–75 (from chapter 10, pp. 131–45.

'The Democratic Calculus', in Henry S. Kariel (ed.) *Frontiers of Democratic Theory*, New York: Random House, 1970, pp. 78–80 (from pp. 266–7, 304–6).

'A Generalized Economic Theory of Constitutions', in Rene and Bruno Frey (eds) *The Economic Approach to Politics* Tubingen, Germany: J. C. B. Mohr, 1972, pp. 63–84.

'Simple Majority Voting', in Rene and Bruno Frey (eds) *The Economic Approach to Politics*, Tubingen, Germany: J. C. B. Mohr, 1972, pp. 131-45.

'Una teoria economica generalizzata delle scelte constituzionali', in Francesco Forte and Gianfranco Mossetto (eds) *Economia del Benessere e Democrazia* Milano: Franco Angeli Editore, 1973, pp. 681–93 (from pp. 63-84).

'Regole di votazione a maggioranza qualificate, rappresentanza, e interdipen-dendenza delle', in Francesco Forte and Gianfranco Mossetto (eds) *Economia del Benessere e Democrazia*, Milano: Franco Angeli Editore, 1973, pp. 681–93 (from pp. 211–22).

'Eine allgemeine okonomische Theorie der Verfassung', in Hans Peter Widmaier (ed.) *Politische Okonomie des Wohlfahrtsstaates: Eine Kirtische Darstellung der Neuen Politischen Okonomie* Frankfurt am Main: Athanaum Taschenbuch Verlag, 1974, pp. 63–84.

'Simple Majority Voting', in Bruce A. Ackerman (ed.) *Economic Foundations of Property Law*, Boston: Little, Brown, 1975, pp. 238–47 (from pp. 131–45).

Articles

'Hyper-inflation in China, 1937–40' (with Colin Campbell), *Journal of Political Economy*, **62**, June 1954, pp. 237–45.

'Paper money: a cycle in Cathay,' *Economic History Review*, **9**, June 1956, pp. 393–407.

'Some little understood aspects of Korea's monetary and fiscal system' (with Colin Campbell) *American Economic Review*, **47**, June 1957, pp. 336–40. Translated into Korean and published in Seoul National University's *Economic Journal*.

'Reply,' *American Economic Review*, **48**, September 1958, pp. 661–2.

'Problems of majority voting', *Journal of Political Economy*, **67**, December 1959, pp. 571–9.

'Reply to a Traditionalist', *Journal of Political Economy*, **69**, April 1961, pp. 200–3.

'Problemi del voto a maggioranza', in Francesco Forte and Gianfranco Mossetto (eds) *Economia del Benessere e Democrazia*, Milano: Franco Angeli Editore, 1973, pp. 459–71.

Reprinted in Kenneth Arrow and Tibor Scitovsky (eds) *Readings in Welfare Economics* (Homewood, Ill.: Irwin 1969, pp. 169–78.

Reprinted in Thomas Schwartz (ed.) *Freedom and Authority: An Introduction to Political Philosophy* (Encino, CA: Dickenson Publishing).

'An economic analysis of political choice', *Il Politico*, 16, 1961, pp. 234–40.

'Hobson's imperialism', *Modern Age*, 7, Spring 1963, pp. 157–61.

'Public debt: who bears the burden?' *Revista di Diritto Finanziario e Scienza dette Finanze*, 22, June 1963, pp. 207–13.

Reprinted in James Ferguson (ed.) *Public Debt and Future Generations*, Chapel Hill: University of North Carolina Press, 1964.

'The irrationality of intransitivity', *Oxford Economic Papers*, 16, October 1964, pp. 401–6.

'The revolution in fiscal theory', *Public Administration Review*, March 1965, pp. 85–9.

'Constitutional Mythology', *New Individualist Review*, 3, Spring 1965, pp. 13–17.

'Entry barriers in politics', *American Economic Review*, 55, May 1965, pp. 458–66.

'Public and Private Interaction Under Reciprocal Externalities' (with James M. Buchanan), in Julius Margolis (ed.) *The Public Economy of Urban Communities*, Washington DC: Resources for the Future, 1965, pp. 52–73.

'Optimality with monopolistic competition', *Western Economic Journal*, 4, Fall 1965, pp. 41–8.

'Information without profit', *Papers on Non-Market Decision Making*, 1, 1966, pp. 141–59.

Reprinted in D. M. Lamberton (ed.) *Economics of Information and Knowledge*, London: Penguin, 1971), pp. 119–38.

'Informacion no Lucrativa', (Information without Profit) in D. M. Lamberton (ed.) *Economia de la Informacion y del Conocimiento*, Mexico City: Fondo de Cultura Economica, 1977, pp. 115–33.

'Inflazione prolongata', *Revista Internazionale di Scienze Economiche e Commerciali*, 13, 7, 1966, pp. 632–45.

'High school economics texts' (with Robert Johnson) *The University Bookman*, Autumn 1966, pp. 3ff.

'The general irrelevance of the general impossibility theorem', *Quarterly Journal of Economics*, 81, May, 1967, pp. 256–70.

'L'irrelevanza generale del theorema della impossibilita generale', in Francesco Forte and Gianfranco Mossetto (eds) *Economia del Benessere e Democrazia*, Milan: Franco Angeli Editore, 1973, pp. 261–76.

'The Welfare Costs of Tariffs, Monopolies and Theft', *Western Economic Journal*, 5, June 1967, pp. 224–32.

Reprinted in Donald S. Watson (ed.) *Price Theory in Action: A Book of Readings*, Boston: Houghton Mifflin, 1969, pp. 201–7.

'Los Costes en Bienestar de los Aranceles, Los Monopolioa y el Robo', *ICE*, January 1980, pp. 89–94.

Reprinted in James M. Buchanan, Robert D. Tollison and Gordon Tullock (eds)

Towards a Theory of the Rent-Seeking Society, Texas A & M University Press, 1981, pp. 39–50.

'The dead hand of monopoly' (with James M. Buchanan) *Anti-Trust Law and Economic Review*, 1, Summer, 1968, pp. 85–96.

'Pareto optimality with risk aversion', *Western Economic Journal*, 6, September, 1968, pp. 227–82.

'Welfare for Whom?' (Velfred for Hven-for De Fattige?) *Farman* 6, December, 1968, pp. 17–25.

'Welfare for Whom?' *Il Politico*, 33, December, 1968, pp. 746-61.

'Federalism: Problems of Scale', *Public Choice*, 6, Spring, 1969, pp. 19–29.

    Reprinted in Ryan C. Amacher, Robert D. Tollison, and Thomas D. Willett (eds) *The Economic Approach to Public Policy*, Ithaca, NY: Cornell University Press, 1976, pp. 511–19.

    Reprinted in Bhajan S. Grewl, Geoffrey Brennan, and Russell L. Mathews (eds) *Economics of Federalism*, Canberra: Australian National University Press, 1980, pp. 39–49.

'The New Theory of Corporations', in Erich Streissler (ed.) *Roads to Freedom: Essays in Honor of Friedrich A. von Hayek*, London: Routledge and Kegan Paul, 1969, pp. 287–307.

'Social cost and government action', *American Economic Review*, 59, May, 1969, pp. 189–97.

'An economic approach to crime', *Social Science Quarterly*, 50, June, 1969, pp. 59–71.

    Reprinted in Lee R. McPheters and William B. Stronge (eds) *The Economics of Crime and Law Enforcement*, Springfield, Ill.: Charles C. Thomas, 1976, pp. 121–37.

    Reprinted in Ryan C. Amacher, Robert D. Tollison, and Thomas D. Willett (eds) *The Economic Approach to Public Policy*, Ithaca, NY: Cornell University Press, 1976, pp. 111–24.

'Control – Law and Regulations – Property Rights', *Economics of Air and Water Pollution*, Blacksburg.: Water Resources Research 'Center, Virginia Polytechnic Institute, 1969, pp. 118–33.

'Computer simulation of a small voting system' (with Colin Campbell) *Economic Journal*, 80, March, 1970, pp. 97–104.

'A simple algebraic logrolling model', *American Economic Review*, 60, June, 1970, pp. 419–26.

'An Application of Economics in Biology', *Towards Liberty*, Vol. II, Menlo Park, CA: Institute for Humane Studies, 1971, pp. 375–91.

'A Model of Social Interaction', in James Herndon and Joseph Bernd (eds) *Mathematical Applications in Political Science*, V Charlottesville: University Press of Virginia, 1971, pp. 4–28 (A revised version of monograph).

'A modest proposal,' *Journal of Money, Credit and Banking*.

    'A Modest proposal: comment,' *Journal of Money, Credit and Banking*, 3, May, 1971, pp. 263–71.

'A different approach to the repeated prisoner's dilemma' (with H. Edwin Overcast), *Theory and Decision*, 1, June, 1971, pp. 350–8.

'Inheritance justified,' *Journal of Law and Economics*, 14, October, 1971, pp. 465–74.

'Inheritance rejustified: a reply,' *Journal of Law and Economics*, **16**, October, 1973, pp. 425–28.

'The paradox of revolution', *Public Choice*, **11**, Fall, 1971, pp. 89–99.

'The cost of transfers', *Kyklos* **24**, (fasc. 4, 1971), pp. 629–43.

'More on the welfare Cost of transfers', *Kyklos* (fasc. 2, 1974), pp. 378–81.

'El Coste de las Transferencias', *Hacienda Publica Espanola* (47), Instituto de Estudios Fiscales, 1977, pp. 231–40.

Reprinted in James M. Buchanan, Robert D. Tollison, and Gordon Tullock (eds) *Towards a Theory of the Rent-Seeking Society*, Texas A & M University Press, 1981, pp. 269–82.

'The charity of the uncharitable', *Western Economic Journal*, **9**, December, 1971, pp. 379–92.

Reprinted in *The Economics of Charity*, London: Institute of Economic Affairs, 1973, pp. 15–32.

Reprinted in *Against Equality: Readings on Economic and Social Policy*, London: Macmillan, 1983, pp. 325–44.

'Biological externalities', *Journal of Theoretical Biology*, **33**, December 1971, pp. 565–76.

'Il Gruppo Sovrano', in Francesco Forte and Gianfranco Mossetto (eds) *Economia del Benessere e Democrazia*, Milano: Franco Angeli Editore, 1973, pp. 729–51.

'Economic Imperialism', in James M. Buchanan, Robert D. Tollison, and Gordon Tullock (eds) *Theory of Public Choice: Political Applications*, Ann Arbor: University of Michigan Press, 1972, pp. 317–29.

'A view from the inside: an individualistic approach to the corporation', in Matthew F. Tuite (ed.) *Interorganizational Decision Making*, Chicago: Aldine, 1972, pp. 133–43.

'The Edge of the Jungle', in Gordon Tullock (ed.) *Explorations in the Theory of Anarchy*, Blacksburg, VA.: Center for Study of Public Choice, 1972, pp. 65–75.

'Paying people not to work', *National Review*, **25**, 3 August, 1973, pp. 831–54.

'Education and equality' (with Robert J. Staaf), *The Annals*, **409**, September, 1973, pp. 125–34.

'Does Punishment Deter Crime?' *The Public Interest*, **36**, Summer, 1974, pp. 103–11.

Reprinted in Arthur Niederhoffer and Abraham Blumberg (eds) *The Ambivalent Force*, 2nd edn (1977).

'Corruption and Anarchy', in Gordon Tullock (ed.) *Further Explorations in the Theory of Anarchy*, Blacksburg, VA.: Center for Study of Public Choice, 1974, pp. 65–70.

'A Neoclassical View of Postwar Europe', in Louis J. Mensonides and James A. Kuhlman (eds) *The Future of Inter-Bloc Relations in Europe*, New York: Praeger, 1974, pp. 181–90.

'The Costs of a Legal System' (with Warren F. Schwartz) *Journal of Legal Studies*, **4**, January, 1975, pp. 75–82.

'Polluter's profits and political response: Direct Controls Versus Taxes' (with James M. Buchanan) *American Economic Review*, **65**, March, 1975, pp. 139–47.

'Reply' (with James M. Buchanan), *American Economic Review*, **66**, December, 1976, pp. 983–84.

'Optimal poll taxes', *Atlantic Economic Journal*, **3**, April, 1975, pp. 1–6.

'Optimal poll taxes: Further Aspects', *Atlantic Economic Journal*, 4, Fall, 1976, pp. 7–9.

'Optimal poll taxes: rejoinder to Gartner's rejoinder', *Atlantic Economic Journal*, 5, July, 1977, pp. 86–7.

'Optimal voting turnouts: a reply' (to Brennan/Miller), *Atlantic Economic Journal*, VIII (3), September, 1979, pp. 69–70.

'The transitional gains trap', *Bell Journal of Economics*, 6, Autumn, 1975, pp. 671–8.
Reprinted in James M. Buchanan, Robert D. Tollison, and Gordon Tullock (eds) *Towards a Theory of the Rent-Seeking Society* (Texas A & M University Press, 1981, pp. 211–21.

'Competing monies', *Journal of Money, Credit and Banking*, 7, November, 1975, pp. 491–7.

'Competing monies: reply', *Journal of Money, Credit and Banking* 8, November, 1976, pp. 521–5.
Reprinted in 'International Perspectives' Column in *The Money Manager*.

'Competing for aid', *Public Choice*, 21, Spring, 1975, pp. 41–51.

'Column war', *Frontiers of Economics*, 1975, pp. 79–98.

'On the efficient organization of trials', *Kyklos*, 28 (fasc. 4, 1975), pp. 745–62.
'On the efficient organization of trials: Reply to McChesney, Ordover and Weitzman', *Kyklos*, 30, (fasc. 3, 1977), pp. 517–19.

'Trial of the Fact', in Robert D. Leiter and Gerald Sirkin (eds) *Economics of Public Choice*, New York: Cyrco, for Department of Economics, City College of New York 1975, pp. 121–36.

'Science's Feet of Clay', in William Breit and William P. Culbertson, Jr (eds) *Science and Ceremony: The Institutional Economics of C. E. Ayres*, Austin: University of Texas Press, 1976, pp. 135–45.

'The Politics of Bureaucracy and Planning' (with James M. Buchanan), in a. Lawrence Chickering (ed.) *The Politics of Planning: a Review and Critique of Centralized Economic Planning*, San Francisco, Ca.: Institute for Contemporary Studies, 1976, pp. 225–73.

'A new and superior process for making social choices' (with T. Nicolaus Tideman), *Journal of Political Economy*, October, 1976, pp. 1145–59.

'Regulating the Regulators', in Svetozar Pejovich (ed.) *Governmental Controls and the Free Market: The US Economy in the 1970s*, College Station; Texas A & M University Press, 1976, pp. 141–59.
'Quien Regula a Los Reguladores?' in Antonio Casahuga Vinardell and Jorge Bacaria Colom (eds) *Teoria de la Politica Economica*, Madrid: Instituto de Estudios Fiscales, 1984, pp. 705–34.

'Rational models, politics, and policy analysis' (with Richard E. Wagner), *Policy Studies Journal*, 4, Summer, 1976, pp. 408–16.

'The social cost of reducing social cost', in Garrett Hardin and John Baden (eds) *Managing the Commons*, San Francisco: W. H. Freeman, 1976, pp. 147–56.
Reprinted in George H. Haines, Jr (ed.) *Problems in Consumer Affairs: A Research Symposium*, Toledo, Oh.: Consumer Affairs Academy/Business Research Center, University of Toledo, 1976, pp. 246–62.

'Energy supply and governmental policy', *Materials and Society*, Vol. 1, December, 1976, pp. 209–14.

'Models in Politics', in Donald M. Freemman (ed.) *Political Science: Research, Methods, and Scope*, New York; Free Press, 1977, pp. 377–99.

'Revealing the Demand for Transfers', in Richard D. Auster (ed.) *American Re-evolution, Papers and Proceedings*, Tucson: University of Arizona, Department of Economics, 1977, pp. 107–23.

'The demand-revealing process as a welfare indicator', *Public Choice*, 29 (2) (Supplement to Spring, 1977), pp. 51–63.

'Demanding revealing process, coalitions, and public goods', *Public Choice*, 29, (2) (Supplement to Spring, 1977), pp. 103–5.

'Practical problems and practical solutions', *Public Choice*, 29, (2) (Supplement to Spring, 1977), pp. 27–35.

'Altruism, malice, and public goods', *Journal of Social and Biological Structures*, I, January, 1978, pp. 3–9.

　'Altruism, Malice, and Public Goods: Reply to Frech', *Journal of Social and Biological Structures*, I, January, 1978, pp. 187–9.

'Welfare effects of sales maximization', *Economic Inquiry*, January, 1978, pp. 113–18.

'Demand Revealing, Groves-Ledyard, and the Seventh Order of Smalls', in Karl W. Roskamp (ed.) *Public Choice and Public Finance*, Proceedings of the 34th Congress of the International Institute of Public Finance, Hamburg, 1978, pp. 69–76.

'The Economics of Revolution', in J. H. Johnson, J. J. Leach, and R. G. Muehlmann (eds) *Revolution, Systems, and Theories* Dordrecht, Holland: D. Reidel, 1979, pp. 47–60.

'Objectives of Income Redistribution', in Louis Levy-Garboua (ed.) *Sociological Economics*, London and Beverly Hills: Sage, 1979, pp. 161–81.

'Courts as Legislatures', edited with an introduction by Robert L. Cunningham, *Liberty and the Rule of Law*, College Station and London: A & M University Press, 1979.

'Avoiding Difficult Decisions' Review Article of *Tragic Choices* Guido Calabresi and Philip Bobbitt, New York: W. W. Norton, and Toronto: George J. McLeod, 1978. In *New York University Law Review*, 54 (1) April, 1979, pp. 267–79.

'Sociobiology and economics', *Atlantic Economic Journal* VIII (3), September, 1979, pp. 1–10.

'Public Choice in Practice', in Clifford S. Russell (ed.) *Collective Decision Making: Applications from Public Choice Theory*, published for Resources for the Future, Baltimore and London: Johns Hopkins, 1979, pp. 27–45.

'Flatland revisited', *Speculations in Science and Technology*, 3 (1) April, 1980, pp. 107–112.

'Efficient Rent-Seeking', in James M. Buchanan, Robert D. Tollison, and Gordon Tullock (eds) *Toward a Theory of the Rent-Seeking Society*, College Station: Texas A & M University Press, 1980, pp. 97–112.

'Why so much stability?' *Public Choice*, 37 (2), 1981, pp. 189–202.

'An American Perspective' (with James M. Buchanan), in Arthur Seldon (ed.) *The Emerging Consensus, IEA 1957–1981*, The Institute of Economic Affairs, London, 1981, pp. 79–97.

'Negligence again', *International Review of Law and Economics*, 1981, pp. 51–62

'The rhetoric and reality of redistribution', *Southern Economic Journal*, 47 (4), April, 1981, pp. 895–907.

'La Fundamentacion de la Redistribucion', *Conferencia Mont Pelerin: Santiago, Chile Centro De Estudios Publicos*, No. 6 Segundo Trimestre 1981, pp. 153–63.

'The Short Way With Dissenters', in Wolfgang Sodeur (ed.) *Okonomische Erklarungen Sozialen Verhaltens* vom 11–13, Wuppertal, W. Germany, Marz 1982, pp. 201–23.

'Welfare and the Law', *International Review of Law and Economics*, Kent, England: Butterworths, 1982, pp. 152–63.

'Income Testing and Politics: a Theoretical Model', in Irwin Garfinckel (ed.) *Income-Tested Transfer Programs: The Case For and Against*, New York: Academic Press, 1982, pp. 97–116.

'The Economics of Dying: The Misapplication of Comments' (with Richard B. McKenzie), *Atlantic Economic Journal*, X (2), 1982, pp. 48–9.

'The political economy of benefits and costs: a neoclassical approach to distributive politics – comment', *Journal of Political Economy* 90 (4), August, 1982, pp. 824–26.

'An economic theory of military tactics' (with Geoffrey Brennan) *Journal of Economic Behavior and Organization* Amsterdam: North-Holland, 1982, pp. 225–42.

'A (partial) rehabilitation of the public interest theory', *Public Choice*, 42 (1), 1984, pp. 89–99.

'Judicial errors and a proposal for reform' (with I. J. Good), *Journal of Legal Studies* XIII (2) June, 1984, pp. 289–98.

'How To Do Well While Doing Good!' in David C. Colander (ed.) *Neoclassical Political Economy* Cambridge, Mass.: Ballinger, 1984, pp. 229–39.

'Concluding Comments', included in 'New Approaches to Labor Economics', proceedings of a conference. *Research and Labor Economics*, 6 (forthcoming).

Comments and Communications

'Japanese modernization and the West', *Prod*, 1, November, 1957, pp. 28–9.

'Publication decisions and tests of significance: Comment', *Journal of the American Statistical Association*, 54, September, 1959, p. 593.

> Reprinted in Denton E. Morrison and Ramon E. Henkel (eds) *The Significane Test Controversy: a Reader*, Chicago: Aldine, 1970, pp. 301–2.

'An introduction to logical models', *Prod*, 3, November, 1959, pp. 9–11.

'Korea', *Collier's Encyclopaedia Yearbook for the Year 1959*, 1960, pp. 371–73.

'Aphorisms for the ambitious', *American Behavioral Scientist* 4, December, 1960, pp. 36–8.

'Korea', *Collier's Encyclopaedia Yearbook for the Year 1960*, 1961, pp. 351–4.

'Utility, strategy, and social decision rules: Comment', *Quarterly Journal of Economics*, 75 August, 1961, pp. 493–7.

'The historic figure: why study ignorance?' *American Behavioral Scientist*, 5, November, 1961, pp. 25–6.

'Our 'Other-Directed' Foreign Policy', *Foreign Policy Bulletin*, 1, November, 1961, pp. 1–2.

'Growth and debt: A suggestion for research', *The Exchange*, 4, July, 1963.

'Effects of stabilization', *Journal of Political Economy*, 71, August, 1963, pp. 413–15.

'The social rate of discount and the optimal rate of investment: Comment', *Quarterly Journal of Economics*, 78, May, 1964, pp. 331–6.

'Economic analogues to the generalization argument' (with James M. Buchanan), *Ethics*, **74**, July, 1964, pp. 300–1.

'A measure of the importance of cyclical majorities' (with Colin Campbell), *Economic Journal*, **75**, December, 1965, pp. 853–75.

'Gains-from-trade in votes' (with James M. Buchanan), *Ethics*, **76**, July, 1966, pp. 305–6.

'The paradox of voting: a possible method of calculation', *American Political Science Review*, **60**, September, 1966, pp. 684–5.

'Asymmetry between bribes and charges: comment', *Water Resources Research*, **2** (4), 1966, pp. 854–5.

'The prisoner's dilemma and mutual trust', *Ethics*, **77**, April, 1967, pp. 229–30.

'Excess benefit', *Water Resources Research*, **3** (2), 1967, pp. 643–4.

'The Rand-Parkinson effect', *Papers on Non-Market Decision Making*, **3**, Fall, 1967, pp. 93–6.

'A Faculty member addresses his students', *The Exchange*, October, 1968.

'A Note on Censorship', *American Political Science Review*, **62**, December, 1968, pp. 1265–7.

'Hereditary Southerners and the 1968 elections', *The Exchange*, January, 1969.

'The Truman-Johnson Syndrome', *The Exchange*, **31**, June, 1969.

'The allocation of the cost of displaced labor and severance pay: comment', *Journal of Human Resources*, **5**, Spring, 1970, pp. 248–9.

'Exhibit II', *American Economic Review*, **60**, May, 1970, pp. 489. (statement made at 82nd Annual Meeting, American Economic Association, December 1969).

'Switching in General Predators: A Comment', *Bulletin of the Ecological Society of America*, **51**, September, 1970, pp. 21–4.

'Local decentralization and the theory of optimal government: comment', in Julius Margolis (ed.) *The Analysis of Public Output*, New York: National Bureau of Economic Research, 1970, pp. 65–8.

'The coal tit as a careful shopper', *The American Naturalist*, **105**, January/February, 1971, pp. 77–80.

'Subsidized Housing in a Competitive Market: Comment', *American Economic Review*, **61**, March, 1971, pp. 218–19.

'Superiority of federalism', *The Alternative*, **4**, April, 1971, pp. 3–4.

'Public decisions as public goods', *Journal of Political Economy*, **79**, July/August, 1971, pp. 913–18.

Reprinted in Frey and Meissner (eds) *Kontroversenbuch zur Politischen Oekonomie*, Frankfurt am Main: Athaneum, 1974.

'Las Decisiones Publicas Como Bienes Publicos', in Antonio Casahuga Vinardell and Jorge Bacaria Colom (eds) *Teoria de la Politica Economica*, Madrid: Instituto de Estudios Fiscales, 1984, pp. 693–703.

'Can You Fool All of the People All of the Time?' *Journal of Money, Credit and Banking*, **4**, May, 1972, pp. 426–30.

Inflation and unemployment: the discussion continues', *Journal of Money, Credit and Banking*, **5**, August, 1973, pp. 826–35.

'Constitutional choice and simple majority rule: reply', *Journal of Political Economy*, **81**, pt 1, March/April, 1973, pp. 480–4.

'The income distribution as a pure public good: comment' (with Harold M.

Hochman and James D. Rogers) *Quarterly Journal of Economics*, **87**, May, 1973, pp. 311–15.

'Universities *Should* Discriminate Against Assistant Professors', *Journal of Political Economy*, **81**, September/October, 1973, pp. 1256–7.

'Further reasons why universities should discriminate against assistant professors ', *Journal of Political Economy*.

'On the economies of theater in Renaissance London and gay nineties Eldora', *Swedish Journal of Economics*, **76**, September, 1974, pp. 366–8.

'On the economies of theater in Renaissance London: further comment', *Scandinavian Journal of Economics*, **78** (1), 1976, pp. 115.

'Dynamic hypothesis on bureaucracy', *Public Choice*, **19**, Fall, 1974, pp. 127–31.

'Letter to the Editor', ('Paradox Lost' comment on Riker-Brams article) *American Political Science Review*, **68**, December, 1974, pp. 1687–8.

'On Mathematics as Decoration', in Roger K. Chisholm (ed.) *Papers in Economic Criticism*, Memphis.: Memphis State University Press,1975, pp. 22–3.

'General discussion', *Journal of Law and Economics*, **18**, December, 1975, pp. 913–18.

'The paradox of not voting for oneself', *American Political Science Review*, **69**, September, 1975, pp. 1295–7.

'The Pathology of Politics: Discussion', *Capitalism and Freedom: Problems and Prospects*, Charlottesville: University Press of Virginia, 1975, pp. 41–51.

'Avoiding the voter's paradox democratically: comment', *Theory and Decision*, **6**, November, 1975, pp. 485–6.

'Economics of crime: punishment or income redistribution – comment', *Review of Social Economy*, **34**, April, 1976, pp. 81–2.

'Is all that's real rational: comment', *Journal of Peace Science*, **2**, Spring, 1976, pp. 161–2.

'Planning: the bureaucrat's dream', *Public Interest Economics Review*, September, 1976, p. 13.

'Current Practices and Suggested Reforms: Commentary', *Blood Policy: Issues and Alternatives*, Washington: American Enterprise Institute for Public Policy Research, 1976, pp. 152–4.

'On the adaptive significance of territoriality: comment', *The American Naturalist*, **113** (5), 1978, pp. 772–5.

'The expanding public sector: Wagner squared' (with James M. Buchanan), *Public Choice*, **31**, Fall, 1977, pp. 147–50.

'Economics and sociobiology: a comment', *Journal of Economic Literature*, June, 1977, pp. 502–6.

'What Gordon Tullock really said', *American Political Science Review*, **70**, September, 1978, p. 924.

'DICTA: the victims of 'victimless crimes'', *Virginia Law Weekly*, **30**, 3 March, 1978, pp. 1–3.

'Why politicians won't cut taxes', *Taxing and Spending*, **13**, October/November, 1978, pp. 12–14.

'Rhigodynamics', *Speculations in Science and Technology*, I, (3), August, 1978, pp. 296–7.

'The economics of public services: comment', *Journal of Economic Literature*, XVI, September, 1978, pp. 1051–2.

254 *Appendix*

'Achieving deregulation – a public choice perspective', *Regulation*, November/December, 1978, pp. 50–4.

'Comment on "The physiological (and sociological) causes of the evolution of man from apes"', *Speculations in Science and Technology*, 1 (5), December, 1978, p. 528.

'Keynesianism: Alive, If Not So Well, At Forty: Comment', in James M. Buchanan and Richard E. Wagner (eds) *Fiscal Responsibility in Constitutional Democracy* (Studies in Public Choice Series, Vol. 1) Leiden/Boston: Martinus Nijhoff Social Sciences Division, 1978, pp. 70–4.

'Monopoly and the Rate of Extraction of Exhaustible Resources: Note', *The American Economic Review*, **69** (1), March, 1979, pp. 231–3.

'When is inflation not inflation?' *Journal of Money, Credit and Banking*, XI (2), May, 1979, pp. 219–21.

'Letter to the editor' (comment on articles by Brams and Fishburn, Balinski and Young), *American Political Science Review*, **73** (2), June, 1979, pp. 551–2.

'Law and economics: an economic invasion of the secret precincts of the law', *Businessman's Law*, **9** (2), 1 November, 1979, pp. 44–6.

'What's wrong with editing', *Speculations in Science and Technology*, 3 (5), 1980, pp. 659–68.

'Imperialismo Economico', *Libertad y Leviatan, Estudios Publicos* No. 1, Centro de Estudios Publicos, Santiago, Chile, Diciembre, 1980, pp. 185–200.

'An approach to empirical measures of voting paradoxes' (with J. Dobra, *Public Choice*, 36, 1981, pp. 193–4.

"Debt limitation: the President's unused weapon', *Journal of Contemporary Studies*, IV (3), Summer, 1981, pp. 101–2.

'Coalitions Under Demand Revealing' (with T. Nicolaus Tideman), *Public Choice*, 36, 1981, pp. 323–28.

'Lobbying and welfare: a comment', *Journal of Public Economics*, 16, 1981, pp. 391–94.

'More thoughts about demand revealing', (Reply to Margolis) *Public Choice*, 38 (2), pp. 167–70.

'Beyond the rent-seeking society', *ESP*, 2 (118), February, 1982, (Japan), pp. 19–23.

Forward for *Underground Government: The Off-Budget Public Sector*, by James T. Bennett and Thomas J. DiLorenzo, Washington, DC: CATO Institute, 1983, pp. xi–xiii.

'A Comment', *Constructive Approaches to the Foreign Debt Dilemma*, a seminar sponsored by the Taxpayer's Foundation, Washington, DC: Taxpayer's Foundation, 1983, pp. 26–30.

"The New Telecommunications Act as a Regulatory Framework, A Comment', *Telecommunications Regulation Today and Tomorrow*, New York: Law & Business, Inc./Harcourt Brace Jovanovich, 1983, pp. 257–64.

"Further Tests of a Rational Theory of the Size of Government', *Public Choice*, 41 (3), 1983, pp. 419–21.

'Long-run equilibrium and total expenditures in rent-seeking: a comment', *Public Choice* 43 (1), 1984, pp. 95–7.

Book Reviews

Soviet Economic Warfare, by Robert A. Allen *Journal of Politics*, **23** (4), November, 1961.

Conflict and Defense, by Kenneth E. Boulding, *Southern Economic Journal*, October, 1962.

Silent Spring, by Rachel Carson, *National Review*, 20 November 1962.

Awakened China, by Felix Greene, *Virginia Qaurterly*, 38, Winter, 1962.

The Economics of the Political Parties, by Seymour E. Harris, *Journal of Political Economy*, October, 1963.

The New States of Asia: A Political Analysis, by Michael Brecher, *The Annals* September, 1964.

A Strategy of Decision: Policy Evolution as a Social Process, by Braybrooke and Lindblom, *Ethics* October, 1964.

The Revolution in Fiscal Theory (3 books) *Public Administration Review*, XXV (1), March, 1965.

Economic Growth and External Debt, by Dragoslav Avramovic, et al., *The Annals*, July, 1965.

The Ombudsman, by Donald C. Rowat, *National Review*, 28 December, 1965.

Private and Public Planning, by Neil W. Chamberlain, *Southern Economic Journal*, XXXII (4), October, 1966.

'In Brief', (several short reviews), *National Review*, 28 June, 1966.

Economics in the High School, with Robert Johnson, *The University*, Autumn, 1966.

Economic Organizations and Social Systems, by Robert A. Solo, *Southern Economic Journal*, 1967.

The Creative Elite in America, by Nathaniel Weyl, *National Review*, 16 May, 1967.

Communist China's Economic Growth and Foreign Trade: Implications for US Policy, by Alexander Eckstein, *Political Science Quarterly*, June, 1967.

Politics, Economics, and the Public: Policy Outcomes in the American State, by Thomas R. Dye, *Journal of Business*, **40** (4), October, 1967.

Politics and the Regulatory Agencies, by William L. Cary, *George Washington Law Review* October, 1967.

Influencing Voters: A Study of Campaign Rationality by Richard Rose, *Papers on Non-Market Decision Making*, III, Fall, 1967.

Who Rules America? by G. William Domhoff, *Modern Age*, Spring, 1968.

Ten Economic Studies in the Tradition of Irving Fisher, by William C. Fellner, *The Journal of Business*, **41** (3), July, 1968.

Politics and Television, by Lang and Lang; and *The Image Candidates*, by Wyckoff, *The Journal of Politics*, **31** (1), 1969.

Bureaucracy and Representative Government, by William Niskanen, Chicago: Aldine-Atherton, 1971, *Public Choice*, **12**, Spring, 1972, pp. 119–24.

Institutional Change in American Economic Growth, by Lance E. Davis and Douglass C. North, Cambridge: Cambridge University Press, 1971, *Public Choice*, **13**, Fall, 1972, pp. 131–2.

Public Planning: Failure and Redirection, by Robert A. Levine, *Journal of Economic Literature*, XI (2), June, 1973, pp. 576–7.

Economic Analysis of Law, by Richard A. Posner, *Public Choice*, **17**, Spring, 1974, pp. 122–3.

Power and the Structure of Society, by James S. Coleman, New York: W. W. Norton, 1974, *Public Choice*, **18**, Fall, 1974, pp. 130–1.

The Limits of Organization, by Kenneth Arrow, *Journal of Economic Literature*, XIII (1), March, 1975.

Sociobiology, The New Synthesis, by Edward Wilson, Cambridge, Mass.: Belknap Press of Harvard University Press, 1975, *Public Choice*, **25**, Spring, 1976, pp. 97–9.

The Economics of Crime and Law Enforcement, by Lee R. McPheters and William B. Strong (eds), Springfield, Ill.: Charles C. Thomas, 1976, *Public Choice*, **27**, Fall, 1976, p. 131.

On Human Nature, by Edwin Wilson, Cambridge, Mass.: Harvard University Press, 1978, *Public Choice*, **34** (2), 1979, pp. 253–4.

Modern Political Economy, by Bruno S. Frey, New York: Halsted Press, 1978, *Public Choice*, **34** (2), 1979, pp. 251–2.

Public Interest Law: An Economic and Institutional Analysis, edited by Weisbrod and Burton, *Journal of Economic Literature*, XVII, March, 1979.

Charge, by Arthur Seldon, *Reason*, May, 1979, pp. 42–3.

Politics and Markets: The World's Political-Economic System, by Charles E. Lindblom, *Policy Review*, Summer, 1979.

Property, Power, and Public Choice: An Inquiry into Law and Economics, by A. Allan Schmid, *The Journal of Politics*, **42**, 1980, pp. 346–7.

The Crossman Diaries: Selections from the Diaries of a Cabinet Minister 1964–1970, by Richard Crossman. Introduced and edited by Anthony Howard, London: Magnum Books, Methuen Paperbacks, 1979, *Policy Review*, **13**, Summer, 1980, pp. 174–9. 'Research in Experimental Economics', edited by Vernon L. Smith, Greenwich: JAI Press, **1**, 1979, *Public Choice*, **35** (2), 1980, p. 253.

Metropolitan Reform: An Annotated Bibliography, P. C. Baker, E. Ostrom, and R. Goehlert. Workshop in Political Theory and Public Analysis, Bloomington: Indiana University Press, 1979, *Public Choice*, **35** (5), 1980, p. 635.

The Organization of Interests: Incentive and the Internal Dynamics of Political Interest Groups, by Terry M. Moe, Chicago and London: The University of Chicago Press, 1980, *Public Choice* **36** (1) 1981, pp. 207–8.

Cutting Back City Hall, by Robert W. Poole, University Books, 1980, *Public Choice*, **36** (2), 1981, p. 370–1.

The Way Out, by Vernon L. Smith, Montreal, Quebec, Canada: The Institute for Research on Public Policy, 1980, *Public Choice*, **36** (2), 1981, pp. 370–1.

The Stalinist Planning for Economic Growth, 1933–1952, by Eugene Zalisky. Translated from the French and edited by Marie-Christine MacAndrew and John H. Moore, Chapel Hills: The University of North Carolina Press, 1980, *Public Choice*, **36** (2), 1981, p. 371.

'Science and Poetry', review article of 'Ecodynamics', by Kenneth Boulding, Beverly Hills: Sage, 1978, *Journal of Social and Biological Structures*, **4** (2), April, 1981, pp. 185–6.

'Two Gurus', book review of *Wealth and Poverty*, by George Gilder, New York: Basic Books, 1981, and *The Zero-Sum Society*, by Lester Thurow, New York: Basic Books, 1980, *Policy Review*, Summer, 1981, pp. 137–44.

A Short History of Electoral Systems in Western Europe, by Andrew Carstaris, London: George Allen & Unwin, 1980, *Public Choice*, **37** (3), 1981, p. 620.

The Economics of Justice, by R. A. Posner, Cambridge: Harvard University Press, 1981, *Public Choice*, **38** (2), 1982, p. 222.

Markets and States in Tropical Africa: The Political Basis of Agricultural Policies, by Robert H. Bates, University of California Press, 1981, *Public Choice*, **39** (2), 1982, pp. 331–3.

Essays in Trespassing: Economics to Politics and Beyond, by Albert O. Hirschman, London and New York: Cambridge University Press, 1981, *The Southern Economic Journal*, **2** (49), October, 1982, p. 596.

The Rise and Decline of Nations, by Mancur Olson, New Haven: Yale University Press, 1982, *Public Choice*, **40** (1), 1983, pp. 111–16.

Locking Up the Range: Federal Land Controls and Grazing, by G. D. Libecap, Cambridge, Mass.: Ballinger, 1981, *Public Choice*, **40** (2), 1983, p. 235.

Approval Voting, by Steven J. Brams and Peter C. Fishburn, Boston: Birkhauser, 1982, *Public Choice*, **44** (2), 1984, pp. 389–90.

The Economic Constitution of Federal States, by Breton and Scott, *The Canadian Journal of Economics*, 1984.

Index

Index by Fiona F. Barr